本书受到上海市浦江人才计划资助（15PJC070）

Greek Classics:
Reading for Discussion

古希腊经典：
阅读和讨论

主　编◎吴诗玉

副主编◎马　拯　葛明永

上海交通大学出版社
SHANGHAI JIAO TONG UNIVERSITY PRESS

内容提要

　　本书为古希腊经典英文译本精读,选篇包括赫西奥德的《神谱》、荷马的《伊利亚特》第一、第六章、希罗多德的《历史》等相关内容、索福克勒斯的《俄狄浦斯王》,以及柏拉图的关于苏格拉底的《论虔诚》哲学对话等经典名篇。本书旨在通过讨论的方法来引导学生形成批判性思维,并通过阅读、思考及口头表达的训练来习得语言。可用作学校通识教育教材,适合各个专业的学生使用。

图书在版编目(CIP)数据

　古希腊经典:阅读和讨论 / 吴诗玉主编.—上海:
上海交通大学出版社,2017
　ISBN 978 - 7 - 313 - 16325 - 7

　Ⅰ.①古…　Ⅱ.①吴…　Ⅲ.①著作-介绍-古希腊
Ⅳ.①Z835

　中国版本图书馆 CIP 数据核字(2016)第 309497 号

古希腊经典:阅读和讨论

Greek Classics:Reading for Discussion

主　　编:吴诗玉
出版发行:上海交通大学出版社　　　　　　地　　址:上海市番禺路 951 号
邮政编码:200030　　　　　　　　　　　　电　　话:021 - 64071208
出 版 人:郑益慧
印　　刷:虎彩印艺股份有限公司　　　　　经　　销:全国新华书店
开　　本:787mm×1092mm　1/16　　　　印　　张:15.5
字　　数:373 千字
版　　次:2017 年 6 月第 1 版　　　　　　　印　　次:2017 年 6 月第 1 次印刷
书　　号:ISBN 978 - 7 - 313 - 16325 - 7/Z
定　　价:48.00 元

前　言

　　首先要问的是：为什么要阅读和讨论？本书所指的阅读主要是指对经典原著的阅读，而讨论则是指在对经典原著进行仔细阅读的基础上，对一些问题以口头的方式广泛地分析、研讨和交流观点。

　　阅读对于个人的成长和教育的重要性怎么强调都不过分。它是我们获取知识，探索世界的重要渠道。而为什么又要强调阅读经典和原著呢？在一个高度技术主义和消费主义的时代，经典阅读似乎早就与时代格格不入。首先，关于经典阅读的重要性，我同意北大吴增定教授的总结，"凡是一个没有经典可读的院系，一定是研究水平最差的。相反，如果是经典源远流长的，跟学术传统能够结合起来的系往往科研水平也较好……"他还指出，"阅读经典不仅能够帮助我们克服学科壁垒和专业界限，而且能够将专业知识本身融会贯通，变成活生生的思想资源，并且使我们有能力思考家国天下和宇宙人生等至关重要的问题。"

　　为什么又强调讨论，甚至把它置于与阅读同等的位置呢？关于讨论，受到广泛认同的一点是，它为学习者提供了探索和发现的通道。这也是提升学生的学习动机，培育学术灵活性和鼓励"民主"习惯的重要策略。它能为学生创造重要的机会，练习和提升许多重要的技能，比如清楚地表达和为自己立场辩护的能力，思考和接受各种不同观点的能力，以及获得和评估各种证据的能力。最终，训练他们能够有效地使用语言，清楚、连贯和具有说服力地进行口头表达和写作。阅读和讨论被视为通识教育质量保证的重要制度，实际上，阅读经典并进行讨论，亦是国外人文教育的主要方式。本质上，阅读和讨论也与通识教育要实现的目标一脉相承，即"拓宽视野，奠定学生的世界观、人生观和价值观，培养学生的独立思考能力、有效交流能力、批判思维能力和价值判断能力，提升学生的责任感，使之成长为健全的公民"。

　　从外语学习的角度看，阅读和讨论的重要性也同样不可低估。依据笔者多年从事英语教学实践的经验，我甚至认为，对于具备一定英语基础的大学生来说，"基于阅读基础上的讨论课"是最理想的外语教学课。一方面，阅读可以为语言学习提供不可或缺的语言输入，帮助词汇的附带习得，也可为写作提供范例等等；另一方面，讨论则能让学习者在交互协作的空间里，通过获得"帮助"，进行意义互动，实现独立地完成超过他们实际语言水平所能完成的任务。第二语言习得研究已经有几十年的历史，但是迄今为止，研究者关于有效的第二语言学习最有把握的结论仍然是让"学习者在一个类似于社会的语境里接触和使用语言，与别人在互动中进行口头的语义交流"。不管是要解决所谓的"费时低效"的问题，还是"哑巴英语"的问题，也不管现代技术如何变迁，为语言学习能够提供多大的便利，坚守"阅读和讨论"恐怕仍然是最有效的方式。而无论第二语言教学的专家和学者提出何种语言教学的方法，所谓的语法翻译法、直接法、听说法，还是新近的交际法或者基于任务的教学法，如果离开了阅读和讨论，无异于舍本逐末。

　　本书正是基于以上理念而编写。它的内容包涵广泛，从神话到史诗、历史学、悲剧及古希腊哲学。而所有这些内容，我们安排和选取的都是经典文本，并提供相应的研究问题供学习和讨论，避免概要式地知识性地讲解。通过对它们的阅读和讨论，帮助读者认识希腊经典时代的神话故事，和它在史诗、哲学、戏剧以及政治思想等方面的创造。此书，既可以作为通识教育的教材，也可以作为语言学习的材料。它的目的与我们在上海交通大学所开设的通识核心课程《古希腊文明演绎》的目的是一致的，即除帮助读者扩充视野，认识世界，培养人文素养以外，重在帮助读者提升批判性阅读、思考和写作的能力。关于本课程的更多内容，可在http://cc.sjtu.edu.cn/中搜索关键字"古希腊文明"找到。

编　者

2016 年 12 月

N.-A. Monsiau 1754-1837：The Olympians Photo © Maicar Forlag-GML

Contents

Introduction   The Rise of Greek Civilization

Bertrand Russell

Bertrand Russell
(1872 — 1970)

IN all history, nothing is so surprising or so difficult to **account**[1] for as the sudden rise of civilization in Greece. Much of what makes civilization had already existed for thousands of years in Egypt and in **Mesopotamia**[2], and had spread thence to neighbouring countries. But certain elements had been lacking until the Greeks supplied them. What they achieved in art and literature is familiar to everybody, but what they did in the purely **intellectual**[3] **realm**[4] is even more **exceptional**[5]. They invented mathematics and science and philosophy; they first wrote history **as opposed to**[6] mere **annals**[7]; they speculated freely about the nature of the world and the ends of life, without being bound in the **fetters**[8] of any **inherited**[9] **orthodoxy**[10]. What occurred was so astonishing that, until very recent times, men were content to **gape**[11] and talk mystically about the Greek genius. It is possible, however, to understand the development of Greece in scientific terms, and it is well worth while to do so. (To be continued)

1. [əˈkaʊnt] vt. 解释
2. [ˌmesəʊpəˈteimjə] n. 美索不达米亚
3. [intəˈlektʃuəl] adj. 智力的
4. [relm] n. 王国；领域
5. [ikˈsepʃənl] adj. 杰出的；独特的
6. 与…相对（或相反），而不是
7. [ˈænlz] n. 编年史；历史记载
8. [ˈfetə(r)] n. 束缚；脚镣
9. [inˈheritid] adj. 通过继承得到的
10. [ˈɔːθədɒksi] n. 正统；正统性
11. [geip] v. 张口结舌地看

* * * * * * * * * * * * * * * * * * * * * * *

❉ **Questions to discussion**:

(1) We begin this textbook by taking an excerpt from Bertrand Russell. What do you know about Bertrand Russell? From which book is this excerpt taken?

(2) Bertrand Russell begins by saying "in all history", is it fair and proper for him to comment on the rise of Greek civilization in such an absolute way by saying "all"? Find in this same passage a word or words with meanings similar to "all".

(3) Russell comments "they [the Greeks] speculated freely about the nature of the world and the ends of life, without being bound in the fetters of any inherited orthodoxy". Please translate this sentence into Chinese and give comments on Russell's views.

* * * * * * * * * * * * * * * * * * * * * * *

Chapter One   Greek Mythology

This chapter concerns Greek mythology, a very important, and also most familiar topic to many Chinese readers. We mostly know about the Ancient Greek people by reading their legendary stories. Greek mythology serves like a window to know and understand Ancient Greek Civilization. However, instead of presenting some very specific stories, this chapter approaches Greek mythology by introducing and discussing two ancient and well-known books, Hesiod's *Theogony* and Homer's epic poetry, *The Iliad*. We do believe that, through reading and discussing these two great books, you will have a good taste of Greek classical mythology. Before that, some background knowledge is first provided.

Background Knowledge

1. Mythology and Myth

The term **mythology** is actually not easy to define. Usually we know that the "-ology" endings means "study of". For example, biology is the study of life, psychology is the study of the mind, and geology is the study of the earth. Then mythology ought to mean the study of myth. In fact, some scholars do use it that way. Yet, in common usage, mythology tends to mean **the whole body of myths** told by a particular culture. Then by Greek mythology, we mean the whole body of myths told by ancient Greek people.

Mythology has, thus, these two separate meanings: the study of myth, and simply the whole body of myth developed within any particular culture. Then, if mythology is the study of myth or the whole body of myth developed by a culture, what is "**myth**?" That is a question that has no easy or obvious answer either. The attempt to define myth is very difficult and scholars are divided as to what actually a myth is. Professor Elizabeth Vandiver from Whitman College provides a simple and straightforward definition, which, we think, works well for this textbook. She defines myth as "**traditional stories a society tells itself that encode or represent the world view, beliefs, principles, and often the fears of that society.**"

Some characteristics of "myth" are also summarized: ① Myths are traditional tales or stories. They are presented in narrative form and are handed down in a society from one generation to the next. It is usually hard to tell who first "invented" a particular myth. ② Myths are set in the past, usually very long time ago. It usually recounts events in the far past. ③ Myths are often seen as true history by its people in a particular culture, as the Greek people see the Trojan War as their real history. ④ Myths often explain, justify, instruct, or warn. Through the myths, people nowadays know why things are as they are or how certain events, entities, or conditions came into being. In the opinion of Andrew Lang (1844—1912), myths were meant to explain the cause of things or how things came to be. ⑤ Myths frequently concern gods and the supernatural.

It will sound natural and fitting that the United States (or other Western countries) name the human spaceflight program as "Apollo Program (or Project Apollo)". However, if we Chinese do the same and name our lunar exploration mission as "Apollo Program", it will sounds rather weird and awkward. Instead the name "Chang'e" sounds very natural and fitting, a name which triggers Chinese people's memory of a too familiar old tale. This illustrates that myths are always linked to a particular culture and society.

Here are two questions for you to think about: (1) If myths are traditional tales or stories that a society tells itself about itself, then which societies use myth and why do they use it? (2) Do you think that all societies have their own myths?

2. The Geography of Greece

In ancient time, Greeks colonized rather extensively. In addition to the mainland Greece, they also lived in **Asia Minor** (小亚细亚), on the islands of **Crete** and Cyprus, on the coasts of North Africa, southern France and Italy, on Sicily and the Black Sea. The civilization of ancient Greece flowered, however, mainly in what is modern Greece.

The geography of Greece is divided and sub-divided by hills, mountains and rivers, with plains and valleys **straggled** (*vi.* 蔓延) in between. As a result of the **rugged terrain** (崎岖的地形), land suitable for farming was limited. Upon the limited land, though, the ancient Greeks grew grain, grapes, and olives, out of which the Greeks produced bread, wine, and olive oil. Mountainous terrain provided plentiful timber for building houses and ships, though later the Greeks might have weathered **deforestation** (*n.* 森林采伐) and began importing lumber (*n.* 木材) from northward regions. Besides, the land of Greece also produced some mineral resources, with some deposits of metal ore scattered throughout the territory. For example, in the Athenian territory, the silver mines helped Athens enter into the so-called Golden Age in the fifth Century BC.

The Greek coastline was so jagged that the Ancient Greeks mostly lived within forty miles of the sea, providing easy access for fishermen and seagoing merchants. The abundance of good harbors enabled the Greeks to have frequents contacts between the Greeks and other people living at the eastern **Mediterranean** (地中海). Sea voyage played a central role in the shaping of the Greek culture, as the Greeks were able to learn new technologies and ideas from the older civilizations, such as the Egyptians.

A map of Ancient Greece

The mountainous **topography** (*n*. 地貌) contributed to the political **fragmentation** (*n*. 分裂) of ancient Greece as the naturally divided landscape was politically divided. Though ancient Greeks recognized they shared the same language（with dialects）, religion（with local variations）, customs, and came together for Olympic games and religious festivals, they still lived in a number of small independent states with different forms of government: palace-centered kingdoms in the Bronze Age; city-states operating under the forms of oligarchy, tyranny or democracy in the later ages.

3. Timeline of Ancient Greece

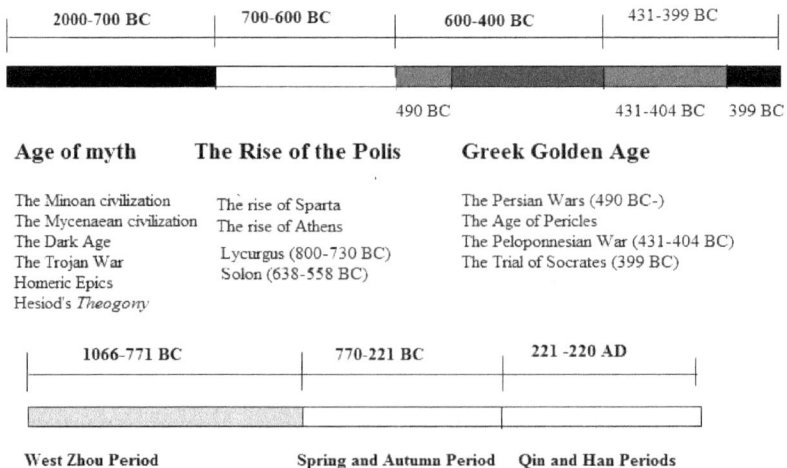

2000-700 BC	700-600 BC	600-400 BC	431-399 BC

490 BC   431-404 BC   399 BC

Age of myth	**The Rise of the Polis**	**Greek Golden Age**
The Minoan civilization The Mycenaean civilization The Dark Age The Trojan War Homeric Epics Hesiod's *Theogony*	The rise of Sparta The rise of Athens Lycurgus (800-730 BC) Solon (638-558 BC)	The Persian Wars (490 BC-) The Age of Pericles The Peloponnesian War (431-404 BC) The Trial of Socrates (399 BC)

1066-771 BC	770-221 BC	221-220 AD
West Zhou Period	**Spring and Autumn Period**	**Qin and Han Periods**

Timeline of Ancient Greece contrasted with the same period in Ancient China

4. Hesiod and His Theogony

Hesiod and the Muse

Ancient Greek people living on such a place had fully developed their imagination. From quite early times, they were interested in the question of the world genesis. Like other ancient societies, they created myths and legends we refer to here as Greek **mythology** to explain natural phenomenon and also the creation of the world. Greek mythology concerns their gods and heroes, the nature of the world, and the origins and significance of their own **cult** and ritual practices.

Origins of the gods and the physical universe have been offered in many even conflicting accounts, yet Hesiod's *Theogony*, an epic history of the divine order, received wide acceptance of the Greeks as the standard mythical account of the earlier history of the world.

Hesiod, born in the 8th century BC, is often considered as one of the earliest Greek poets. He was generally thought by scholars to have been active between 750 and 650 BC, about the same time as Homer. He and Homer were credited with establishing Greek religious customs. Modern scholars recognize him as a main source on Greek mythology, farming techniques, early economic thought, archaic Greek astronomy and ancient time-keeping.

Hesiod is best known for his two poems, *The Theogony* and *Works and Days*. *The Theogony* is commonly considered as his earliest work, composed circa 700 B.C. Written in the Epic dialect of Homeric Greek, it describes the origins and genealogies (or birth) of the Greek gods. Origins of the gods and the physical universe have been offered in many even conflicting accounts, yet according to Herodotus (Greek first historian), Hesiod's *Theogony* has gained most influences far and wide, and been accepted as the standard mythical account that linked all Hellenes.

While reading *Theogony*, it is advisable, first of all, to understand how Zeus and the twelve Olympic gods come to power and become the ruler of the universe. In order to do so, you can choose the followings lines to read at first. They include lines 1—34, 115—506, and 616—end.

Theogony
Hesiod

Muses of **Helicon**[1]，let us begin our song with them，   1
who hold the great and **holy**[2] mountain of Helicon，
and around its **violet**[3]-like spring and **altar**[4] of
exceedingly strong Zeus, dance on **dainty**[5] feet，and
who，after **bathing**[6] their soft skin in the Permessos   5
or the spring of the Horse or holy Olmeios
on the peak of Helicon，form their dances，beautiful
dances that arouse desire，and they move **erotically**[7].
From Helicon they rise up **veiled**[8] in a deep mist and walk
through the night，**sending forth**[9] their voice most   10
beautiful，**hymning**[10] aegis-bearing Zeus and Lady Hera
the Argive **clad**[11] in **sandals**[12] of gold，and
the daughter of Zeus of the aegis，gray-eyed Athena，and
Phoebus Apollo and Artemis，who **pour forth**[13] arrows，and
Poseidon，holder and shaker of Gaia，and   15
august[14] Themis and Aphrodite of the glancing eyes and
and Hebe with her golden crown and beautiful Dione，and
Leto and Iapetos and Kronos of **crooked counsel**[15] and
Eos and great Helios and shining Selene and
Gaia and great Okeanos，and black Night and the   20
sacred[16] clan of the other deathless ones who are for always.

The Muses once taught Hesiod beautiful song   22
while he was **shepherding**[17] sheep at the foot of holy Helicon.
The goddesses first spoke this word to me，
the Muses of Olympus，daughters of **aegis-bearing**[18] Zeus.   25
"**Rustic**[19] shepherds，worthless **reproaches**[20]，mere stomachs，
we know how to say many lies like the truth，
and，whenever we wish，we know how to tell the truth."

Thus spoke the fluent daughters of mighty Zeus，and
they gave me a **scepter**[21]，a branch of flourishing **laurel**[22]
that they had **plucked**[23]，a thing of wonder. They breathed

1.［ˈhelɪkən］*n*.赫利孔山
2.［ˈhəʊli］*adj*.神圣的
3.［ˈvaɪələt］*n*.紫罗兰
4.［ˈɔːltə(r)］*n*.圣坛
5.［ˈdeɪnti］*adj*.精致的
6.［beɪð］*vt*.沐浴
7.［ɪˈrɒtɪkəɪ］*adv*.色情地
8.［veɪl］*vt*.用面纱遮盖
9.发出
10.［hɪm］*vt*.赞美、赞歌
11.［klæd］*n*.族
12.［ˈsændl］*n*.凉鞋
13.大量地发射出
14.［ɔːˈɡʌst］*adj*.威严的
15.狡猾的计划
16.［ˈseɪkrɪd］*adj*.神圣的
17.［ˈʃepəd］*vt*.放牧
18.神盾持有者
19.［ˈrʌstɪk］*adj*.粗俗的
20.［rɪˈprəʊtʃ］*n*.耻辱
21.［ˈseptə］*n*.权杖
22.［ˈlɒrəl］*n*.月桂
23.［plʌk］*vt*.摘下

in me an **inspired**[1] voice so I might celebrate what will be and
what has been, and they **bid**[2] me to hymn the **clan**[3] of the blessed
ones who always are and to sing of them first and last.   34

But what has this to do with **an oak or a rock**?[4]   35
You, let us begin from the Muses who in hymning their
father Zeus, delight his mighty mind within Olympus,
saying what is and what will be and what has been,
with voices **in tune**[5], and a sound flows tirelessly
and sweet from their mouths. The halls of father Zeus   40
loud-thundering laugh as their delicate sound fragments,
and the peaks of snow-covered Olympus **resound**[6] as do
the halls of the immortals. They **emit**[7] their immortal
tones and first celebrate the august clan of the gods
in song from the beginning, whom Gaia and wide Ouranos 45
bore, and those born from them, gods, givers of good things.
Secondly, they celebrate Zeus, father of gods and men,
so much is he the foremost of the gods and greatest in power.
Again, by hymning the clan of men and powerful Giants,   50
they **delight**[8] the mind of Zeus within Olympus.

1. [ɪnˈspaɪə(r)] *adj.* 有灵感的
2. [bɪd] *vt.* 命令
3. [klæn] *n.* 族群
4. 离题,偏题
5. 合调子
6. [rɪˈzaʊnd] *vi.* 回响
7. [ɪˈmɪt] *vt.* 发出
8. [dɪˈlaɪt] *vt.* 使…愉快

❋ ❋ ❋   ❋ ❋ ❋   ❋ ❋ ❋   ❋ ❋ ❋   ❋ ❋ ❋   ❋ ❋ ❋   ❋ ❋ ❋   ❋ ❋ ❋

❋Questions for discussion:

(1) Read the beginning of the poetry. How was Hesiod inspired to compose *The Theogony*?
    For what purpose is the poetry composed?
(2) The key to understand the first paragraph is to understand the two important verb phrases
    "sending forth" and "hymning". Translate these two phrases into Chinese and then

answer "To whom are Muses hymning in their beautiful voices?" Please list all the names.

(3) Translate the words spoken by Muses to Hesiod.

＊＊＊　　＊＊＊　　＊＊＊　　＊＊＊　　＊＊＊　　＊＊＊　　＊＊＊　　＊＊＊

Muses of Olympus, daughters of aegis-bearing Zeus,
whom Mnemosyne **mingled**[1] with father Zeus and bore
in Pieria, while she was **guarding**[2] the fields of Eleutheros
to be forgetfulness of troubles and **cessation**[3] of worries.　　55
For nine nights, the counselor Zeus was **mingling with**[4] her
apart from the immortals, going up into her sacred bed.
But when it had been a year, and the seasons of the **withering**[5]
months turned, and the many days were fulfilled,
she bore nine **maidens**[6], alike in mind, who care for song　　60
in their breasts and whose spirits are free of pain,
down a little from the highest peak of snow covered Olympus.
There are their shining dancing places and beautiful halls,
and beside them the Graces and Desire have their **dwellings**[7]
amid **festivities**[8]. Sending forth their lovely voice　　65
they sing songs and celebrate the **ordinances**[9] and trusty ways
of all the immortals, sending forth their lovely voice.
Then they go to Olympus, glorying in their beautiful voice
amid **ambrosial**[10] song. All around them as they hymn, black
Gaia laughs, and a lovely **din**[11] rises up from their feet　　70
as they are coming to their father. He is king in Ouranos,
holding the thunder and **gleaming**[12] lightning bolt and
after **conquering**[13] his father Kronos by power. Fairly in each
did he **distribute**[14] to the **immortals**[15] their ordinances and devise
their **provinces**[16]. These things the Muses who have their hall　　75
on Olympus, sing, the nine daughters **sired**[17] by mighty Zeus,
Kleio and Euterpe and Thaleia and Melpomene and
Terpsichore and Erato and Polymnia and Ourania and
Kalliope. The last is the foremost of them all,
for she accompanies and attends **revered**[18] kings　　80
Whomever the daughters of **mighty**[19] Zeus honor and
see being born from kings **nurtured**[20] by Zeus,
upon his tongue they pour **dews**[21] wetter than honey and
from his mouth flow **soothing**[22] words. All the people

1. ['mɪŋgl] vi. 交配
2. [gɑːd] vt. 看守
3. [se'seɪʃn] n. 中断
4. 与…交配
5. ['wɪðə(r)] adj. 枯萎的
6. ['meɪdn] n. 少女
7. [dwel] n. 居住地
8. [fe'stɪvəti] n. 欢庆
9. ['ɔːdɪnəns] n. 神职
10. [æm'brəʊʒɪəl] adj. 芬香的
11. [dɪn] n. 响声
12. [gliːm] v. 闪烁
13. ['kɒŋkə(r)] vt. 征服
14. [dɪ'strɪbjuːt] vt. 分配
15. [ɪ'mɔːtl] n. 神仙
16. ['prɒvɪns] n. 职责
17. ['saɪə(r)] vt. 做…的父亲
18. [rɪ'vɪə(r)] vt. 敬畏
19. ['maɪti] adj. 强有力的
20. ['nɜːtʃə(r)] vt. 养育
21. [djuː] n. 露水
22. [suːθ] vt. 安慰

look to him as he decides between opposing claims   85
with straight judgments. He **addresses**[1] them without **erring**[2]
and quickly and knowingly ends a great quarrel.
For this reason, kings are wise, because for people
injuring one another in **assembly**[3], they end actions that call
for **vengeance**[4] easily, **appeasing**[5] the parties with soft words. 90
As he walks in the marketplace, they **glorify**[6] him as if a god
with soothing **deference**[7], and he stands out in the gathering.
Such is the sacred **bounty**[8] of the Muses to men.

From the Muses and **far-shooting Apollo**[9]   94
are singers and guitar-players across the earth
but kings are from Zeus. Blessed is he whom the Muses
love. From his mouth the **streams**[10] *flow sweeter than honey*. 97
If anyone holds sorrow in his spirit from fresh **grief**[11] and
is dried out in his heart from **grieving**[12], the singer,
servant of the Muses, hymns the deeds of men of the past 100
and the blessed gods who hold Olympus and right away
he forgets his troubles and does not remember a single
care. Quickly do the gifts of the goddess **divert**[13] him.

Hail[14], children of Zeus, and give your song that excites desire.
Celebrate the holy race of immortals who are for always,   105
those born from Gaia and starry Ouranos, and
from dark Night and those whom **salty**[15] Pontos bore.
Tell how the gods and Gaia first came into being and
rivers and the **boundless**[16] ea raging with swell and
the shining stars and wide Ouranos above   110
[*The ones born of them, gods, givers of good things*] and
how they divided the wealth and **apportioned**[17] provinces,
also how they first came to hold Olympus of many glens.
Tell me these things, Muses who hold your halls on Olympus.
From the beginning, also tell the one of them who came first. 115

1. [ə'dres] v. 向…说话
2. [ɜː(r)] vi. 犯错
3. [ə'sembli] n. 集会
4. ['vendʒəns] n. 仇恨
5. [ə'piz] vt. 安抚
6. ['glɔːrɪfaɪ] vt. 颂扬
7. ['defərəns] n. 尊重
8. ['baʊnti] n. 奖金
9. 远射神阿波罗
10. [striːm] n. 溪流
11. [griːf] n. 悲痛
12. [griːv] vi. 悲伤
13. [daɪ'vɜːt] vt. 转移注意力
14. [heɪl] vt. 赞扬
15. ['sɔːlti] adj. 辛辣的;咸的
16. ['baʊndləs] adj. 无边际的
17. [ə'pɔːrʃn] vt. 分配

＊＊＊　　＊＊＊　　＊＊＊　　＊＊＊　　＊＊＊　　＊＊＊　　＊＊＊　　＊＊＊

❈**Questions for discussion:**

(4) Tell the birth story of Muses in your own words.

(5) Who is the mother of the nine Muses? Search the name in the internet. What kind of

goddess is Mnemosyne? Is Mnemosyne the most natural and reasonable mother for the Muses, these lovely and talented and creative singers?

(6) Who are the neighbors of the Muses? What features do they have?

(7) Translate the sentence in lines 94—96 into Chinese. What is special with this sentence?

＊＊＊　　＊＊＊　　＊＊＊　　＊＊＊　　＊＊＊　　＊＊＊　　＊＊＊　　＊＊＊

First of all **Chaos**[1] came into being. But then

Gaia broad-chested, always the unshakable seat of all

the immortals who hold the peaks of snowy Olympus,

and dark Tartaros in the **recesses**[2] of the wide-wayed earth,

and Eros, the most beautiful among the immortal gods,　　120

loosener of **limbs**[3], who **subdues**[4] the mind and **prudent**[5]

counsel in the chests of all gods and of all men.

From Chaos were born Erebos and black Night.

From Night, again, were born Aether and Day, whom she

conceived[6] and bore after mingling with Erebos in philotês. 125

Gaia first bore equal to herself **starry**[7] Ouranos

so that he may cover her all over like a **veil**[8],

to be always the unshakable seat for the blessed gods.

She bore the large mountains, pleasant **haunts**[9] of the goddess

Nymphs[10] who **dwell**[11] up along the woody mountains,　　130

and he produced the **unplowed**[12] open waters raging

with **swell**[13], Pontos, without philotês. But then bedded

by Ouranos, she produced **deep-eddying**[14] Okeanos and

and Koios and Kreios and Hyperion and Iapetos and

Thea and Rheia and Themis and Mnemosyne and　　135

golden-garlanded Phoebe and lovely Tethys.

And after them born last Kronos of the **crooked**[15] **scheme**[16],

most fearful of children, and he hated his **lusty**[17] father.

She further bore the Kyklopes with **exceeding**[18] forceful hearts,

Brontes and Steropes and Arges mighty of spirit,　　140

who gave to Zeus the thunder sound and **fashioned**[19] the **thunderbolt**[20].

They were like the gods in all respects except

the single eye that lay in the middle of their foreheads.

They are named Kyklopes from this feature,

1. ['keɪɒs] n. 混沌

2. [rɪ'ses] n. 隐蔽处

3. [lɪm] n. 四肢

4. [səb'djuː] vt. 制服

5. ['pruːdnt] adj. 精明的;稳健的

6. [kən'siːv] vt. 孕育;

7. ['stɑːrɪ] adj. 星光闪耀的;繁星点点的

8. [veɪl] n. 面纱

9. [hɔːnt] n. 常去之地

10. [nɪmf] n. 小神仙

11. [dwel] vt. 居住

12. [ʌn'plɒʊd] adj. 不能耕种的

13. [swel] v. 膨胀起来;爱欲

14. ['edɪɪŋ] n. 涡流

15. ['krʊkɪd] n. 狡猾

16. [skiːm] n. 计划

17. ['lʌstɪ] adj. 性欲旺盛的

18. [ɪk'siːdɪŋ] adj. 特别的

19. ['fæʃn] v. 制作

20. ['θʌndəbɒʊlt] n. 雷电

21. ['sɜːkjələ(r)] adj. 圆形的

because one **circular**[21] eye lay in the forehead of each.   145
Strong is their brute force，and designs are upon their deeds.

Others were born from Gaia and Ouranos，
three great and mighty children **not to be named**[1]，   1. (强大得)无法形容的
Kottos and Briareos and Gyges, exceedingly **arrogant**[2] children.   2. ['ærəgənt] *adj.* 傲慢的
A hundred arms shot forth from their shoulders，   150
not to be **molded**[3] into an image，and on each fifty   3. [məʊld] *v.* 塑造
heads grew upon the fifty shoulders on **sturdy**[4] **limbs**[5].   4. ['stɜːdi] *adj.* 强壮的
Strong, immense, powerful in their shape.   5. [lɪm] *n.* 四肢

✳ ✳ ✳   ✳ ✳ ✳   ✳ ✳ ✳   ✳ ✳ ✳   ✳ ✳ ✳   ✳ ✳ ✳   ✳ ✳ ✳   ✳ ✳ ✳

❀**Questions for discussion：**

（8）According to Hesiod，who came first in the Universe? What is its meaning?

（9）Did Hesiod say Gaia is given birth by Chaos?

（10）What are the epithets used to describe mother earth?

（11）Why is the birth of Eros very important for the coming into being of the Universe?

（12）Uranus mated with Gaia who then gave birth to twelve wonderful children. Who are these wonderful children? What is the name of the youngest child? Uranus uses one common name for these twelve children. Refer to line 208，what is that name? It seemed that people in England made a mistake for naming that huge ship as "Titanic"，why?

（13）What are special with the Kyklopes，the three children of Gaia and Uranus? Are they wonderful engineers?

（14）What are very remarkable with the other three children，Kottos，Briareos，and Gyges? Can you use your pens and pencils to give a sketch of these three wonderful children of Gaia and Uranus?

✳ ✳ ✳   ✳ ✳ ✳   ✳ ✳ ✳   ✳ ✳ ✳   ✳ ✳ ✳   ✳ ✳ ✳   ✳ ✳ ✳   ✳ ✳ ✳

So many were born of Gaia and Ouranos，   154
most dreadful of children，and they hated their father
from the beginning. As soon as one of them was born，
Ouranos would **conceal**[6] them all in hiding place in Gaia and   6. [kən'siːl] *vt.* 隐藏
did not sent them back into the light，and he **delighted**[7] in his   7. [dɪ'laɪt] *vt.* 以…为乐
evil deed. **Monstrous**[8] Gaia was **groaning**[9] within，   8. ['mɒnstrəs] *adj.* 巨大的
congested[10]. She **conceived**[11] a cunning, evil trick.   160   9. [grəʊn] *vi.* 痛苦呻吟
Quickly she made the element of grey **adamant**[12] and   10. [kən'dʒest] *vt.* 堵塞
fashioned a great **sickle**[13] and showed it to her children. Then   11. [kən'siːv] *vt.* 构想
she spoke，encouraging them，though sorrowing in her heart.   12. ['ædəmənt] *n.* 坚硬的物质

"My children with a **reckless**[14] father, if only you agree
to obey me. We would **avenge**[15] the evil **outrage**[16] of this   165
father of yours, for he first devised **unseemly**[1] deeds."

Thus she spoke, and **binding**[2] fear grabbed them all, and none
of them spoke. Then great Kronos of crooked counsel,
embolden[3], quickly addressed his dear mother with words:
"Mother, I promise that I will bring to completion,   170
this deed, since I do not care for that ill-named father
of ours. For he first **devised**[4] unseemly deeds."

Thus he spoke, and **monstrous**[5] Gaia laughed loudly in her heart.
She hid him in an **ambush**[6] and placed in his hands
a sickle, and **apprised**[7] him **of** her whole cunning.   175
Great Ouranos came, bringing the night,
and spread out around Gaia, **desiring philotês**[8],
and was extended. His son reached out from ambush
with his left hand, and in his right he held the sickle,
long and **serrated**[9] and the **genitals**[10] of his father   180
he quickly **reaped**[11] and threw them behind his back
to be carried away. But they did not flee from his hand fruitlessly.
As many drops of blood spurted forth,
all of them Gaia received. In the **revolving**[12] years,
she bore the powerful **Erinyes**[13], and great Giants,   185
gleaming in their **armor**[14], holding long **spears**[15] in their hands,
and the **nymphs**[16] whom they call the Ash Tree Nymphs across
endless Gaia. As soon as Kronos **lopped off**[17] the genitals with
the sickle, they fell from the mainland into the **much-surging**[18]
sea, so that the sea carried them for a long time. Around them
a white **foam**[19] from the immortal skin began to arise.   190
In it, a **maiden**[20] was **nurtured**[21]. First, she drew near holy Kythera,
and from there she arrived at Kypros surrounded by water.
From within, a **majestic**[22] and beautiful goddess stepped, and
all around grass grew beneath her **slender**[23] feet. Aphrodite 195
[foam-born goddess and fair-wreathed Kythereia]
gods and men call her because she was nurtured in **foam**[24].
But they call her Kythereia because she happened upon Kythera,
and Kyprogenes because she was born in much-surging Kypros,
and Philommeides because she appeared out of genitals.   200
Eros was her constant companion, and beautiful Desire

13. ['sɪkl] n. 镰刀
14. ['rekləs] adj. 莽撞的
15. [ə'vendʒ] vt. 报仇
16. ['aʊtreɪdʒ] n. 暴行
1. [ʌn'siːmli] adj. 不得体的
2. ['baɪndɪŋ] vt. 捆绑
3. [ɪm'bəʊldən] adj. 有胆量的
4. [dɪ'vaɪz] vt. 设计
5. ['mɑːnstrəs] adj. 巨大的
6. ['æmbʊʃ] n. 埋伏
7. [ə'praɪz] vt. 告知
8. 渴望爱欲
9. [sə'reɪtɪd] adj. 锯齿状的;
10. ['dʒenɪtlz] n. 生殖器;
11. [riːp] vt. 收割
12. [rɪ'vɒlv] v. 循环
13. 复仇女神
14. ['ɑːmə] n. 盔甲
15. [spɪə] n. 长矛
16. [nɪmf] n. 仙女
17. [lɒp] vi. 砍伐
18. 波涛汹涌的
19. [fəʊm] n. 泡沫
20. ['meɪdn] n. 少女
21. ['nɜːtʃə(r)] vt. 养育
22. [mə'dʒəstɪk] adj. 庄重的
23. ['slendə(r)] adj. 苗条的
24. [fəʊm] n. 泡沫

followed her when she was being born and when she was entering

the **throng**[1] of the gods. From the beginning she **held sway**[2] 205

and obtained this province among men and immortal gods:

a young girl's whispers and smiles and **deceits**[3] and

sweet delight and philotês and **graciousness**[4].

1. [θrɒŋ] *n*. 群

2. 支配

3. [dɪˈsiːt] *n*. 欺骗

4. [ˈɡreɪʃəsnɪs] *n*. 优雅

Kronos with sickle

Father great Ouranos, quarreling with the children he sired

himself, gave them the name Titans, **Stretchers**[5]. He said that

they stretched with a great **recklessness**[6] to accomplish a huge

deed, and for it **retribution**[7] shall be laid up for the future. 210

5. [ˈstretʃə] *n*. 紧张者

6. [ˈrekləsnəs] *n*. 莽撞

7. [ˌretrɪˈbjuːʃn] *n*. 报应

﹡﹡﹡   ﹡﹡﹡   ﹡﹡﹡   ﹡﹡﹡   ﹡﹡﹡   ﹡﹡﹡   ﹡﹡﹡   ﹡﹡﹡

❋**Questions for discussion:**

(15) The name of Kronos is linked to time, and Kronos is the god of time. In English there are some words linked to the name of Kronos (time), for example, chronology. Can you find other English words related to Kronos?

(16) What is the weapon used by Kronos to castrate his father? What is it like? Is it materially possible at that time?

(17) What is the symbolic implication for Kronos to overthrow his father and replace him? Is it just or outrage for him to do so? First come up with a working definition of justice, and then present your analyses and comments.

(18) Tell the birth story of Aphrodite, goddess of love, in your own words. What is special with her? In Chinese culture, we use the term "窈窕" to praise a beautiful woman. Do you find differences from the Greeks by looking at the image of Aphrodite?

﹡﹡﹡   ﹡﹡﹡   ﹡﹡﹡   ﹡﹡﹡   ﹡﹡﹡   ﹡﹡﹡   ﹡﹡﹡   ﹡﹡﹡

Night bore hateful Death Appointed and black Doom

and Death，and she bore Sleep and the **tribe**[8] of Dreams.
Then dark Night bore Blame and painful Woe，
not lying with any of the gods，and
the Hesperides who live beyond **renowned**[1] Okeanos and   215
care for the beautiful golden apples and the trees bearing fruit.
She gave birth to the Appointers of Death and Goddesses of
Doom who punish **relentlessly**[2]. She also bore Klotho，
Spinner of Life's Thread，and Lachesis，**Dispenser**[3] of Lots，
Atropos，Unturnable One，who give to mortals
as they are born what is good and bad to have，
who **pursue**[4] the **transgressions**[5] of men and gods，   220
and the goddess never cease from their dreadful **wrath**[6]
until whoever **transgresses**[7] pays someone back evil punishment.
Destructive Night also bore Retribution，a **bane**[8] for mortal
men. Then she bore Deceit and Passion and
destructive[9] Old Age and mighty-hearted Strife.   225

But hateful Strife bore painful Toil and
Forgetfulness and Famine and tearful Sorrows and
Discord and Battles and Murders and Homicides and
Dissension and Lies and Arguments and Disputes and
Quarrels and Ruin，**bosom**[10] companions these two，and   230
Oath who causes pain the most for men on earth
whenever some one of them willingly swears falsely.

＊＊＊   ＊＊＊   ＊＊＊   ＊＊＊   ＊＊＊   ＊＊＊   ＊＊＊   ＊＊＊

✤Questions for discussion：

（19）Draw the family tree of Night.

（20）What do the gods of fate look like?

＊＊＊   ＊＊＊   ＊＊＊   ＊＊＊   ＊＊＊   ＊＊＊   ＊＊＊   ＊＊＊

Pontos sired **straightforward**[11] and truthful Nereus，   233
eldest of his children. But they call him Old Man
because he is **unerring**[12] and gentle and does not forget   235
what is right but knows just and gentle **counsels**[13].
Then，Pontos mingled with Gaia and sired great Thaumas and
excessively **manly**[14] Phorkys and Keto of the beautiful
cheeks and Eurybia，having a spirit of iron in her breast.

Numberless children who were goddesses were born   240

8. [traɪb] *n*. 部族

1. [rɪˈnaʊnd] *adj*. 有声望的

2. [rɪˈlentləsli] *adv*. 无情地
3. [dɪˈspensə(r)] *n*. 分配者

4. [pəˈsjuː] *vt*. 追赶；追捕
5. [trænsˈɡreʃn] *n*. 违反
6. [rɒθ] *n*. 愤怒
7. [trænzˈɡres] *v*. 违反
8. [beɪn] *n*. 祸根
9. [dɪˈstrʌktɪv] *adj*. 毁灭性的

10. [ˈbʊzəm] *n*. 胸怀

11. [ˌstreɪtˈfɔːwəd] *adj*. 坦率的

12. [ʌnˈɜːrɪŋ] *adj*. 一贯正确的
13. [ˈkaʊnsl] *n*. 建议

14. [ˈmænli] *adj*. 有男人气概的

to Nereus and fair-haired Doris in the **unplowed**[15] sea,
Doris the daughter of Okeanos, the **encircling**[1] river:
Protho and Eukrate and Sao and Amphitrite and
Eudore and Thetis and Galene and Glauke and
Kymothoe and Speio and Thoe and lovely Halia and   245
Pasithea and Erato and Eunike of the rosy arms and
graceful[2] Melite and Eulimene and Agave and
Doto and Proto and Pherousa and Dynamene and
Nesaia and Aktaia and Protomedeia,
Doris and Panope and beautiful Galateia and   250
lovely Hippothoe and Hipponoe of the rosy arms and
Kymodoke, who, with Kymatolege and Amphitrite
of the fair ankles, calms the waves on the **murkey**[3] sea
and the **blasts**[4] of stormy winds easily, and
Kymo and Eione and Halimede with a beautiful **crown**[5]   255
and Glaukonome who loves to laugh and Protoporeia and
Leiagora and Euagora and Laomeideia and
Poulynoe and Autonoe and Lysianassa and
Euarne lovely of **stature**[6] and **blameless**[7] shape and
Psamathe graceful of body and shining Menippe and   260
Nesso and Eupompoe and Themisto and Pronoe and
Nemertes who has he mind of her immortal father.
These were the daughters born of blameless
Nereus, fifty in all and knowing blameless works.

Thaumas took as his wife the daughter   265
of deep flowing Okeanos, Electra, and she bore him **swift**[8]
Iris and **the Harpies** with beautiful hair, Aello and Okypete,
who follow the blasts of the winds and birds
on swift wings. They fly high up in the air.

To Porkys Keto bore **fair-cheeked**[9] old women   270
gray haired from birth, whom the immortals call
the Old Women as do men who walk the earth, and
Pemphredo of the lovely dress and Enyo of the **saffron**[10] dress;
She bore too the Gorgons who dwell near renowned Okeanos
at the **borders**[11] of the night beside the clear-toned Hesperides, 275
Sthenno, Euryale and Medusa who suffered **grievously**[12].

15. [ˌʌnˈploud] adj. 不能耕的
1. [ɪnˈsɜːkl] vt. 包围，围绕

2. [ˈgreɪsfl] adj. 优雅的

3. [ˈmɜːki] adj. 阴暗的
4. [blɑːst] n. 阵阵
5. [kraʊn] n. 王冠

6. [ˈstætʃə(r)] n. 身材
7. [ˈbleɪmləs] adj. 无可指责的

8. [swɪft] adj. 敏捷的

9. 美颊的

10. [ˈsæfrən] adj. 橘黄色的

11. [ˈbɔːdə(r)] n. 边界
12. [ˈgriːvəsli] adv. 严重地
13. [ˈmɔːtl] adj. 会死的

She was **mortal**[13], while they were immortal and ageless,
the two. With the one, Medusa, **dark-maned**[1] Poseidon lay
in a soft **meadow**[2] and amid the spring flowers.
When Perseus cut her head from her neck,   280
mighty Chrysaor **leaped**[3] out and the horse Pegasos.
The latter had this name because he was born beside the Pagae,
while the other was born holding a golden sword in his hands.
Pegasos, flying upwards, left the earth mother of **flocks**[4],
reached the immortals. He lives in the halls of Zeus   285
and brings to Zeus the **counselor**[5] his thunder and flash.
Chrysaor bore three-headed Geryones,
having mingled with Kallioroe, daughter of renowned Okeanos.
The brutal force of Herakles **slew**[6] him
beside the rolling-**gaited**[7] cows at sea-girt Erytheia   290
on that day when he was driving his broad-headed **cattle**[8]
to **sacred**[9] Tiryns, having crossed Okeanos' stream.
He killed Orthos and the **cowherd**[10] Eurytion
in their murky **stable**[11] on the other side of renowned Okeanos.

Then Keto bore another **monstrous**[12] and unmanageable thing,   295
like neither to mortal men or immortal gods,
in a hollow cave, the **divine**[13] strong-hearted Echnida,
half glancing-eyed maiden with beautiful **cheeks**[14], and
half monstrous **serpent**[15], dreadful and huge,
swift eater of raw flesh, beneath the ways of holy Gaia.   300
There is her cave below a hollow rock
far from the immortal gods and mortal men, where
the gods have apportioned her renowned halls to dwell in.
Baneful Echnida **stands guard**[16] in Arima beneath the earth,
a maiden immortal and ageless all days.   305
With her they say Typhaon mingled in philotês,
a dreadful and lawless raper with the glancing-eyed maiden.
She **conceived**[17] and bore strong-hearted children.
First she gave birth to Orthos, Geryones' dog. Secondly,
she bore an unmanageable thing, not to be spoken   310
about, raw-eating Kerberos the **bronze**[18]-voiced, fifty-headed
dog of Hades, shameless and powerful,
Third, she gave birth to the Hydra who knew **baneful**[19] things,

1. 黑色鬃毛的
2. ['medəu] n. 草地
3. [li:p] v. 跳跃
4. [flɒk] n. 群集
5. ['kaʊnsələ] n. 顾问
6. [slu:] vt. 杀死
7. ['geɪtɪd] adj. 某种步态的
8. ['kætl] n. 牛
9. ['seɪkrɪd] adj. 神圣的
10. ['kaʊhɜːd] n. 牧牛者
11. ['steɪbl] n. 马厩
12. ['mɒnstrəs] adj. 巨大的
13. [dɪ'vaɪn] adj. 神圣的
14. [tʃiːk] n. 脸颊
15. ['sɜːpənt] n. 蛇
16. 站岗；放哨
17. [kən'siːv] vt. 怀孕
18. [brɒnz] adj. 青铜的
19. ['beɪnfl] adj. 有害的

the Hydra of Lerna, whom Hera of the white arms **nurtured**[1],

when she was **insatiably**[2] wrathful at the brutal force of　315

Herakles. The son of Zeus slew her with his **pitiless**[3] bronze,

Herakles, son of Amphitryon, along with Iolaos, dear to Ares,

in **accord**[4] with the plans of Athena, Driver of Booty.

Hydra bore Chimaira, who breathes fire not to be resisted,

a dreadful, great thing, swift of foot and powerful.　320

She has three heads. One is that of a fierce lion,

another of a goat, and the last of a mighty serpent snake.

[In front a lion, behind a serpent and, in the middle, a goat,

breathing out the dreadful power of gleaming fire.]

Her Pegasos and noble Bellerophon slew.　325

She bore Sphinx as a **destructive**[5] destruction for Cadmeians,

subdued[6] by Orthos, and the lion of Nemea,

whom Hera, renowned wife of Zeus, having nurtured,

set up in the fields of Nemea, a pain to men.

There he dwelled and destroyed the tribes of men,　330

holding sway over Nemean Tretos and Apesas.

But the **violence**[7] of the might of Heracles subdued him.

Keto mingled with Phorkys in philotês and gave birth

to her last, a dreadful serpent that in the depths of

gloomy[8] Gaia on the great ends guards all-golden apples.　335

This is the family of Keto and Phorkys.

Tethus to Okeanos bore the **whirling**[9] rivers,

Neilos and Alpheios and deep-whirling Eridanos and

Strymon and Maiandros and beautifully flowing Istros and

Phasis and Rhesos and Acheloios of the silver **whirls**[10] and　340

Nessos and Rhodios and Haliakmon and Heptaporos and

Grenikos and Aispepos and divine simoeis and

Peneios and Hermos and fair-flowing Kaikos and

great Sangarios and Ladon and Parthenios and

Euenos and Ardeskos and divine Skamandros.　345

She gave birth to a family of holy daughters who across

the Gaia, with lord Apollo and the rivers bring men

to adulthood, and they have this lot by Zeus's **dispensation**[11].

They are Peitho and Admete and Ianthe and Elektra and

1. ['nɜːtʃə(r)] vt. 培育
2. [ɪn'seɪʃəbli] adv. 贪得无厌地
3. ['pɪtɪləs] adj. 无情的
4. [ə'kɔːd] n. 一致
5. [dɪ'strʌktɪv] adj. 毁灭性的
6. [səb'djuː] vt. 征服
7. ['vaɪələns] n. 暴力
8. ['gluːmi] adj. 黑暗的
9. ['wɜːlɪŋ] adj. 涡流的
10. [wɜːl] vi. 旋转
11. [ˌdɪspen'seɪʃn] n. 分配

Doris and Prymno and godlike Ouranie and   350
Hippo and Klymene and Rhodeia and Kalliroe and
Zeuzo and Klutie and Iduia and Pasithoe and
Plexaure and Galaxaure and lovely Dione and
Melobosis and Thoe and **comely**[1] Polydore and

1. ['kʌmli] *adj.* 英俊的

Kerkeis with the lovely **stature**[2] and cow-eyed Plouto and   355
Perseis and Ianeira and Akaste and Xanthe and

2. ['stætʃə(r)] *n.* 身材

charming[3] Petraia and Menestho and Europe and
Metis and Eurynome and Telesto of the **saffron**[4] dress and

3. ['tʃɑːmɪŋ] *adj.* 迷人的
4. ['sæfrən] *adj.* 橘黄色的

Chryseis and Asie and desirable Kalypso and
Eudrore and Tyche and Amphiro and Okyroe and   360
Styx, who is the most **preeminent**[5] of all.

5. [prɪ'emɪnənt] *adj.* 卓越的

These were born of Okeanos and Tethyos,
their eldest daughters. Yet, there are many others,
for three thousand are the **slender**[6]-ankled Okeanids,

6. ['slendə(r)] *adj.* 柔弱的

who, spread wide, **haunt**[7] the Gaia and the waters' depths 365
everywhere alike, the **glorious**[8] children of goddesses.

7. [hɔːnt] *vt.* 时常出没于
8. ['glɔːrɪəs] *adj.* 辉煌的

Again there are as many other rivers **roaring**[9] loudly,

9. [rɔː(r)] *vi.* 咆哮

sons of Okeanos, whom Lady Tethys bore.
Their names a mortal man would be hard put to tell.
Each of them knows those who dwell nearby.   370
Theia bore mighty Helios and **gleaming**[10] selene

10. [gliːm] *v.* 闪烁

and Eos who shines for all those on Gaia and
for the immortal gods who hold wide Ouranos,
having been **subdued**[11] in Hyperion's philotês.

11. [səb'djuː] *vt.* 制服;征服

With Kreio, Eurybie mingled in philotês and bore   375
mighty Astraios and Pallas and Perses, that one
shining among goddesses. Perses **surpassed**[12] all in skills.

12. [sə'pɑːs] *vt.* 超过

Eos bore to Astraios the strong spirited winds and
the cleanser Zephyr and **swiftly**[13] speeding Boreas, and

13. [swɪftli] *adv.* 迅速地

Notos, a goddess bedded with a god in philotês.   380
After them, early born Eos brought forth the star
Eosphoros and the shining stars that crown Ouranos.

Styx, daughter of Okeanos, mingled with Pallas and
bore Zelos and slender-ankled Nike in the halls and
Kratos and Bia, **conspicuous**[14] children.   385

14. [kən'spɪkjʊəs] *adj.* 明显的

Their home is never far from Zeus，nor is there

any **abode**[1] or journey for which the god is not their guide，

but always beside deep **thundering**[2] Zeus they have their abode.

For so Styx，the **unwithering**[3] daughter of Okeanos，planned

on that day when the Olympian Lightener　　　　390

summoned all the immortal gods to **lofty**[4] Olympus and

said that whoever of the gods fought the **Titans**[5] on his side

would not be **deprived**[6] of their prerogatives，and each

would have the honor as before among the immortal gods.

Zeus said that he who was dishonored and without **privileges**[7]　395

under Kronos would gain honor and privileges，as is right.

Styx，the unwithering daughter of Okeanos，was first to go

to Olympus with her children through the **counsels**[8] of her father.

Zeus honored her and gave her countless gifts.

He made her the mighty **oath**[9] of the gods and　　　　400

for her children to dwell beside him for all days.

Thus he **accomplished**[10]，as he promised，through and

through，but he himself is very powerful and **lords**[11] over all.

Phoebe went to Koios' bed of much desire.

Then the goddess **conceived**[12] in philotês with a god and　　405

bore dark-robbed Leto，always **gracious**[13]，

gentle to men and immortal gods，

gracious from the beginning，most kindly within Olympus.

She bore Asterie，of whom it is good to speak，whom Perses

once led to his great house to be called his wife.　　　410

Asterie conceived and bore Hekate，whom above all

Zeus honored. He **granted**[14] her glorious gifts and

to have a portion of the Gaia and unplowed sea.

She has a **portion**[15] also of the starry Ournaos as her province.

She is especially honored among the immortals gods.　　415

For even now，when some one of men on earth，

sacrificing beautiful victims，**propitiates**[16] the gods

in the **customary**[17] way，he calls upon Hekate. Much honor

follows him easily whose prayers the goddess eagerly

accepts. She gives him **blessings**[18]，since it is in her power. 420

She has a share with all the immortals

who were born from Gaia and Ouranos and received honor.

1. [ə'bəʊd] *n*.住所

2. ['θʌndə(r)] *vi*.打雷

3. [ʌn'wɪðərɪŋ] *adj*.不凋谢的

4. ['lɒfti] *adj*.高耸的

5. ['taɪtn] *n*.巨人

6. [dɪ'praɪv] *vt*.剥夺

7. ['prɪvəlɪdʒ] *n*.特权

8. ['kaʊnsl] *n*.建议

9. [əʊθ] *n*.誓言

10. [ə'kʌmplɪʃ] *vt*.完成

11. [lɔːd] *vt*.统治

12. [kən'siːv] *vi*.孕育

13. ['greɪʃəs] *adj*.和蔼的

14. [grɑːnt] *vt*.授予

15. ['pɔːʃn] *n*.一部分

16. [prə'pɪʃieɪt] *vt*.使息怒

17. ['kʌstəməri] *adj*.照惯例的

18. ['blesɪŋs] *n*.赐福

Kronides never did her violence or took from her

what she had from the **distribution**[1] among the former Titans,

but she **retained**[2] all as the distribution was first done.　　425

Although only-begotten, the goddess did not receive

a lesser share of honor and privileges in the earth and

Ouranos and sea, but yet even more, since Zeus honors her.

She comes and greatly aids whatever man she prefers

and at trials sits beside **revered**[3] kings.　　430

In the marketplace, that man whom she prefers is **preeminent**[4]

among people. Whenever men arm for **man-slaying**[5]

war, then the goddess comes beside those whom

she prefers, eagerly granting victory and holding out glory.

Good is she at standing beside horsemen she prefers.　　435

Good again is she when men compete in the contest.

There the goddess comes beside and aids them.

He who has won by **brute**[6] force and power carries the

beautiful prize off lightly and joyfully and **confers**[7] honor

upon his parents. Upon those who work the rough grey　　440

sea and pray to Hekate and loud- **rumbling**[8] Earth Shaker,

easily does the glorious goddess confer a larger catch.

Lightly, too, if it is her wish, she takes away one appearing

before them. Noble is she in the **stables**[9] with Hermes to increase

the herds. Herds of cattle, broad **flocks**[10] of goats and　　445

wooly sheep, if it is her wish in her spirit, she enlarges from

small and **diminishes**[11] from many. Thus, even being the only

begotten[12] of her mother, she is honored with privileges among

all the immortals. Kronides made her Nurturer of Youths who

after her with their eyes saw the light of much-seeing Dawn.　　450

Thus from the beginning she was Nurturer of Youths, and

these are her provinces.　　453

1. [ˌdɪstrɪˈbjuːʃn] n. 分配
2. [rɪˈteɪn] vt. 保持
3. [rɪˈvɪəd] adj. 可敬的
4. [prɪˈemɪnənt] adj. 卓越的
5. 杀人的
6. [bruːt] adj. 残忍的
7. [kənˈfɜː(r)] vt. 授予
8. [ˈrʌmbl] vi. 隆隆作响
9. [ˈsteɪbl] n. 马厩
10. [flɒk] n. 兽群
11. [dɪˈmɪnɪʃ] v. 变小或减少
12. [bɪˈɡɒtn] v.〈文〉为…之父

＊＊＊　　＊＊＊　　＊＊＊　　＊＊＊　　＊＊＊　　＊＊＊　　＊＊＊　　＊＊＊

❀Questions for discussion:

(21) In this section (lines 233-453), many stories of the gods and goddesses were told. It takes time and effort to read through the lines. However, if you take the trouble to read them through, you will reap great benefits, both in English and in your understanding of *Theogony*. Please name a god or goddess narrated in this section you feel like most.

(22) Before reading this book, have you heard of the story of Medusa? Tell the story about her.

※※※　　※※※　　※※※　　※※※　　※※※　　※※※　　※※※　　※※※

Rheia, subdued by Kronos, bore **illustrious**[1] children, Hestia and Demeter and golden-sandaled Hera and **mighty**[2] Hades who dwells in houses **beneath**[3] the earth, having a pitiless heart, 455 and loud rumbling Earth Shaker, and Zeus of counsels, father of gods and men, beneath whose thunder the wide earth **quivers**[4].

Great Kronos kept swallowing them as each arrived at his mother's knees from her sacred **womb**[5], intending that no other one of the illustrious children of Ouranos hold the kingly province among the immortals for he learned from Gaia and starry Ouranos that it was fated for him to be **subdued**[6] by his son, although he himself was powerful, through the plans of great Zeus. Therefore, he kept no blind **vigilance**[7] but, 465 awaiting each, he would swallow his children. Rheia had pain not to be forgotten. But when she was about to bear Zeus, father of gods and men, she **beseeched**[8] her parents, Gaia and starry Ouranos, to **contrive**[9] a **scheme**[10] so that she might 470 give birth to her son in secret and make great Kronos of **crooked**[11] counsel pay her father's **avenging**[12] Fury and that of the children he swallowed. They listened to their daughter and obeyed, and informed her what was fated to happen for Kronos, king 475 and powerful hearted son. They sent Rheia to Lyktos, to the fat country of **Krete**[13], when she was about to give birth to the last of her children, great Zeus. **Monstrous**[14] Gaia received him in broad Krete to **nourish**[15] and foster. There she arrived, 480 carrying him through the swift black night, first to Lyktos.

Holding him in her arms, she hid him in a high cave, beneath the ways of divine Gaia, on **densely**[16] wooded Mount Aigiaon. She wrapped a stone in **swaddling**[17] clothes **entrusted**[18] it to 485 Ouranos' son and great lord, king of gods before, He took it and put in down into his **womb**[19], cruel one, and he did not realize it in his mind, so that in return for a stone, his son remained **unconquered and unconcerned**[20], who was going to subdue him by brute force and his hands and drive him 490 from his province and **lord**[21] among immortals. Rapidly the strength and the **limbs**[22] in their glory of the lord grew, and when the year in its cycle came around, deceived by Gaia's **sagacious**[23]

1. [ɪˈlʌstrɪəs] *adj.* 著名的
2. [ˈmaɪti] *adj.* 强大的
3. [bɪˈniːθ] *prep.* 在…下面
4. [ˈkwɪvə(r)] *v.* 颤抖;摇晃
5. [wuːm] *n.* 子宫
6. [səbˈdjuːd] *vt.* 征服
7. [ˈvɪdʒɪləns] *n.* 警觉
8. [bɪˈsiːtʃ] *vt.* 请求
9. [kənˈtraɪv] *vt.* 构想
10. [skiːm] *n.* 图谋
11. [ˈkrʊkɪd] *adj.* 狡猾的
12. [əˈvendʒɪŋ] *adj.* 报仇的
13. 克里特岛(希腊南部)
14. [ˈmɒnstrəs] *adj.* 巨大的
15. [ˈnʌrɪʃ] *vt.* 哺育
16. [densli] *adj.* 浓密的
17. [ˈswɒdl] *n.* 襁褓
18. [ɪnˈtrʌst] *vt.* 托付
19. [wuːm] *n.* 肚子里
20. 毫发无损的
21. [lɔːd] *n.* 主
22. [lɪm] *n.* 四肢
23. [səˈgeɪʃəs] *adj.* 精明的
24. 吐出了他的孩子

advice, Kronos of crooked counsel **sent up his offspring** again, 495

conquered by the schemes and brute force of his son.

He **vomited**[1] the stone first, swallowing it last.

And it Zeus fixed in the broad-wayed earth, in **hallowed**[2] Pytho beneath the vales of Parnassos, to be a sign hereafter, a wonder for mortal men.   500

He **loosened**[3] his father's brothers from destructive **bonds**[4], sons of Ouranos, whom their father bound in his **folly**[5]. They remembered gratitude for his **benefactions**[6] and gave him thunder and gleaming lightning and flash. Before, monstrous Gaia hid them.   505

Relying upon these, Zeus **lords**[7] over mortals and immortals.

1. ['vɒmɪt] *vt*. 吐
2. [hæləʊd] *adj*. 神圣的
3. ['luːsn] *vt*. 解放
4. [bɒnd] *n*. 捆绑
5. ['fɒli] *n*. 愚蠢
6. [ˌbenɪ'fækʃn] *n*. 慈善行为
7. [lɔːd] *vi*. 统治

Kronos devouring one of his children

❋ ❋ ❋   ❋ ❋ ❋   ❋ ❋ ❋   ❋ ❋ ❋   ❋ ❋ ❋   ❋ ❋ ❋   ❋ ❋ ❋   ❋ ❋ ❋

❋ Questions for discussion:

(23) Who are the children of Rheia and Kronos? Zeus is said to be their youngest and also the oldest child. How is it possible?

(24) What wrongs did Kronos do to his children? Why did he repeat his father's outrage when his children were born? How was he overthrown by his child Zeus?

(25) Tell the birth story of Zeus in your own words.

＊＊＊　　＊＊＊　　＊＊＊　　＊＊＊　　＊＊＊　　＊＊＊　　＊＊＊　　＊＊＊

Iapetos led the daughter of Okeanos，**beautiful-ankled**[1]
Klymene and went with her up to the same bed.
She gave birth to a son Atlas and produced
the exceedingly glorious Menoitios and Prometheus，510
changeful，slippery-counseled，and **erring**[2]-minded Epimetheus
who proved an evil for men who eat what the soil yields.
He was first to receive under his roof Zeus's **molded**[3] woman
virgin. Wide-seeing Zeus sent **insolent**[4] Menoitios down
into Erebos，striking him with **smoldering**[5] lightning，515
because of his rashness and **excessive**[6] manliness.
Atlas holds wide Heaven beneath powerful necessity，
standing on the boundaries of the Gaia before the clear-toned
Hesperides，on his head and weariless arms. This portion
counselor Zeus distributed to him. He **bound**[7] 520
the changeful-planning Prometheus with unbreakable **fetters**[8]，
painful bonds，and drove them through the middle of a **pillar**[9].
And he sent a long-winged **eagle**[10] upon him. Further，it ate
his deathless **liver**[11]，but there grew back all over during the night
as much as the bird of long wings had eaten during the whole 525
whole day. The stout son of Alkmene of the beautiful ankles，
Heracles，**slew**[12] it，and **warded off**[13] the evil sickness
for Iapetos' son and released him from troubles，
not against Olympian Zeus's will，who was **contriving**[14] on high
in order that the renown of Theban-born Heracles 530
might be more than before over the much-**nourishing**[15] earth.
So respecting him，he honored his **conspicuous**[16] son.
Although angry，he let off the **wrath**[17] he had before against
Prometheus because he rivaled the very mighty Zeus in designs.

For when gods and mortal men were making a settlement at 535
Mekone，at that time Prometheus divided with eager spirit a
great **ox** and set it before him，seeking to **beguile**[18] the mind of
Zeus. For him，Prometheus covered flesh and **innards**[19] rich in fat
with the ox's stomach and set them down wrapped in the **hide**[20].
For them，he covered the ox's white bones with shining fat 540
and，well arranging them for his cunning trick，set them down.

1. 美踝的

2. ［ɜː(r)］adj. 犯错

3. ［ˈməʊldɪd］adj. 铸造的
4. ［ˈɪnsələnt］adj. 侮慢的
5. ［ˈsməʊdərɪŋ］vi. 熏烧，慢燃
6. ［ɪkˈsesɪv］adj. 过度的

7. ［baʊnd］vt. 绑住
8. ［ˈfetə(r)］n. 枷锁
9. ［ˈpɪlə(r)］n. 柱，台柱
10. ［iːɡl］n. 老鹰
11. ［ˈlɪvə(r)］n. 肝脏

12. ［sluː］vt. 杀死
13. 阻挡
14. ［kənˈtraɪv］vt. 策划，设计

15. ［ˈnʌrɪʃ］vt. 滋养
16. ［kənˈspɪkjʊəs］adj. 惹人注意的

17. ［ræθ］n. 愤怒

18. ［bɪˈɡaɪl］vt. 欺骗；愚弄
19. ［ˈɪnədz］n. 内脏
20. ［haɪd］n. 皮

Then the father of men and gods **addressed**[1] him:
"Son of Iapetos, most **conspicuous**[2] of all lords,
dear sir, how **partially**[3] you divided the portions." Thus
spoke Zeus who knows imperishable counsels, **chiding**[4] him.　545

Again, Prometheus of crooked counsel addressed him,
smiling slightly, and he did not forget his **cunning trick**[5]:
"Very noble Zeus, greatest of the gods who are for always,
choose whichever of these the spirit in your breast **bids**[6] you."
He spoke, planning cunning. Zeus who knows **imperishable**[7]　550
counsels recognized and was not **ignorant**[8] of the cunning, but he
eyed evils with his mind for mortal men, that he intended to fulfil.
With both hands, he took the white fat, and grew
angry around his breast, and bitter **bile**[9] entered his mind
when he saw the ox's white bones in a cunning trick.　555
From then on, for the immortals the tribes of men on earth
burn white bones on fragrant **altars**[10].

Outraged[11], the cloud-gatherer Zeus addressed him:
"Son of Iapetos, knowing counsels above all others,
dear sir, you did not yet forget your trick."　560
Thus spoke Zeus who knows imperishable counsels, angered.
From this time, always **mindful of**[12] his wrath,
he would not give the strength of **weariless**[13] fire
to the ash trees for mortal men who dwell on earth.
But good son of Iapetos deceived him,　565
stealing the far-seen **beam**[14] of weariless fire
in a hollow **fennel stalk**[15]. It **stung**[16] anew Zeus
high thunderer in his spirit, and he **raged**[17] in his heart
when he saw among men the far-seen beam of fire. Straightway,
in return for[18] fire he fashioned an evil for men.　570
For the renowned Lame One **molded**[19] from Gaia a likeness
of majestic maiden through the plans of Zeus.
Goddess gray-eyed Athena **girded and dressed**[20] her in a
silvery white garment. Down from her head, she drew with
her hands a veil skillfully **wrought**[21], a wonder to **behold**[22].　575
[About her head Pallas Athena put fresh-budding garlands,
flowers of the **meadow**[23], desirable things, around her head.]

1. [ə'dres] vt. 对…说话
2. [kən'spɪkjuəs] adj. 明显的
3. ['pɑːʃəli] adv. 不平均
4. [tʃaɪd] vt. 斥责

5. 狡猾的伎俩

6. [bɪd] vt. 恳求；命令
7. [ɪm'perɪʃəbl] adj. 不灭的
8. ['ɪɡnərənt] adj. 无知的

9. [baɪl] n. 胆汁；坏脾气

10. ['ɔːltə(r)] n. 圣坛

11. ['aʊtreɪdʒəd] adj. 暴怒

12. 记住的；不忘的
13. [wɪrɪlɪs] adj. 不疲倦的

14. [biːm] n. 束
15. ['fenl] [stɔːk] n. 茴香杆
16. [stʌŋ] vt. 激怒
17. [reɪdʒ] vi. 暴怒
18. 为了回报
19. ['məʊldɪd] vt. 塑造；浇铸；用模子做
20. 打扮，穿衣

21. [rɔːt] vt. 编织
22. [bɪ'həʊld] vt. 看到，注视
23. ['medəʊ] n. 草地

About her, she put a golden band on her head
that the **renowned**[1] Lame One himself had made,
working it with his hands, while pleasing his father Zeus.　580
On it he had fashioned many skillful things, a wonder to behold,
beasts as many as land and sea nourish, dreadful things.
He put many of them on it, and grace breathed in all,
wondrous, very like to living animals with voices.
When he fashioned a good evil in return for something　　585
noble, he led her out to where the other gods and men were, her
adorned[2] in the garment the gray-eyed Daughter of a Mighty Father.
Wonder held immortal gods and mortal men,
when they saw a sheer cunning, unmanageable for men.
For from her is the **descent**[3] of female women　　590
[for the race and tribes of women are destructive,]
a great pain for mortals, living with men,
companions not of destructive Poverty but of Plenty.

As when, in **hives**[4] overhung from above, bees
feed **drones**[5], conspirators in evil deeds,　　595
all day until the setting sun,
they busy themselves and pack white **honeycombs**[6],
while the drones, staying within the sheltered nest,
scrape[7] into their stomachs the fruits of another's weariness,
thus women, **conspirators**[8] of grievous deeds,　　600
Zeus high thunderer **ordained**[9] to be an evil for mortal men.
He gave another evil in return for something noble.
Whoever, fleeing marriage and women's **mischievous**[10] deeds,
chooses not to marry comes to destructive old age
without someone to tend to his old age. He lives in want　　605
of nothing, but when he dies, distant relatives divide up
his property. For that man whose lot it is to marry
and have a trusty wife, one suited to his ways,
evil unceasingly rivals good from his prime.
Whoever gets a **baneful**[11] type lives with an unremitting　　610
sorrow on his spirit and heart, and it is an evil **incurable**[12].
Thus, there is no deceiving Zeus's mind nor getting by it.
For not even the son of Iapetos, akakêta Prometheus
escaped his heavy bile, but beneath necessity him,

1. [rɪˈnaʊnd] *adj.* 有名的

2. [əˈdɔːn] *adj.* 被修饰的

3. [dɪˈsent] *adj.* 血统

4. [haɪvz] *n.* 蜂巢

5. [drəʊn] *n.* 雄蜂

6. [ˈhʌnɪkəʊm] *n.* 蜂窝

7. [skreɪp] *v.* 刮破；挖空

8. [kənˈspɪrətə] *n.* 共谋者

9. [ɔːˈdeɪn] *vt.* 任命；判定

10. [ˈmɪstʃəvəs] *adj.* 淘气的；有害的

11. [beɪnfl] *adj.* 有害的

12. [ɪnˈkjʊərəbl] *adj.* 无法治愈的

although very clever, a great bond restrained.   615

* * *   * * *   * * *   * * *   * * *   * * *   * * *   * * *

❋Questions for discussion:

(26) Iapetos and Klymene gave birth to several children. Who are those children? Almost each child suffered from Zeus' punishments. What are the punishments by each child?

(27) What did Hesiod say about Prometheus and Epimetheus?

(28) Prometheus is said to be man's dear friend. What did he do to help man? Why fire was important for man? What punishments did man suffer from for his help?

(29) For what purpose was Pandora created? What was very special about her?

* * *   * * *   * * *   * * *   * * *   * * *   * * *   * * *

When first father Ouranos was angered in his spirit at
Obriareus and Kottos and Gyges, he **bound**[1] them in evil
chains, envying their **excessive**[2] manhood and shape and
size. He settled them beneath broad-wayed earth.
There dwelling beneath the earth in pain, they sat   620
at the farthest ends on the limits of great Gaia,
grieving[3] deeply and having great sorrow in their heart.

But Zeus and the other immortal gods whom
beautiful-haired Rheia bore in philotês with Kronos, in accord
with Gaia's advice, brought them into the light again.   625
She herself **recounted**[4] for them everything in clear fashion:
with them, they would win victory and **vault**[5] of renown.
For all too long they had been fighting with **toil**[6]
that pains the spirit against one another in **strong encounters**[7],
the Titans gods and those born of Kronos,   630
the **illustrious**[8] Titans from lofty Othryos and from Olympus
the gods, givers of good things, those whom
beautiful-haired Rheia bore after being bedded by Kronos.
They had battles against one another that bring pain to the
spirit, constantly battling for ten full years.   635
No loosening of harsh **strife**[9] was there or end for
either side, and the decision of war was pulled fast and **even**[10].

But when Zeus supplied them with what they needed, **nectar**[11]
and **ambrosia**[12], things gods themselves eat,
their manly spirit grew in the breasts of them all   640

1. [baʊnd] vt. 困绑住(bind)
2. [ɪkˈsesɪv] adj. 过度的
3. [griːv] vi. 悲痛
4. [rɪˈkaʊnt] vt. 详细讲述
5. [vɔːlt] n. 拱顶,穹窿
6. [tɔɪl] vi. 辛苦地工作
7. [ɪnˈkaʊntə] n. 遭遇战
8. [ɪˈlʌstrɪəs] adj. 卓越的
9. [straɪf] n. 争执
10. [ˈiːvn] adj. 平均的
11. [ˈnektə(r)] n. 花蜜
12. [æmˈbrəʊzɪə] n. 美味食品
(神的食物)

[after they **consumed**[1] nectar and lovely ambrosia.]
Then to them spoke the father of men and gods：
"Hear me，brilliant children of Gaia and Ouranos，
that I may say what the spirit in my breast **bids**[2] me.
Already now for too long against one another　　645
for victory and power we have been fighting all days，
the Titan gods and those of us born from Kronos.
You，**reveal**[3] your great brute force and untouchable
hands to the Titans，opposing them **in the dire fray**[4].
Remember kind philotês and what you suffered　　650
before you came into the light again from **bondage**[5]
from the **murky**[6] darkness in accord with our plans."

Thus Zeus spoke，and **blameless**[7] Kottos answered him：
"Strange one，you do not reveal what is unknown，but we　655
ourselves know that your mind is **superior**[8] and your purpose，
and you are the defender for the immortals against icy cold
harm，and by your advice from the **gloomy**[9] darkness
and **harsh**[10] chains we have come back again，
lord son of Kronos，having suffered the unexpected.　　660
Now with stubborn mind and ready spirit，
we will defend your power in dread battle-**strife**[11]，
fighting against the Titans in strong **encounters**[12]."
So spoke Kottos，and the gods，givers of good things，
heard and praised his words. Their spirit **craved**[13] war　　665
even more than before. They moved **wretched**[14] battle，
all of them，females and males，on that day，
Titan gods and those who were born from Kronos and those
whom Zeus from Erebos beneath the earth brought into light.
These were dreadful and strong，possessing excessive force.670
A hundred arms **shot forth**[15] from their shoulders，
for all of them alike，and each had fifty heads
grown out from their shoulders on **sturdy**[16] limbs.
Then，they settled themselves against the Titans **in the dire fray**[17]，
holding huge rocks in their sturdy hands.　　675

1.［kənˈsjuːm］vt.吃光

2.［bɪd］vt.命令

3.［rɪˈviːl］vt.展示出
4.激战一场

5.［ˈbɒndɪdʒ］n.奴役；束缚
6.［ˈmɜːki］adj.阴暗的，昏暗的

7.［ˈbleɪmləs］adj.无可指责的

8.［suːˈpɪərɪə(r)］adj.更高级

9.［ˈgluːmi］adj.黑暗的；悲观的
10.［hɑːʃ］adj.苛苦的

11.［straɪf］n.争斗
12.［ɪnˈkaʊntə(r)］n.遭遇战

13.［kreɪv］vt.渴望
14.［ˈretʃɪd］adj.悲惨的，不幸的

15.长出

16.［ˈstɜːdi］adj.强壮的
17.激战一场

From the other side，the Titans strengthened their ranks
eagerly，and both sides were revealing the works of forceful
hands，and the boundless sea **resounded**[1] dreadfully，and
the earth screamed loudly，and wide Ouranos **groaned**[2]，when
heaved[3]，and from the foundations lofty Olympus shook   680
beneath the **fury**[4] of the immortals. The heavy pounding
of their feet reached **murky**[5] Tartaros，as did the shrill screams
of the terrible pursuit and powerful missiles.
Thus they **hurled**[6] mournful **darts**[7] at one another.
The sound of both reached starry Ouranos   685
as they cried out. They clashed with a great war cry.
No longer did Zeus **restrain**[8] his might but straightaway
his heart filled with **might**[9]，and he showed all
his brute force. From Ouranos and Olympus together
he came **striding**[10]，flashing lightning constantly. His bolts   690
were flying in close **array**[11] with thunder and flash
from his sturdy hands，**whirling**[12] the flame
thickly. Life-bearing Gaia screamed as she burned，and
the immense forest **crackled**[13] loudly all round.
All the earth was boiling as well as the streams of Ouranos   695
and the unplowed sea. Hot blasts **encompassed**[14]
the **nether**[15] Titans，and immense flame reached
the shining aether. Although the Titans were **stalwart**[16]，
the gleaming light of the lightning and flash **deprived**[17]
them of their eyes. **Ineffable**[18] heat gripped Chaos.   700
It seemed to the eyes for the seeing and ears for the hearing
exactly as if Gaia and wide Ouranos from above
were drawing near one another. Such a loud **din**[19] would rise up
with Gaia being fallen upon and Ouranos falling from above.
Such was the din that sounded as the gods **clashed**[20] in **strife**[21].   705
The winds produced shaking and **whipped up**[22] dust，and
abetted[23] thunder and flashing and gleaming lightning，
shafts[24] of Great Zeus，and they carried swift uproar and clamor
into the midst of both sides. A terrible din arose from their
dreadful **wrath**[25]，and the work of power was revealed.   710

Battle **inclined**[26]. Before they had launched at one another
and battled constantly through strong **encounters**[27].

1. [rɪ'zaʊnd] *vi.* 回响
2. [grəʊn] *n.* 呻吟
3. [hi:v] *v.* 喘息
4. ['fjʊəri] *n.* 狂怒
5. ['mɜ:ki] *adj.* 黑暗的
6. [hɜ:l] *vt.* 投掷
7. [dɑ:t] *n.* 标枪
8. [rɪ'streɪn] *vt.* 抑制(力量)
9. [maɪt] *n.* 力量
10. [straɪd] *v.* 大踏步
11. [ə'reɪ] *n.* 队列
12. [wɜ:l] *vt.* 旋转着
13. ['krækl] *vi.* 爆裂
14. [ɪn'kʌmpəs] *vt.* 包围
15. ['neðə(r)] *adj.* 下面的
16. ['stɔ:lwət] *adj.* 强壮的
17. [dɪ'praɪv] *vt.* 剥夺
18. [ɪn'efəbl] *adj.* 不可言喻的
19. [dɪn] *n.* 喧闹声
20. [klæʃ] *v.* 冲突
21. [straɪf] *n.* 斗争
22. 激起、鞭打
23. [ə'bet] *vt.* 煽动
24. [ʃɑ:ft] *n.* 箭
25. [rɒθ] *n.* 愤怒
26. [ɪn'klaɪn] *vi.* 倾斜
27. [ɪn'kaʊntə] *n.* 遭遇战

Then among the foremost they aroused bitter battle，

Kottos and Briareos and Gyges，**insatiate of**[1] war.

Three hundred rocks from their sturdy hands

they were hurling，one on another，and they **cast shadows**[2]

over the Titans with **missiles**[3]. They sent them beneath

broad-wayed earth and **bound**[4] them in painful **bonds**[5]，

having conquered them by hands，though they were **bold**[6]，

as far beneath the earth as Ouranos is above Gaia

so far from earth to murky Tartaros.

1. [ɪnˈseɪʃɪeɪt] adj. 不知足的，贪得无厌的

2. 投射阴影

3. [ˈmɪsaɪl] n. 导弹；投射物

4. [baʊnd] vt. 捆绑

5. [bɒnd] n. 枷锁

6. [bəʊld] adj. 勇敢的；无畏的

✻ ✻ ✻   ✻ ✻ ✻   ✻ ✻ ✻   ✻ ✻ ✻   ✻ ✻ ✻   ✻ ✻ ✻   ✻ ✻ ✻   ✻ ✻ ✻

❇**Questions for discussion**：

（30）During the ten years' war against the Titans，Zeus and his brothers and sisters got the support and help from the three one-hundred handers. Why and how?

（31）In order to call on the one-hundred handers to fight bravely against the Titans，Zeus made a speech to them. Please read the speech very carefully and put each line into Chinese. Beautiful and powerful language，do you think so?

（32）Retell the story of the ten-full-year's war. Why do you think that Zeus could be victorious?

✻ ✻ ✻   ✻ ✻ ✻   ✻ ✻ ✻   ✻ ✻ ✻   ✻ ✻ ✻   ✻ ✻ ✻   ✻ ✻ ✻   ✻ ✻ ✻

For nine days and nights a bronze **anvil**[7]，that was

going down from Ouranos，would arrive at Gaia on the tenth.　　722

For nine days and nights a bronze anvil that was going

down from Gaia would arrive at Tartaros on the tenth.　　725

A bronze wall runs around Tartaros. Around its neck，

night in three rows is spread. From above

grow the roots of earth and the unplowed sea.

There the Titan gods beneath the murky darkness

have been hidden by the plans of **cloud-gathering**[8] Zeus，　　730

in that **squalid**[9] place，the ends of monstrous Gaia.

There is no exit for them，but Poseidon put on gates

of bronze，and a wall runs on around from both sides.

［There Gyges and Kottos and great-spirited Obriareos，

dwell，faithful guards of **aegis-bearing**[10] Zeus.　　735

There are **the sources and limits**[11] in order of dark night

and murky Tartaros and the unplowed sea and starry

Ouranos，painful and squalid places，that gods **shudder at**[12].

There is a great Chawos. In one entire year，one would　　740

not reach its floor，once he were within the gates，

7. [ˈænvɪl] n. 砧

8. 集云的

9. [ˈskwɒlɪd] adj. 污秽的

10. [ˈiːdʒɪs] n. 神盾持有者

11. 源头和尽头

12. [ˈʃʌdə(r)] vt. 颤抖

but **gust**[1] after racking **gust** would carry him

here and there，dreadful even for immortal gods.]

[This **portent**[2]：the dreadful dwelling of dark Night

is there，veiled in **tenebrous**[3] clouds.]　　　　　　745

Before the gates stands Iapetos' son and holds

on his head and **weariless**[4] arms broad Ouranos

without moving，where Night and Day，**drawing nigh**[5]，

address one another as they cross over the great **threshold**[6]

of bronze. One will go down inside，and the other outside　750

is going，and never does the house **enclose**[7] both within.

But always the one，being outside the houses，

traverses[8] Gaia，and the other，being inside the house，

waits the hour of her journey until it arrives.

The one has much-seeing light for those on earth.　　　　755

The other has Sleep in her hands，brother of Death，

the other being destructive Night，veiled in dark clouds.

There pitch-dark Night's children have houses，

Sleep and Death，dreadful gods. Never does

radiant[9] Helios look upon them with his rays　　　　　760

as he goes up into Ouranos or comes down from Ouranos.

Of them，the one goes and dwells in the earth and sea's

broad back quietly and graciously for men，

but the other's heart is of iron，and his heart is of pitiless

bronze in his chest. He holds any of men whom he first　　765

seizes. He is hated even by the immortal gods.

There the **echoing**[10] houses of the **nether**[11] god

[of stalwart Hades and very awful Persephone]

stand. A dreadful dog guards in front，

remorseless[12]，and he has an evil trick. Those entering　770

he **fawns**[13] upon with his tail and both ears，

but he does not allow them to go out again.

Waiting，he **devours**[14] whomever he catches going out the gates.

There dwells a goddess hated by the immortals，　　　　　775

dreadful **Styx**[15]，daughter of Okeanos of back-flowing streams，

his eldest. Apart from the gods，she dwells in renowned

halls **roofed**[16] over by large rocks. All around it is firmly

rooted by silver **pillars**[17] reaching to Ouranos.

1. [gʌst] n . 狂风

2. ['pɔːtent] n . 奇物；征兆

3. ['tenɪbrəs] adj . 黑暗，晦涩的

4. ['wɪərɪlɪs] adj . 不疲倦的

5. [naɪ] adv . 走近

6. ['θreʃhəʊld] n . 门槛

7. [ɪn'kləʊz] vt . 把…围起来

8. [trə'vɜːs] vt . 穿越

9. ['reɪdɪənt] adj . 闪耀的

10. ['ekəʊ] n . 回音

11. ['neðə] adj . 下界的

12. [rɪ'mɔːsləs] adj . 无情的

13. [fɔːn] vt . 摇尾乞怜

14. [dɪ'vaʊə(r)] vt . 吞吃

15. [stɪks] n . 冥河

16. [ruːf] vt . 给…盖顶

17. ['pɪlə(r)] n . 柱子

Seldom does the daughter of Thaumas，swift-footed Iris，　　780
messenger[1]，go there over the sea's broad back.
Whenever **strife**[2] and quarrels arise among the immortals
and if someone of those having halls on Olympus is lying，
Zeus sends Iris to bring the gods' great **oath**[3]
from afar in a golden jar—**the water of many names**[4]，　　785
cold water that drips down from a huge rock
on high. Far beneath the wide-wayed earth
from a **sacred**[5] river，it flows through the black night.
A branch of Okeanos, it is **allotted**[6] a tenth part of the water.
Nine parts，**coiling**[7] around earth and the sea's broad back　790
in silver whirlings fall into the **brine**[8]. But this one flows
forward from the rock，a great pain for gods.

Whoever pours it in **libation**[9] and swears a false oath，
some one of those who hold the **pinnacles**[10] of snowy Olympus，
lies breathless for a completed year.　　　　　　　795
Never does he go near **ambrosia and nectar**[11]
by way of food but lies breathless and speechless
on covered beds，and an evil magic sleep **envelops**[12] him.
But when he completes his great sickness at the end of a great year，
another and harsher labor after the other awaits him.　　800
For nine years he is **deprived of**[13] the gods who always are.
Never does he mingle with them in **council**[14] or in **feasts**[15] for
nine whole years. In the tenth，he mingles again in the
assembly place of the immortals who have halls on Olympus.
Such an oath did the immortal gods make Styx's　　805
unwithering[16] waters，primeval. It **gushes**[17] through a rugged place.

There are the sources and limits in order
of dark night and murky Tartaros
and the unplowed sea and starry Ouranos，
painful and squalid places，that the gods **shudder**[18] at.　810
There are shining gates and a floor of bronze，
fast with roots that reach far and are gripped in the ground，
grown by their own growing. Before them away from all gods
dwell[19] the Titans on the other side of pitch-dark Chawos.
Moreover，the renowned **allies**[20] of loud-thundering Zeus　815

1. ['mesɪndʒə(r)] n. 信使
2. [straɪf] n. 不和
3. [əʊθ] n. 誓言
4. 著名的水
5. ['seɪkrɪd] adj. 神圣的
6. [ə'lɒt] vt. 分配
7. ['kɔɪlɪŋ] vt. 环绕
8. [braɪn] n. 海水
9. [laɪ'beɪʃn] n. 奠酒
10. ['pɪnəkl] n. 顶峰
11. (古希腊)神的食物
12. [ɪn'veləp] vt. 笼罩
13. [dɪ'praɪv] vt. 剥夺
14. ['kaʊnsl] n. 开会
15. [fiːst] n. 聚餐
16. [ˌʌn'wɪðərɪŋ] adj. 不枯萎的
17. [gʌʃ] vi. 喷涌
18. ['ʃʌdə(r)] vt. 颤抖
19. [dwel] vi. 居住
20. ['ælaɪ] n. 同盟

dwell in halls at the bases of Okeanos,

Kottos and Gyges. Briareos, being good,

the heavy-sounding Earth Shaker made his son-in-law and

gave him Kymopoleia to marry, his daughter.   819

* * *   * * *   * * *   * * *   * * *   * * *   * * *   * * *

✤Questions for discussion:

(33) This section (lines 722-819) is very hard to read and follow. This is a great test of readers' patience and English proficiency. Do you make sense of the lines? What difficulties do have in reading the lines?

(34) Hesiod gave very detailed and vivid description of Tartaros, the underworld. What was it like? Compare Hesiod's underworld with the one in other mythologies like the one Chinese mythology.

(35) A dreadful dog guards in front of Tartaros. What is special with the dog?

(36) What punishments god will suffer from if he swears false oath?

* * *   * * *   * * *   * * *   * * *   * * *   * * *   * * *

When Zeus drove the Titans from Olympus,   820

monstrous Gaia bore her last child Typhoeus

in philotês with[1] Tartaros through golden Aphrodite.   1. 与…在爱欲之中

His hands were strong.

The feet of the powerful god were **weariless**[2]. From his shoulders   2. ['wɪərɪlɪs] adj. 不知疲倦的

were a hundred head of a dreadful serpent dragon,   825

licking[3] with dark tongues. The eyes   3. [lɪk] vt. 舔

on the monster's **ineffable**[4] heads flashed fire beneath their **brows**[5]   4. [ɪn'efəbl] adj. 不可言喻的

[From all the heads, as he looked, burned fire.]   5. [braʊz] n. 眉毛

Voices were in all his dreadful heads, **emitting**[6]   6. [ɪ'mɪt] vt. 发出

sounds of all sorts, **unutterable**[7] by gods.   830   7. [ʌn'ʌtərəbl] adj. 说不出的

Sometimes they spoke so gods could comprehend. Sometimes

they emitted the cry of a bull, **unchecked**[8] in might, proud of   8. [ˌʌn'tʃekt] adj. 未受抑制的

voice, sometimes the cry of a lion having a shameless spirit,

sometimes sounds like **puppies**[9], a wonder to hear,   9. ['pʌpi] n. 小狗

sometimes he hissed, and the lofty mountains **rumbled**[10].   835   10. ['rʌmbl] vi. 轰隆隆

A unmanageable deed would have been done that day, and

Typhoeos would have become lord for mortals and immortals,

had not the father of men and gods keenly attended.

He thundered harsh and strong, and all around, Gaia

resounded[11] awfully, and the wide Ouranos above and   840   11. [rɪ'zaʊnd] vi. 回响

the sea and streams of Okeanos and Gaia's Tartaros.

Beneath the god's immortal feet as he moved

was **quivering**[1] great Olympus. Gaia was groaning.

Heat from both of them **gripped**[2] the **violet**[3]-like sea,

heat from the thunder and flash and fire from the monster 845

and thunderbolts and winds and **scorching**[4] lightning.

All the earth boiled and Ouranos and the sea.

Huge waves **raged**[5] along the shores round and about,

at the fury of the immortals, and an endless quaking arose.

Hades, lording over the wasted dead men, 850

and the Titans under Tartaros who around Kronos,

trembled[6] with the endless **din**[7] and terrible battle-strife.

When Zeus lifted up his might and seized his weapons,

thunder, flash, and gleaming lightning,

he leaped up from Olympus and **smote**[8] them. 855

All about he set fire to the dread monster's divine heads.

But when he had **subdued**[9] him, **flogging**[10] him with blows,

Typhoeos collapsed, crippled, and **monstrous**[11] Gaia was groaning.

From the lightning-smote lord, a flame **shot forth**[12]

in the mountain **glens**[13] dark and **craggy**[14] 860

as he was struck. And monstrous Gaia was burning all over

with an ineffable blast and melted like **tin**[15] heated

beneath the skill of craftsmen in bellowed **crucibles**[16]

or iron, which is the strongest of all things,

being subdued in the mountain glens by **blazing**[17] fire, 865

melts in the shining earth beneath **Hephaestos**[18]' hands.

In this way, Gaia was melting from the flame of the **blazing**[19] fire.

And Zeus in terrible anger threw Typhoeus into wide Tartaros.

From Typhoeus comes the **moist**[20] might of the blowing winds,

apart from Notos and Boreas and the **cleanser**[21] Zephyr. 870

They are in **descent**[22] from gods, a great **boon**[23] to mortals.

The other winds blow fruitlessly over the sea,

who falling upon the murky sea,

a great **bane**[24] to mortals, **howl**[25] with evil gales.

They blow at varying times and scatter ships and 875

destroy sailors. There is no **remedy**[26] for this evil

for men who happen upon them across the sea.

Moreover, across the boundless, flowering Gaia,

they destroy the lovely works of earth-born men,

filling Gaia with dust and painful **uproar**[27]. 880

1. ['kwɪvə(r)] vt. 颤抖
2. [grɪp] vt. 抓牢
3. ['vaɪələt] n. 紫罗兰
4. [skɔːtʃ] v. 炙热
5. [reɪdʒ] vi. 愤怒
6. ['trembl] vi. 颤抖
7. [dɪn] n. 喧闹
8. [sməʊt] vt. 重击
9. [səb'djuː] vt. 征服
10. [flɒg] vt. 抽打
11. ['mɒnstəs] adj. 巨大的
12. 喷射而出
13. [glen] n. 峡谷
14. ['krægi] n. 陡峭的
15. [tɪn] n. 锡
16. ['kruːsɪbl] n. 坩锅
17. ['bleɪzɪŋ] adj. 炙烤
18. [hi'fiːstəs] n. 火神
19. ['bleɪzɪŋ] adj. 炙热的
20. [mɒɪst] adj. 潮湿的
21. ['klenzə˞] n. 清洁剂
22. [dɪ'sent] n. 血统
23. [buːn] n. 恩惠
24. [beɪn] n. 祸害
25. [haʊl] n. 嚎叫
26. ['remədi] n. 药方
27. ['ʌprɔː(r)] n. 喧嚣; 吵闹

＊＊＊　　＊＊＊　　＊＊＊　　＊＊＊　　＊＊＊　　＊＊＊　　＊＊＊　　＊＊＊

❀**Questions for discussion：**

（37）What did Typhoeus look like?

（38）In this section（lines 820—880），there are several sentences beginning with "sometimes".
Read these sentences very carefully and translate them into Chinese.

（39）Locate two English words in this section，"boon" and "bane". These two words
begin with the same English letter. But they are antonyms. Make up sentences using
these two words.

＊＊＊　　＊＊＊　　＊＊＊　　＊＊＊　　＊＊＊　　＊＊＊　　＊＊＊　　＊＊＊

But when the blessed gods completed their **toil**[1] and

made settlement of honors for the Titans by brute force，

they urged wide-seeing Olympian Zeus

in accord with[2] the advice of Gaia to be king and lord，

and he **apportioned**[3] **provinces**[4] to them well.　　　　　885

1. [tɒɪl] *n*. 劳作

2. 根据；听从

3. [ə'pɔːʃn] *vt*. 分配

4. ['prɒvɪns] *n*. 神职

Zeus，king of gods，made Metis his first wife，

most knowledgeable of gods and **immortal**[5] men.

But when she was about to bear Athena of **gleaming**[6] eyes，890

then by a **cunning**[7] he deceived her mind

with **coaxing**[8] words and put her down into his **womb**[9]，

in accord with the advice of Gaia and starry Ouranos.

Thus they told him in order that the kingly province no

other of the gods who are for always **might**[10] hold instead of Zeus.

For it was fated that from her would be born

thoughtful children. First，a **maiden**[11]，gleaming-eyed　　895

Tritogeneia who has might and keen plans equal to her father.

Then Metis was going to bear a son to be

king of gods and men，having a very forceful heart.

But Zeus sent her down into his womb before then

so that the goddess might advise him on good and evil.　　900

5. [ɪ'mɔːtl] *adj*. 不死的

6. [gliːm] *adj*. 闪闪发光的

7. ['kʌnɪŋ] *n*. 欺骗

8. [kəʊks] *v*. 欺骗

9. [wuːm] *n*. 肚子，子宫

10. [maɪt] *n*. 力量

11. ['meɪdn] *n*. 少女

＊＊＊　　＊＊＊　　＊＊＊　　＊＊＊　　＊＊＊　　＊＊＊　　＊＊＊　　＊＊＊

❀**Questions for discussion：**

（40）Who is Zeus's first wife? Hesiod said she was the most knowledgeable. But in the next line，
Hesiod said Zeus deceived her mind and put her down into his womb. How was it possible?

（41）Zeus is the only one who defies the fate and prophecy that "he will be replaced by
his greater son". How did Zeus succeeded in doing so and thus become the ruler
（CEO）of the Universe?

(42) Write a review in about 500 words of *Theogony*. Please entitle your writing as "My Reading of *Theogony*".

* * *   * * *   * * *   * * *   * * *   * * *   * * *   * * *

Genesis

Background Knowledge

Genesis is the first book of the Old Testament of the Bible. The word "genesis" means the origin or the beginning, and the book Genesis tells about the beginning of the world and the origin of human beings.

Both the world and the human beings are created by God. Then Human beings begin to reproduce, meanwhile exposing their sins, so God decides to wipe out human beings. Out of sympathy, he instructs the righteous Noah to save his family with an ark, who survives the flood sent by God.

As human beings prosper again, they begin to cooperate to build a great tower, named the Tower of Babel, yet God divides human beings with many languages and sets them apart with confusion, leaving them unable to finish the construction of the tower.

God promises Abraham that his descendants will be as numerous as stars, but the people will undergo much oppression and hardship, after which they will inherit the land from the river of Egypt to the river Euphrates. As the sign of the covenant with Abraham, circumcision of all males is instituted. When Abraham is later tested by God, he passes the test, and God again promises him numberless descendants.

One of the descendants, Joseph, Jacob's son, is sold into slavery in Egypt, but he prospers after much suffering hardship. Through his agency, the Jacob family descends into Egypt, and Joseph manages to be reunited with his father and brothers in Egypt. As he is dying, he urges his brothers to go out of Egypt and take his bones with them.

Genesis ends with Jacob, who has changed his name into Israel, ready for the coming of Moses, who later leads the Exodus of the Israelites out of Egypt and across the Red Sea.

Genesis
(Excerpted from *The Bible*)

The Origin of the World and of the Human Race

A: The Creation and the Fall

In the beginning God created heaven and earth.	1
Now the earth was a formless **void**[1]; there was darkness over	2
the deep, with a **divine**[2] wind sweeping over the waters.	3
God said, 'Let there be light,' and there was light.	4
God saw that light was good, and God divided light from	5

1. [vɒɪd] *n.* 空白
2. [dɪˈvaɪn] *adj.* 神的

darkness.

God called light 'day', and darkness he called 'night'.

Evening came and morning came: the first day.

God said, 'Let there be a **vault**¹ through the middle of the   6
waters to divide the waters in two.' And so it was.

God made the vault, and it divided the waters under the   7
vault from the waters above the vault.

God called the vault 'heaven'. Evening came and morning   8
came: the second day.

God said, 'Let the waters under heaven come together into   9
a single **mass**², and let dry land appear.' And so it was.

God called the dry land 'earth' and the mass of waters   10
'seas', and God saw that it was good.

God said, 'Let the earth produce **vegetation**³: seed-bearing   11
plants, and fruit trees on earth, bearing fruit with their seed
inside, each **corresponding to**⁴ its own species.' And so it was.

The earth produced vegetation: the various   12
kinds of **seed-bearing**⁵ plants and the fruit trees with seed
inside, each corresponding to its own species. God saw
that it was good.

Evening came and morning came: the third day.   13

God said, 'Let there be lights in the vault of heaven to   14
divide day from night, and let them **indicate**⁶
festivals, days and years. Let them be lights in the vault of
heaven to shine on the earth.' And so it was.   15

God made the two great lights: the greater light to **govern**⁷   16
the day, the smaller light to govern the night, and the stars.

God set them in the vault of heaven to shine on the earth,   17
to govern the day and the night and to divide light from   18
darkness. God saw that it was good.

Evening came and morning came: the fourth day.   19

God said, 'Let the waters be alive with a **swarm**⁸ of living   20

1. [vɔːlt] n. 拱顶

2. [mæs] n. 块,堆,团

3. [ˌvedʒəˈteɪʃn] n. 植物

4. [kɒrəˈspɒndɪŋ] vi. 与…一致

5. 长种子的

6. [ˈɪndɪkeɪt] vt. 表明,标示,指示

7. [ˈɡʌvn] vt. 支配;管理

8. [swɔːm] n. 一大群

creatures, and let birds wing their way above the earth across the vault of heaven.' And so it was.

God created great sea-**monsters**[1] and all the creatures that　21
glide[2] and **teem**[3] in the waters in their own species, and winged birds in their own species. God saw that it was good.

God blessed them, saying, 'Be fruitful,　22
multiply[4], and fill the waters of the seas; and let the birds multiply on land.'

Evening came and morning came: the fifth day.　23

God said, 'Let the earth produce every kind of living　24
creature in its own species: cattle, **creeping**[5] things and wild animals of all kinds.' And so it was.

God made wild animals in their own species, and cattle in　25
theirs, and every creature that **crawls**[6] along the earth in its own species. God saw that it was good.

God said, 'Let us make man in our own image, in the　26
likeness of ourselves, and let them be masters of the fish of the sea, the birds of heaven, the cattle, all the wild animals and all the creatures that creep along the ground.'

God created man in the image of himself, in the image of　27
God he created him, male and female he created them.

God blessed them, saying to them, 'Be fruitful, **multiply**[7],　28
fill the earth and **subdue**[8] it. Be masters of the fish of the sea, the birds of heaven and all the living creatures that move on earth.'

God also said, 'Look, to you I give all the seed-bearing　29
plants everywhere on the surface of the earth, and all the trees with **seed-bearing**[9] fruit; this will be your food.

And to all the wild animals, all the birds of heaven and all　30
the living creatures that creep along the ground, I give all the **foliage**[10] of the plants as their food.' And so it was.　31
God saw all he had made, and indeed it was very good.
Evening came and morning came: the sixth day.

Thus heaven and earth were completed with all their **array**[11].　32

1. ['mɒnstə] *n.* 怪物；庞然大物
2. [ɡlaɪd] *v.* 滑翔，滑动
3. [tiːm] *v.* 充满
4. ['mʌltɪplaɪ] *vi.* 繁殖
5. [kriːp] *adj.* 爬行的
6. [krɔːl] *vi.* 爬行
7. ['mʌltɪplaɪ] *vi.* 繁殖
8. [səb'djuː] *vt.* 征服
9. 长种子的
10. ['fəʊlɪdʒ] *n.* 叶子
11. [ə'reɪ] *n.* 队列

On the seventh day God had completed the work he had   33
been doing. He rested on the seventh day after all the work he had
been doing. God blessed the seventh day and made it holy，   34
because on that day he rested after all his work of creating.
Such was the story of heaven and earth as they were created.   35

Paradise，and the test of free will
At the time when Yahweh God made earth and heaven
there was as yet no wild bush on the earth nor had any wild 36
plant yet **sprung up**[1], for Yahweh God had not sent rain on the   1. 生根发芽
earth，nor was there any man to **till**[2] the soil.   2. [tɪl] *vt*. 耕种
Instead，water flowed out of the ground and watered all the   37
surface of the soil.
Yahweh God shaped man from the soil of the ground and blew   38
the breath of life into his **nostrils**[3], and man became a living being.   3. ['nɒstrəl] *n*. 鼻孔

Yahweh God planted a garden in Eden，which is in the   39
east，and there he put the man he had **fashioned**[4].   4. ['fæʃn] *vt*. 创作
From the soil，Yahweh God caused to grow every kind of   40
tree，**enticing**[5] to look at and good to eat，with the tree of life   5. [ɪn'taɪs] *vt*. 引诱
in the middle of the garden，and the tree of the knowledge of
good and evil.

A river flowed from Eden to **water**[6] the garden，and from   41   6. ['wɔːtə] *vt*. 浇灌
there it divided to make four streams.
The first is named the **Pishon**[7], and this winds all through   42   7. 比逊河
the land of **Havilah**[8] where there is gold.   8. 哈维拉
The gold of this country is pure；**bdellium**[9] and **cornelian**[10]   43   9. ['delɪəm] *n*. 宝石
stone are found there.   10. [kɔː'niːlɪən] *n*. 红玛瑙
The second river is named the Gihon，and this winds all   44
through the land of Cush.
The third river is named the Tigris，and this flows to the   45
east of Ashur. The fourth river is the Euphrates.

Yahweh God took the man and settled him in the garden   46
of Eden to **cultivate**[11] and take care of it.   11. ['kʌltɪveɪt] *vt*. 培育；耕种
Then Yahweh God gave the man this **command**[12], 'You are   47   12. [kə'mænd] *n*. 命令
free to eat of all the trees in the garden.

But of the tree of the knowledge of good and evil you are   48
not to eat; for, the day you eat of that, you are doomed to die.'

Yahweh God said, 'It is not right that the man should be   49
alone. I shall make him a helper.'

So from the soil Yahweh God **fashioned**[1] all the wild   50   1. ['fæʃən] *vt.* 创作
animals and all the birds of heaven. These he brought to the
man to see what he would call them; each one was to bear the
name the man would give it.

The man gave names to all the cattle, all the birds of   51
heaven and all the wild animals. But no helper suitable for the
man was found for him.

Then, Yahweh God made the man fall into a deep sleep.   52
And, while he was asleep, he took one of his **ribs**[2] and closed   2. [rɪb] *n.* 肋骨
the flesh up again forthwith.

Yahweh God **fashioned**[3] the rib he had taken from the man   53   3. ['fæʃn] *vt.* 制作
into a woman, and brought her to the man.   54
And the man said: This one at last is bone of my bones and
flesh of my flesh!
She is to be called Woman, because she was taken from Man.

This is why a man leaves his father and mother and   55
becomes **attached to**[4] his wife, and they become one flesh.   4. [ə'tætʃ] *v.* 联在一起

Now, both of them were **naked**[5], the man and his wife, but   56   5. ['neɪkɪd] *adj.* 赤裸的
they felt no shame before each other.

The Fall

Now, the snake was the most **subtle**[6] of all the wild animals   1   6. ['sʌtl] *adj.* 狡猾的
that Yahweh God had made. It asked the woman, 'Did God
really say you were not to eat from any of the trees in the garden?'
The woman answered the snake, 'We may eat the fruit of   2
the trees in the garden.
But of the fruit of the tree in the middle of the garden God   3
said, "You must not eat it, nor touch it, under pain of death."'

Then the snake said to the woman，'No! You will not die!　4
God knows in fact that the day you eat it your eyes will be　5
opened and you will be like gods，knowing good from evil.'
The woman saw that the tree was good to eat and pleasing　6
to the eye，and that it was **enticing**[1] for the wisdom that it could

1. [ɪn'taɪs] *vt*. 引诱

give. So she took some of its fruit and ate it. She also gave some
to her husband who was with her，and he ate it.
Then the eyes of both of them were opened and they　7
realised that they were naked. So they **sewed**[2] fig-leaves

2. [səʊ] *vt*. 缝纫

together to make themselves **loin**[3]-cloths.

3. [lɔɪn] *n*. 腰部

The man and his wife heard the sound of Yahweh God　8
walking in the garden in the cool of the day，and they hid from
Yahweh God among the trees of the garden.
But Yahweh God called to the man. 'Where are you?' he asked. 9
'I heard the sound of you in the garden,' he replied. 'I　10
was afraid because I was naked，so I hid.'
'Who told you that you were naked?' he asked. 'Have you　11
been eating from the tree I **forbade**[4] you to eat?'

4. [fə'bæd] *vt*. 禁止

The man replied，'It was the woman you put with me；she　12
gave me some fruit from the tree，and I ate it.'
Then Yahweh God said to the woman，'Why did you do　13
that?' The woman replied，'The snake **tempted**[5] me and I ate.'

5. [tempt] *vi*. 引诱

Then Yahweh God said to the snake，　14
'Because you have done this，**Accursed**[6] be you of all animals

6. [ə'kɜːsɪd] *adj*. 被诅咒的

wild and **tame**[7]! On your **belly**[8] you will go and on dust you will

7. [teɪm] *adj*. 驯服的

feed as long as you live.

8. ['beli] *n*. 肚子

I shall put **enmity**[9] between you and the woman，and between

9. ['enməti] *n*. 敌意

your **offspring**[10] and hers；it will **bruise**[11] your head and you will

10. ['ɒfsprɪŋ] *n*. 后代

strike its heel.'

11. [bruːz] *vt*. 使…挫伤

To the woman he said：　16

I shall give you **intense**[12] pain in childbearing，

12. [ɪn'tens] *adj*. 剧烈的

you will give birth to your children in pain.
Your **yearning**[13] will be for your husband，

13. ['jɜːnɪŋ] *n*. 渴望

and he will **dominate**[14] you.

14. ['dɒmɪneɪt] *v*. 主宰，支配

To the man he said, 'Because you listened to the voice of   17
your wife and ate from the tree of which I had forbidden you to
eat; Accursed be the soil because of you!
Painfully will you get your food from it as long as you live.
It will yield you **brambles** and thistles[1], as you eat the   18   1. ['bræmbl] *n.* 荆棘
produce of the land. By the sweat of your face will you earn
your food, until you return to the ground, as you were taken
from it.   19
For dust you are and to dust you shall return.'

The man named his wife 'Eve' because she was the mother 20
of all those who live. Yahweh God made **tunics**[2] of skins for the   2. ['tju:nɪk] *n.* 外衣;短上衣
man and his wife and clothed them. Then Yahweh God   21
said, 'Now that the man has become like one of us in   22
knowing good from evil, he must not be allowed to reach out
his hand and pick from the tree of life too, and eat and live for
ever!'
So Yahweh God **expelled**[3] him from the garden of Eden, to 23   3. [ɪk'spel] *vt.* 驱赶
till[4] the soil from which he had been taken.   4. [tɪl] *vt.* 耕种
He **banished**[5] the man, and in front of the garden of Eden   24   5. ['bænɪʃ] *vt.* 驱赶
he posted the great winged creatures and the **fiery**[6] flashing   6. ['faɪəri] *adj.* 炽热的;燃烧的
sword, to guard the way to the tree of life.

＊＊＊　　＊＊＊　　＊＊＊　　＊＊＊　　＊＊＊　　＊＊＊　　＊＊＊　　＊＊＊

❋Questions for discussion:

(1) Both Hesiod's *Theogony* and *Book of Genesis* tell stories about the beginning of the
world. Is there anything in common? What is the beginning of the world in Chinese
myths?

(2) In Hesiod's *Theogony*, which came to the world first, Night or Day? Is it the same in
Book of Genesis?

(3) On which day were the sun and the stars created by God? On which day were living
creatures created?

(4) On which day was man created? How was the man created? Please put sentences in
line 28 in section one into Chinese.

(5) Where is the Eden garden located? What grows there?

(6) For what reason was the woman created? How was she created?

(7) Why did God forbid the man and the woman to eat the fruit of the tress in the middle
of Eden garden? What happened when the man the woman ate the fruit?

(8) What punishments did God give to the snake, the woman, and the man respectively?

Read lines 14-20 very carefully, word by word, learn these words by heart, and then put them into Chinese.

(9) In Greek mythology, Pandora is the first woman in the world. In *Book of Genesis*, Eve, however, is the first woman. Compare these two women, what similarities and differences about them do you find?

* * *   * * *   * * *   * * *   * * *   * * *   * * *   * * *

Gain and Abel

The man had **intercourse**[1] **with** his wife Eve, and she   1   1. [ˈɪntəkɔːs] *n*. 交配
conceived and gave birth to Cain. 'I have **acquired**[2] a man   2. [əˈkwaɪə(r)] *vt*. 获得
with the help of Yahweh,' she said. She gave birth to
a second child, Abel, the brother of Cain.   2
Now Abel became a shepherd and kept flocks,
while Cain tilled the soil.
Time passed and Cain brought some of the produce of   3
the soil as an offering for Yahweh,
while Abel for his part brought the first-born of his   4
flock and some of their fat as well. Yahweh looked with
favour on Abel and his offering.
But he did not look with favour on Cain and his offering,   5
and Cain was very angry and **downcast**[3].   3. [ˈdaʊnkɑːst] *adj*. 气馁的
Yahweh asked Cain, 'Why are you angry and downcast?   6
If you are doing right, surely you ought to hold your head   7
high! But if you are not doing right, Sin is crouching
at the door hungry to get you. You can still master him.'
Cain said to his brother Abel, 'Let us go out'; and while   8
they were in the open country, Cain set on his brother
Abel and killed him.

Yahweh asked Cain, 'Where is your brother Abel?' 'I do   9
not know,' he replied. 'Am I my brother's **guardian**[4]?'   4. [ˈɡɑːdɪən] *n*. 监护人
'What have you done?' Yahweh asked. 'Listen! Your   10
brother's blood is crying out to me from the ground.
Now be cursed and banned from the ground that has   11
opened its mouth to receive your brother's blood at your hands.
When you till the ground it will no longer **yield**[5] up its   12   5. *vt*. 产出
strength to you. A restless wanderer you will be on earth.'
Cain then said to Yahweh, 'My punishment is greater   13

than I can bear.

Look, today you drive me from the surface of the earth.   14
I must hide from you, and be a restless wanderer on earth.
Why, whoever comes across me will kill me!'

'Very well, then,' Yahweh replied, 'whoever kills Cain   15
will suffer a sevenfold **vengeance**[1].' So Yahweh put a mark   1. ['vendʒəns] n. 报复
on Cain, so that no one coming across him would kill him.

Cain left Yahweh's presence and settled in the land of Nod, 16
east of Eden.

The descendants[2] of Cain   2. [dɪ'sendənt] n. 后代

Cain had intercourse with his wife, and she **conceived**[3] and   17   3. [kən'siːv] vi. 怀孕
gave birth to Enoch. He became the founder of a city and
gave the city the name of his son Enoch.

Enoch fathered Irad, and Irad fathered Mehujael; Mehujael 18
fathered Methushael, and Methushael fathered Lamech.

Lamech married two women: the name of the first was   19
Adah and the name of the second was Zillah.

Adah gave birth to Jabal: he was the ancestor of   20
tent-dwelling **herdsmen**[4].   4. ['hɜːdzmən] n. 牧人

His brother's name was Jubal: he was the ancestor of all   21
who play the **harp**[5] and the **pipe**[6].   5. [hɑːp] n. 竖琴

As for Zillah, she gave birth to Tubal-Cain: he was the   22   6. [paɪp] n. 管乐器
ancestor of all who work copper and iron. Tubal-Cain's
sister was Naamah.

Lamech said to his wives: Adah and Zillah, hear my voice, 23
wives of Lamech, listen to what I say:
I killed a man for wounding me,
a boy for striking me.

Sevenfold vengeance for Cain, but seventy-sevenfold   24
for Lamech.

Seth and his descendants

Adam had intercourse with his wife, and she gave birth to   25
a son whom she named Seth, 'because God has granted
me other offspring', she said, 'in place of Abel, since
Cain has killed him.'

A son was also born to Seth, and he named him Enosh. 26
This man was the first to **invoke**[1] the name Yahweh.

The patriarchs[2] before the flood

This is the roll of Adam's **descendants**[3]: On the day that 1
God created Adam he made him in the likeness of God.
Male and female he created them. He blessed them and 2
gave them the name Man, when they were created.

When Adam was a hundred and thirty years old he 3
fathered a son, in his likeness, after his image, and he
called him Seth.
Adam lived for eight hundred years after the birth of 4
Seth and he fathered sons and daughters.
In all, Adam lived for nine hundred and thirty years; 5
then he died.

When Seth was a hundred and five years old he 6
fathered Enosh.
After the birth of Enosh, Seth lived for eight hundred 7
and seven years, and he fathered sons and daughters.
In all, Seth lived for nine hundred and twelve years; 8
then he died.

When Enosh was ninety years old he fathered Kenan. 9

After the birth of Kenan, Enosh lived for eight hundred and
fifteen years and he fathered 10
sons and daughters.In all, Enosh lived for nine hundred and
five years; then 11
he died.

When Kenan was seventy years old he fathered Mahalalel. 12
After the birth of Mahalalel, Kenan lived 13
for eight hundred and forty years and he fathered
sons and daughters.
In all, Kenan lived for nine hundred and ten years; 14
then he died.

1. [ɪn'vəʊk] *vt.* 引起;求告;乞
灵于
2. ['peɪtrɪɑːk] *n.* 家长、元老
3. [dɪ'sendənt] *n.* 后代

When Mahalalel was sixty-five years old he   15
fathered Jared.

After the birth of Jared, Mahalalel lived   16
for eight hundred and thirty years and he fathered
sons and daughters.

In all, Mahalalel lived for eight hundred and   17
ninety-five years; then he died.

When Jared was a hundred and sixty-two years old   18
he fathered Enoch.

After the birth of Enoch, Jared lived for eight hundred   19
years and he fathered sons and daughters.

In all, Jared lived for nine hundred and sixty-two years;   20
then he died.

When Enoch was sixty-five years old he   21
fathered Methuselah.

Enoch walked with God. After the birth of   22
Methuselah, Enoch lived for three hundred years and
he fathered sons and daughters.

In all, Enoch lived for three hundred and sixty-five years.   23

Enoch walked with God, then was no more, because   24
God took him.

When Methuselah was a hundred and   25
eighty-seven years old he fathered Lamech.

After the birth of Lamech, Methuselah lived for seven   26
hundred and eighty-two years and he fathered sons and daughters.

In all, Methuselah lived for nine hundred and sixty-nine   27
years; then he died.

When Lamech was a hundred and eighty-two years old he   28
fathered a son. He gave him the name Noah because, he said,   29
'Here is one who will give us, in the midst of
our **toil**[1] and the labouring of our hands, a **consolation**[2] out
of the very soil that Yahweh cursed.'

1. [tɔɪl] *n.* 耕种、劳作
2. [ˌkɒnsəˈleɪʃn] *n.* 安慰

After the birth of Noah, Lamech lived for five hundred 30
and ninety-five years and fathered sons and daughters.

In all, Lamech lived for seven hundred and seventy-seven 31
years; then he died.

When Noah was five hundred years old he fathered 32
Shem, Ham and Japheth.

Sons of God and women

When people began being numerous on earth, 1
and daughters had been born to them,

the sons of God, looking at the women, saw how beautiful 2
they were and married as many of them as they chose.

Yahweh said, 'My spirit cannot be indefinitely responsible 3
for human beings, who are only flesh; let the time
allowed each be a hundred and twenty years.'

The Nephilim were on earth in those days (and even 4
afterwards) when the sons of God **resorted**[1] **to** the women,
and had children by them. These were the heroes of days
gone by, men of **renown**[2].

1. [rɪ'zɔːt] v. 诉诸于

2. [rɪ'naʊn] n. 名望,声望

B: The Flood

The corruption[3] of humanity

Yahweh saw that human **wickedness**[4] was great on earth and 5
that human hearts **contrived**[5] nothing but wicked schemes all
day long.

Yahweh regretted having made human beings on earth and 6
was **grieved**[6] at heart.

And Yahweh said, 'I shall rid the surface of the earth 7
of the human beings whom I created—human and
animal, the **creeping**[7] things and the birds of heaven—
for I regret having made them.'

But Noah won Yahweh's favour. 8

This is the story of Noah: 9
Noah was a good man, an **upright**[8] man among his
contemporaries[9], and he walked with God.

Noah fathered three sons, Shem, Ham and Japheth. 10

3. [kə'rʌpʃn] n. 腐败
4. ['wɪkɪdnəs] n. 邪恶
5. [kən'traɪv] vt. 构想

6. [griːvd] vi. 悲痛

7. [kriːp] vi. 爬行

8. ['ʌpraɪt] adj. 正直的
9. [kən'temprərɪz] n. 同时代
的人

God saw that the earth was corrupt and full of lawlessness.   11
God looked at the earth: it was corrupt, for corrupt were   12
the ways of all living things on earth.

Preparations for the flood

God said to Noah, 'I have decided that the end has   13
come for all living things, for the earth is full of
lawlessness because of human beings. So I am now
about to destroy them and the earth.
Make yourself an **ark**¹ out of **resinous**² wood.   14
Make it of reeds and **caulk**³ it with **pitch**⁴ inside and out.
This is how to make it: the length of the ark is   15
to be three hundred cubits, its breadth fifty cubits,
and its height thirty cubits. Make a roof to the ark, building it
up to a cubit higher.   16
Put the entrance in the side of the ark, which is to be
made with lower, second and third decks.

1. [ɑːk] *n*. 方舟
2. ['rezɪnəs] *adj*. 含树脂的
3. [kɔːk] *vt*. 填塞
4. [pɪtʃ] *n*. 树脂

For my part I am going to send the flood, the waters,   17
on earth, to destroy all living things having the breath
of life under heaven; everything on earth is to perish.
But with you I shall establish my **covenant**⁵ and you   18
will go aboard the ark, yourself, your sons, your wife,
and your sons' wives along with you.
From all living creatures, from all living things, you   19
must take two of each kind aboard the ark, to save
their lives with yours; they must be a male and a female.
Of every species of bird, of every kind of animal and of   20
every kind of creature that creeps along the ground,
two must go with you so that their lives may be saved.
For your part, provide yourself with eatables of all   21
kinds, and lay in a store of them, to serve as food for
yourself and them.'
Noah did this; exactly as God commanded him, he did.   22

5. ['kʌvənənt] *n*. 协议;誓约

Yahweh said to Noah, 'Go aboard the ark, you and   1
all your household, for you alone of your **contemporaries**⁶
do I see before me as an upright man.

6. [kən'temprəri] *n*. 同代人

Of every clean animal you must take seven pairs,　　2
a male and its female; of the unclean animals you
must take one pair, a male and its female
(and of the birds of heaven, seven pairs, a male and its　　3
female), to preserve their species throughout the earth.
For in seven days' time I shall make it rain on　　4
earth for forty days and forty nights, and I shall wipe
every creature I have made off the face of the earth.'
Noah did exactly as Yahweh commanded him.　　5
Noah was six hundred years old when the flood came,　　6
the waters over the earth.
Noah with his sons, his wife, and his sons' wives　　7
boarded the ark to escape the waters of the flood.
(Of the clean animals and the animals that are　　8
not clean, of the birds and all that creeps along
the ground,one pair boarded the ark with Noah,　　9
one male and one female, as God had commanded Noah.)
Seven days later the waters of the flood appeared on earth.　10

In the six hundredth year of Noah's life, in the second　　11
month, and on the seventeenth day of the month,
that very day all the springs of the great deep burst
through, and the **sluices**[1] of heaven opened.　　　　　　1.[slu:s] *n*. 水闸
And heavy rain fell on earth for forty days　　12
and forty nights.
That very day Noah and his sons Shem, Ham　　13
and Japheth boarded the ark, with Noah's wife and
the three wives of his sons, and with them every species of wild
animal, every　　14
species of cattle, every species of creeping things
that creep along the ground, every species of bird,
everything that flies, everything with wings.
One pair of all that was alive and had the breath of life　　15
boarded the ark with Noah, and those that went aboard were a
male and female　　16
of all that was alive, as God had commanded him.
Then Yahweh shut him in.

The flood

The flood lasted forty days on earth. The waters   17
swelled[1], lifting the ark until it floated off the ground.

The waters rose, swelling higher above the   18   1. [swel] *vi.* 膨胀;汹涌
ground, and the ark drifted[2] away over the waters.

The waters rose higher and higher above the ground   19   2. [drift] *vi.* 漂流
until all the highest mountains under the whole of
heaven were submerged.

The waters reached their peak fifteen cubits[3]   20
above the submerged[4] mountains.   3. ['kjuːbɪt] *n.* 腕尺

And all living things that stirred on earth perished[5];   21   4. [səb'mɜːdʒ] *vt.* 淹没,把…浸入
birds, cattle, wild animals, all the creatures swarming[6]   5. ['perɪʃ] *vi.* 消失
over the earth, and all human beings.   6. [swɔːm] *vi.* 挤满

Everything with the least breath of life in its nostrils,   22
everything on dry land, died.

Every living thing on the face of the earth was   23
wiped out, people, animals, creeping things and
birds; they were wiped off the earth and only Noah
was left, and those with him in the ark.

The waters maintained their level on earth for a   24
hundred and fifty days.

The flood subsides[7]

But God had Noah in mind, and all the wild animals and   1   7. [səb'saɪd] *vi.* 退潮
all the cattle that were with him in the ark. God sent a
wind across the earth and the waters began to subside.

The springs of the deep and the sluices of heaven were   2
stopped up and the heavy rain from heaven was held back.

Little by little, the waters ebbed from the earth. After a   3
hundred and fifty days the waters fell, and in

the seventh month, on the seventeenth day of the month,   4
the ark came to rest on the mountains of Ararat.

The waters gradually fell until the tenth month when, on   5
the first day of the tenth month, the mountain tops appeared.

At the end of forty days Noah opened the window he had   6
made in the ark and released a raven[8], which flew back
and forth as it waited for the waters to dry up on earth.   7   8. ['reɪvn] *n.* 乌鸦

He then released a **dove**[1] , to see whether the waters were   8

receding[2] from the surface of the earth.

But the dove, finding nowhere to **perch**[3] , returned to   9

him in the ark, for there was water over the whole

surface of the earth; putting out his hand he took hold

of it and brought it back into the ark with him.

After waiting seven more days, he again released the   10

dove from the ark.

In the evening, the dove came back to him and there in   11

its **beak**[4] was a freshly-picked olive leaf! So Noah realised

that the waters were **receding**[5] from the earth.

After waiting seven more days, he released the dove,   12

and now it returned to him no more.

It was in the six hundred and first year of Noah's life,   13

in the first month and on the first of the month,

that the waters began drying out on earth. Noah lifted

back the hatch of the ark and looked out. The surface

of the ground was dry!

In the second month, on the twenty-seventh day of the   14

month, the earth was dry.

They disembark[6]

Then God said to Noah, 'Come out of the ark, you,   15

your wife, your sons, and your sons' wives with you.   16

Bring out all the animals with you, all living things, the   17

birds, the cattle and all the creeping things that creep

along the ground, for them to swarm on earth, for them

to breed and multiply on earth.'

So Noah came out with his sons, his wife, and   18

his sons' wives. And all the wild animals, all the cattle,

all the birds and all the creeping things that creep   19

along the ground, came out of the ark,

one species after another.

Then Noah built an altar to Yahweh and, choosing   20

from all the clean animals and all the clean birds he

1. [dʌv] *n*. 鸽子

2. [rɪˈsiːd] *vi*. 后退，减弱

3. [pɜːtʃ] *vi*. 栖息

4. [biːk] *n*. 嘴

5. [rɪˈsiːd] *vi*. 退潮

6. [ˌdɪsɪmˈbɑːk] *vi*. 下船

presented burnt offerings on the altar.

Yahweh smelt the pleasing smell and said to himself,　　　　21
'Never again will I curse the earth because of human
beings, because their heart **contrives**[1] evil from their
infancy. Never again will I strike down every living
thing as I have done. As long as earth endures:　　　　22
seed-time and harvest, cold and heat, summer and winter, day
and night will never cease.'

1. [kən'traɪv] *vt*. 构想

The new world order

God blessed Noah and his sons and said to them,　　　　1
'Breed, multiply and fill the earth.
Be the terror and the dread of all the animals on　　　　2
land and all the birds of heaven, of everything
that moves on land and all the fish of the sea;
they are placed in your hands.
Every living thing that moves will be yours to eat,
no less than the foliage of the plants.　　　　3
I give you everything, with this exception: you must
not eat flesh with life, that is to say blood, in it.　　　　4
And I shall demand account of your life-blood, too. I shall　　　　5
demand it of every animal, and of man. Of man as regards his
fellow-man, I shall demand account for human life.

He who sheds the blood of man,　　　　6
by man shall his blood be shed,
for in the image of God was man created. Be fruitful then and
multiply,　　　　7
teem over the earth and subdue it!'

God spoke as follows to Noah and his sons,　　　　8
'I am now establishing my **covenant**[2] with you and with　　　　9
your descendants to come, and with every
living creature that was with you: birds,　　　　10
cattle and every wild animal with you; everything
that came out of the ark, every living thing on earth.
And I shall maintain my covenant with you: that never　　　　11
again shall all living things be destroyed by the waters

2. ['kʌvənənt] *n*. 协议

of a flood, nor shall there ever again be a flood to **devastate**[1] 　　1. ['devəsteɪt] *vt*. 毁灭
the earth.'

'And this', God said, 'is the sign of the covenant　　　12
which I now make between myself and you and
every living creature with you for all ages to come:
I now set my bow in the clouds and it will be the　　　13
sign of the covenant between me and the earth.
When I gather the clouds over the earth and the bow　　14
appears in the clouds, I shall recall the covenant
between myself and you and every living creature,　　　15
in a word all living things, and never again will
the waters become a flood to destroy all living things.
When the bow is in the clouds I shall see it and call to　　16

mind the eternal covenant between God and every
living creature on earth, that is, all living things.'

'That', God told Noah, 'is the sign of the covenant　　17
I have established between myself and all living things
on earth.'

C: From the Flood to Abraham
Noah and his sons

The sons of Noah who came out of the ark were Shem,　　18
Ham and Japheth-Ham being the father of Canaan.
These three were Noah's sons, and from these the whole　　19
earth was peopled.
Noah, a tiller of the soil, was the first to plant the vine.　　20
He drank some of the wine, and while he was drunk, he　　21
lay uncovered in his tent.
Ham, father of Canaan, saw his father naked and　　22
told his two brothers outside.
Shem and Japheth took a cloak and they both put it over　　23
their shoulders, and walking backwards, covered their
father's nakedness; they kept their faces turned away,
and they did not look at their father naked.
When Noah awoke from his **stupor**[2] he learned what his　　24　　2. ['stjuːpə(r)] *n*. 昏迷,恍惚

youngest son had done to him,

and said: Accursed be Canaan,   25

he shall be his brothers' meanest slave.

He added: Blessed be Yahweh, God of Shem,   26

let Canaan be his slave!

May God make space for Japheth,   27

may he live in the tents of Shem,

and let Canaan be his slave!

After the flood Noah lived three hundred and fifty years.   28

In all, Noah's life lasted nine hundred and fifty years;   29

then he died.

The peopling of the earth

These are the descendants of Noah's sons, Shem,   1

Ham and Japheth, to whom sons were born after the flood:

Japheth's sons: Gomer, Magog, the Medes, Javan,   2

Tubal, Meshech, Tiras.

Gomer's sons: Ashkenaz, Riphath, Togarmah.   3

Javan's sons: Elishah, Tarshish, the Kittim, the Dananites.   4

From these came the **dispersal**[1] to the islands of the nations.   1. [dɪˈspɔːsl] *n.* 分散

These were Japheth's sons, in their respective countries,   5

each with its own language, by **clan**[2] and nation.   2. [klæn] *n.* 宗族

Ham's sons: Cush, Mizraim, Put, Canaan.   6

* * *   * * *   * * *   * * *   * * *   * * *   * * *   * * *

❉Questions for discussion:

(10) What has made God so angry that he decides to wipe out human beings with flood? What wickedness do you think human beings possess?

(11) Why does God select Noah to be the one spared from the flood? What qualities should an upright man have?

(12) What does Noah take into the ark? If you were Noah, what would you take?

(13) What is the content of the covenant that God establishes after the flood? What consequences do you think it would have?

* * *   * * *   * * *   * * *   * * *   * * *   * * *   * * *

The Iliad
By Homer

Background Knowledge

1. Homer

It was generally believed that Homer (Ancient Greek: οͧηρͦs [hómεːros], Hómēros) lived around 850 B.C., about 400 years after the Trojan War narrated in his two great epic poetries *The Iliad* and *The Odyssey*. With the collapse of the Mycenaean civilization (1600—1100 B.C.), the Greek world was in its Dark Ages. Population sharply declined and people had no books or schools. Then how could the old Greek culture continue its stories and legends? The oral transmission of the traditions of the past, then, played a significant role. Oral poets, like Homer, often wandered about from place to place. They chanted and recited stories skillfully in verse before an audience while playing their lyre, a stringed instrument. They seemed to have a store of traditional plots, characters, and themes that grew out of centuries of such oral performances.

As the composer of the two great epic poems, the *Iliad* and the *Odyssey*, *Homer* was revered as their greatest poet by Greeks. It was said that people like Socrates and Plato got their education by reciting the works of Homer. However, no reliable biographical information about Homer has been handed down. The island of Chios is said to be where he was born. Many scholars have also worked to derive meaning from the name of the poet, Homer. Homer is homophonous with "*hómēros*", meaning "hostage", long understood as "he who accompanies: he who is forced to follow", or, in some dialects, "blind". Thus, Homer is often depicted as a blind wandering bard, singing traditional tales.

Portrayal of Homer

In Plato's "Republic", Homer is portrayed as "first teacher" of the tragedians, "leader of Greek culture", and "teacher of [all] Greece". Mastery of the speaking art was considered valuable in Greece. This tradition may date back to Homer. For example, Achilles the greatest hero in *Iliad*, was depicted as "a speaker of words" and "a doer of deeds". *A* large portion of Homer's works is in speeches. These wonderful speeches provided models in persuasive speaking and writing for later generations.

2. The Iliad and The Odyssey

The term "epic" came to mean long narrative poems, which deal with such themes as gods, heroes, warfare, and adventures. It is generally written in one poetic meter. Good examples are the *Iliad*, and the *Odyssey*. They were written in dactylic hexameter. *The Iliad* (sometimes referred to as the Song of Ilion or Song of Ilium), a poem of nearly sixteen thousand lines, and the *Odyssey*, about twelve thousand lines long, are both set in the Age of Heroes and narrated about the legendary Trojan War. The tale of the Trojan War is a classically simple legendary story. Paris, the son of King Priam of Troy, seduced and brought

Achilles tending Patroclus

back to Troy the most beautiful woman Helen, the wife of Menelaus, ruler of the Spartans. To take revenge for such an insult, Menelaus and his brother, Agamemnon, king of Mycenae, gathered a huge army of Greek warriors. The sailed across the sea and reached Troy, ravaged the city after a ten-year siege, and then they dispersed, each contingent returning to their own homeland.

The *Iliad* covers, however, only a few weeks in the final year of the war. When the *Iliad* begins, the Trojan War had been going on for over nine years. The poem starts off with death of many Greek soldiers caused by a terrible plague sent by god Apollo. It then tells of the battles and events during the weeks of a quarrel between King Agamemnon and the warrior Achilles. The poetry ends with death with the Trojans holding the funeral rites to mark the death of their greatest warrior Hector. But reading through the whole poem, one will find that the *Iliad* mentions or alludes to many of the Greek legends about the siege of Troy; the earlier events, such as the gathering of warriors for the siege, the cause of the war, and related concerns tend to appear near the beginning. By focusing on only several days of the Trojan War, the poet Homer, however, achieved the transcendence of ethical, poetic beauty.

The Iliad is paired with something of a sequel, *the Odyssey*, also attributed to Homer. Along with *the Odyssey*, *the Iliad* is among the oldest extant works of Western literature, and its written version is usually dated to around the eighth century BC. Recent statistical modelling based on language evolution has found it to date to 760—710 BC. In the modern vulgate (the standard accepted version), the Iliad contains 15,693 lines; it is written in Homeric Greek, a literary amalgam of Ionic Greek and other dialects.

The Odyssey, generally regarded as a sequel to the *Iliad*, mainly centers on Greek hero Odysseus and his long journey home. The epic begins in the middle of the overall story, and prior events are described through storytelling. After the ten-year-long war in

Troy, it took Odysseus another ten years to reach home, Ithaca, his kingdom. In his absence, it was assumed he had died, and his wife Penelope and son Telemachus must deal with a group of unruly suitors, who tried to persuade Penelope that her husband was dead and that she should marry one of them. Telemachus, who was just born when Odysseus left home for Troy, was then grown up. He tried to assert control of the household and went out to search news of his father. Penelope managed to refuse the suitors, hoping her husband would eventually return to her.

Odysseus experienced quite a lot during the 10 years. In the end, he managed to return to his home. Plotting with his son Telemachus, he entered the palace disguised as a beggar, killed all the suitors and reunited with his wife.

Even if we do not know about the life of Homer, there can be no doubt about the far-reaching influences of his two epic poems. It is said that there was almost as much Homer as was everybody else combined. When the later authors speak of "the poet", usually they have only one poet in mind, that is Homer. Greeks used memorized large sections of Homer for their education and the poems remained for philosophical, ethical, religious and historical examples. Episodes from Homeric epics were among the most popular themes for art. The social structure of Homeric society illustrated certain values, certain habits of thoughts, and characteristics among the Greeks.

Iliad, Book VIII, lines 245—253, Greek manuscript, late 5th, early 6th centuries AD.

The Rage of Achilles

（Book 1 of *The Iliad* Translated by Robert Fagles）

Rage[1]—Goddess，sing the rage of Peleus' son Achilles，
murderous[2]，doomed，that cost the Achaeans countless losses，
hurling down to the House of Death so many **sturdy**[3] souls，
great fighters' souls，but made their bodies **carrion**[4]，
feasts[5] for the dogs and birds，and the will of Zeus was moving
toward its end.
Begin，Muse，when the two first broke and **clashed**[6]，
Agamemnon lord of men and **brilliant**[7] Achilles.

What god drove them to fight with such a **fury**?[8]
Apollo the son of Zeus and Leto. **Incensed**[9] at the king   10
he swept a fatal **plague**[10] through the army—men were dying
and all because Agamemnon **spurned**[11] Apollo's priest.
Yes，Chryses **approached**[12] the Achaeans' fast ships
to win his daughter back，bringing a priceless **ransom**[13]
and bearing high in hand，wound on a golden **staff**[14]，
the **wreaths**[15] of the god，the distant deadly **Archer**[16].
He begged the whole Achaean army but most of all
the two **supreme**[17] **commanders**[18]，Atreus' two sons，
"Agamemnon，Menelaus—**all Argives geared for war**！
May the gods who hold the halls of Olympus give you   20
Priam's city to **plunder**[19]，then safe passage home.

1. ［reɪdʒ］*n*. 愤怒
2. ［'mɜːdərəs］*adj*. 要命的
3. ［'stɜːdi］*adj*. 健壮的
4. ［'kærɪən］*n*. 腐肉
5. ［fiːst］*n*. 大餐
6. ［klæʃ］*vi*. 爆发冲突
7. ［'brɪlɪənt］*adj*. 杰出的
8. ［'fjʊəri］*n*. 狂怒；暴怒
9. ［'ɪnsens］*vt*. 使愤怒；激怒
10. ［pleɪg］*n*. 瘟疫
11. ［spɜːn］*vt*. 蔑视
12. ［ə'prəʊtʃ］*vt*. 走近
13. ［'rænsəm］*n*. 赎金
14. ［stɑːf］*n*. 权杖
15. ［riːθ］*n*. 花冠
16. ［'ɑːtʃə］*n*. 射手
17. ［suː'priːm］*adj*. 至高无上
18. ［kə'mɑːndə］*n*. 统帅；带胫甲的阿开亚人
19. ［'plʌndə(r)］*v*. 掠夺

Agamemnon and the old man

Just set my daughter free，my dear one... here，
accept these gifts，this ransom. Honor the god

who strikes from worlds away-the son of Zeus，Apollo！"

And all **ranks**[1] of Achaeans cried out their **assent**：
"Respect the priest，accept the shining ransom！"
But it brought no joy to the heart of Agamemnon.
The king dismissed the priest with a **brutal**[2] order
ringing[3] in his ears："Never again，old man，
let me catch sight of you by the **hollow**[4] ships   30
Not **loitering**[5] now，not **slinking back**[6] tomorrow.
The staff and the wreaths of god will never save you then.
The girl—I won't give up the girl. Long before that，
old age will **overtake**[7] her in my house，in Argos，
far from her fatherland，**slaving back and forth**[8]
at the **loom**[9]，forced to share my bed！

                                        Now go，
don't **tempt**[10] my wrath-and you may **depart**[11] alive."

The old man was terrified. He obeyed the order，
turning，**trailing away**[12] in silence down the shore
where the battle lines of breakers **crash and drag**[13].   40
And moving off to a safe distance，over and over
the old priest prayed to the son of **sleek**[14]-haired Leto，
lord Apollo，"Hear me，Apollo！ God of the **silver bow**[15]
who **strides**[16] the walls of Chryse and Cilla **sacrosanct**[17]—
lord in power of Tenedos—Smintheus，god of the plague！
If I ever roofed a **shrine**[18] to please your heart，
ever burned the long rich bones of bulls and goats
on your **holy altar**[19]，now，now bring my prayer to pass.
Pay the Danaans back-your arrows for my tears！"

His prayer went up and Phoebus Apollo heard him.   50
Down he **strode**[20] from Olympus' peaks，**storming**[21] at heart
with his bow and hooded **quivers**[22] lung across his shoulders.
The arrows **clanged**[23] at his back as the god quaked with rage，
the god himself on the march and down he came like night.
Over against the ships he dropped to a knee，let fly a **shaft**[24]
and a terrifying clash rang out from the great silver bow.

1. ［ræŋk］ *n*. 各级别；［ə'sent］ *n*. 同意

2. ['bruːtl] *adj*. 残暴的

3. [rɪŋɪŋ] *vi*. 铃铛般的响

4. ['hɒləʊ] *adj*. 空心的

5. ['lɔɪtə(r)] *vi*. 逗留

6. 偷偷地回来

7. [ˌəʊvə'teɪk] *vt*. 压倒

8. 劳作

9. [luːm] *n*. 织布机

10. [tempt] *vt*. 引诱

11. [dɪ'paːt] *vi*. 离开

12. [treɪl] *vi*. 拖沓而行

13. 碰撞和拖动

14. [sliːk] *adj*. 美发的

15. 银弓之神

16. [straɪd] *vt*. 跨过

17. ['sækrəʊsæŋkt] *adj*. 神圣的

18. [ʃraɪn] *n*. 神龛

19. 圣坛

20. [strəʊd] *v*. 大踏步

21. [stɔːm] *vi*. 风暴

22. ['kwɪvə(r)] *n*. 箭筒

23. [klæŋ] *v*. 铿锵作响

24. [ʃɑːft] *n*. 箭

First he went for the mules and circling dogs but then，

launching a **piercing**[1] shaft at the men themselves，

he cut them down in **droves**[2]—and the

corpse-fires[3] burned on，night and day，no end in sight.　　60

1．［piəs］*vt*. 穿透

2．［drəʊv］*n*. 成群

3．（焚烧尸体）的火

＊＊＊　　＊＊＊　　＊＊＊　　＊＊＊　　＊＊＊　　＊＊＊　　＊＊＊　　＊＊＊

❋Questions for discussion：

（1）What are the three beginning words of *The Iliad*？Is it in some way similar to the beginning of Hesiod's *Theogony*？Who does "Goddess" here refer to？

（2）Homer's beginning of *The Iliad* has won wide recognition and great admirations from literary critics. Rage is the subject matter of *The Iliad* and also the clue that helps glue together all the events narrated in the poetry. Many first-time readers，especially readers in China，are surprised when told that rage is the subject matter of the epic poem. How could such a literary masterpiece concern itself about the rage of one Greek war warrior？Search more information about it，and give your comments on it.

（3）The word "hubris" is originated from Ancient Greece. Look it up in the dictionary and figure out its meaning. Hubristic behaviors are what the Greeks were against. But what Agamemnon did in this section was hubristic. Please cite the words he said which were regarded as hubristic by the Greek people.

（4）The first paragraph (stanza) of this poetry is short (with only 8 lines). Many readers are able to recite these lines through one or two times of rehearsal. Please have a try.

（5）Homer is highly praised for his use of metaphors. Read lines 50-60，comments on Homer's metaphoric use of language.

＊＊＊　　＊＊＊　　＊＊＊　　＊＊＊　　＊＊＊　　＊＊＊　　＊＊＊　　＊＊＊

Nine days the arrows of god **swept through**[4] the army.

On the tenth Achilles called all ranks to **muster**[5]—

the **impulse**[6] seized him，sent by white-armed Hera

grieving[7] to see Achaean fighters drop and die.

Once they'd gathered，crowding the meeting grounds，

the swift runner Achilles rose and spoke among them：

"Son of Atreus，now we are beaten back，I fear，

the long campaign[8] is lost. So home we sail...

if we can escape our death—if war and plague

are joining forces now to **crush**[9] the Argives.　　70

But wait：let us question a holy man，

a **prophet**[10]，even a man skilled with dreams—

dreams as well can come our way from Zeus—

4．席卷

5．［ˈmʌstə(r)］*vi*. 集合

6．［ˈɪmpʌls］*n*. 冲动

7．［griːv］*vi*. 痛苦

8．长征

9．［krʌʃ］*vt*. 压垮

10．［ˈprɒfɪt］*n*. 预言师

come, someone to tell us why Apollo rages so,
whether he blames us for a vow we failed, or **sacrifice**[1].
If only the god would share the smoky **savor**[2] of lambs
and full-grown goats, Apollo might be willing, still,
somehow, to save us from this plague."

So he proposed[3]

and down he sat again as Calchas rose among them,
Thestor's son, the clearest by far of all the **seers**[4]   80
who scan the **flight**[5] of birds. He knew all things that are,
all things that are past and all that are to come,
the seer who had led the Argive ships to Troy
with the second sight that god Apollo gave him.
For the armies' good the seer began to speak:
"Achilles, dear to Zeus...you order me to explain Apollo's anger,
the distant deadly Archer?[6] I will tell it all:
But **strike a pact with**[7] me, swear you will defend me
with all your heart, with words and strength of hand.   90
For there is a man I will **enrage**[8]—I see it now—
a powerful man who **lords it over**[9] all the Argives,
one the Achaeans must obey... A **mighty**[10] king,
raging against an **inferior**[11], is too strong.
Even if he can swallow down his **wrath**[12] today,
still he will nurse the burning in his chest
until, sooner or later, he sends it **bursting forth**[13].
Consider it closely, Achilles. Will you save me?"

And the matchless runner **reassured**[14] him: "Courage!
Out with it now, Calchas. **Reveal**[15] the will of god,   100
whatever you may know. And I swear by Apollo
dear to Zeus, the power you pray to, Calchas,
when you reveal god's will to the Argives—no one,
not while I am alive and see the light on earth, no one
will lay his heavy hands on you by the **hollow**[16] ships.
None among all the armies. Not even if you mean
Agamemnon here who now claims to be, by far,
the best of the Achaeans."

1. ['sækrɪfaɪs] n. 祭祀
2. ['seɪvə] n. 滋味
3. [prə'pəuz] vi. 正式提议
4. [sɪə(r)] n. 预言师
5. [flaɪt] n. 飞翔
6. 致命的远射神
7. 践行承诺
8. [ɪn'reɪdʒ] vt. 触怒
9. vt. 统治
10. ['maɪtɪ] adj. 强大的
11. [ɪn'fɪərɪə(r)] n. 更低级别
12. [rɒθ] n. 愤怒
13. 爆发
14. [ˌriːə'ʃʊə(r)] vt. 使…放心
15. [rɪ'viːl] vt. 泄露；揭露
16. ['hɒləʊ] adj. 空心的

The seer **took heart**[1]
and this time he spoke out，bravely："**Beware**[2]—he casts no
blame for a vow we failed，a sacrifice.   110
The god's enraged because Agamemnon **spurned**[3] his priest，
he refused to free his daughter，he refused the **ransom**[4].
That's why the Archer sends us pains and he will send us more
and never drive this shameful **destruction**[5] from the Argives，
not till we give back the girl with **sparkling**[6] eyes
to her loving father-no price，no ransom paid—
and carry a **sacred**[7] hundred bulls to Chryse town.
Then we can calm the god，and only then **appease**[8] him."

So he declared and sat down. But among them rose the
fighting son of Atreus，lord of the **far-flung**[9] kingdoms，   120
Agamemnon—furious，his dark heart filled to the **brim**[10]，
blazing[11] with anger now，his eyes-like searing fire.
With a sudden，killing look he **wheeled on**[12] Calchas first：
"Seer of misery! Never a word that works **to my advantage**[13]!
Always misery warms your heart，your **prophecies**[14]—
never a word of profit said or brought to pass.
Now，again，you divine god's will for the armies，
bruit[15] it about，as fact，why the deadly Archer
multiplies[16] our pains：because I，I refused
that **glittering**[17] price for the young girl Chryseis.   130
Indeed，I prefer her by far，the girl herself，
I want her mine in my own house! I rank her higher
than Clytemnestra，my **wedded wife**[18]—she's nothing less
in build or **breeding**[19]，in mind or works of hand.
But I am willing to give her back，even so，
if that is best for all. What I really want
is to keep my people safe，not see them dying.
But **fetch**[20] me another prize，and straight off too，
else I alone of the Argives go without my honor.
That would be a **disgrace**[21]：You are all **witness**[22]，   140
look-my prize is **snatched**[23] away!"

But the swift runner

1．鼓起勇气
2．[bɪ'weə] vi.当心
3．[spɜːn] vt.驱赶
4．['rænsəm] n.赎金；赎身
5．[dɪ'strʌkʃ(ə)n] n.破坏
6．[spɑːklɪŋ] adj.闪闪发亮的
7．['seɪkrɪd] adj.神圣的
8．[ə'piːz] vt.安抚
9．[fɑːflʌŋ] adj.辽阔的
10．[brɪm] n.边缘
11．[bleɪz] vi.猛烈燃烧
12．批评
13．有利于我
14．['prɒfəsi] n.预言
15．[bruːt] vi.散播；传播
16．['mʌltɪplaɪ] vt.增加
17．['glɪtərɪŋ] adj.有吸引力的
18．结发妻子
19．['briːdɪŋ] n.教养
20．[fetʃ] v.取来
21．[dɪs'greɪs] n.耻辱
22．[w'ɪtnɪs] n.见证
23．[snætʃ] vt.抢夺，夺得

Achilles answered him at once, "Just how, Agamemnon,

great field **marshal**[1] ... most **grasping**[2] man alive,

how can the generous Argives give you prizes now?

I know of no **troves**[3] of treasure, piled, lying **idle**[4],

anywhere. Whatever we dragged from towns we

plundered[5], all's been **portioned**[6] out. But collect it, call it back

from **the rank and file**? That would be the **disgrace**[7].

So return the girl to the god, at least for now.

We Achaeans will pay you back, three, four times over,   150

if Zeus will **grant**[8] us the gift, somehow, someday;

to raze Troy's **massive**[9] **ramparts**[10] to the ground."

But King Agamemnon **countered**[11], "Not so quickly,

brave as you are, godlike Achilles-trying to cheat me.

Oh no, you won't get past me, take me in that way!

What do you want? To **cling**[12] to your own prize

while I sit calmly by-empty-handed here?

Is that why you order me to give her back?

No—if our **generous**[13] Argives will give me a prize,

a match for my desires, equal to what I've lost,   160

well and good. But if they give me nothing

I will take a prize myself-your own, or Ajax'

or Odysseus' prize-I'll **commandeer**[14] her myself

and let that man I go to visit **choke**[15] with rage!

Enough. We'll deal with all this later, in due time.

Now come, we **haul**[16] a black ship down to the bright sea,

gather a decent number of **oarsmen**[17] along her **locks**[18]

and put aboard a sacrifice, and Chryseis herself,

in all her beauty... we **embark**[19] her too.

Let one of the leading captains **take command**[20].   170

Ajax, Idomeneus, **trusty**[21] Odysseus or you, Achilles,

you—the most violent man alive-so you can perform

the **rites**[22] for us and calm the god yourself."

A dark glance

and the **headstrong**[23] runner answered him in kind:

"Shameless—**armored**[24] in shamelessness-always

shrewd[25] with greed!

How could any Argive soldier obey your orders, freely and

1. ['mɑːʃl] n. 元帅
2. ['grɑːspɪŋ] adj. 贪心的
3. [trəʊv] n. 战利品
4. ['aɪdl] 闲置
5. ['plʌndə] vi. 掠夺
6. ['pɔːʃn] vt. 分派,各级士兵
7. [dɪs'greɪs] n. 耻辱
8. [grɑːnt] vt. 授予
9. ['mæsɪv] adj. 强大的
10. ['ræmpɑːt] n. 防御土墙
11. ['kaʊntə] vi. 反驳
12. [klɪŋ] vt. 抓紧
13. ['dʒenərəs] adj. 大方的
14. [ˌkɒmən'dɪə(r)] vt. 征用
15. [tʃəʊk] v. 哽咽;使窒息
16. [hɔːl] vt. 拖
17. ['ɔːzmən] n. 桨手
18. [lɒks] n. 船闸
19. [ɪm'bɑːk] vt. 启航
20. 挂帅
21. ['trʌsti] adj. 可靠的
22. ['raɪtiːz] n. 仪式
23. ['hedstrɒŋ] adj. 刚愎自用的
24. ['ɑːməd] vt. 武装遮盖
25. [ʃruːd] adj. 奸诈的

gladly do your sailing for you or fight your enemies, full force?
Not I, no. It wasn't Trojan spearmen who brought me here to
fight. The Trojans never did me damage, not in the least, 180
they never stole my cattle or my horses, never in Phthia where
the rich soil breeds strong men did they **lay waste**[1] my crops.   1. 破坏
How could they? Look at the endless miles that lie between
us... shadowy mountain ranges, seas that surge and thunder.
No, you **colossal**[2], shameless-we all followed you, to please   2. [kə'lɒsl] *adj.* 巨大的
you, to fight for you, to win your honor back from the
Trojans—Menelaus and you, you dog-face! What do you care?
Nothing. You don't look right or left. And now you threaten to
strip[3] me **of** my prize in person—the one I fought for long 190   3. [strɪp] *vt.* 剥夺
and hard, and sons of Achaea handed her to me.

My honors never equal yours,
whenever we **sack**[4] some wealthy Trojan **stronghold**[5]—my arms   4. [sæk] *vt.* 洗劫
bear the **brunt**[6] of the raw, savage fighting, true, but when it   5. ['strɒŋhəʊld] *n.* 据点,要塞
comes to dividing up the **plunder**[7] the lion's share is yours, and   6. [brʌnt] *n.* 冲击;撞击
back I go to my ships, clutching some **scrap**[8], some **pittance**[9]   7. ['plʌndə] *n.* 战利品
that I love, when I have fought to **exhaustion**[10].   8. [skræp] *n.* 小块
     9. ['pɪtns] *n.* 少量
     10. [ɪg'zɔːstʃən] *n.* 精疲力竭

No more now—
back I go to Phthia. Better that way by
far, to journey home in the **beaked**[11] ships of war.   200   11. [biːkt] *adj.* 乌嘴状的
I have no mind to **linger**[12] here disgraced,   12. ['lɪŋgə] *vi.* 徘徊
brimming[13] your cup and piling up your plunder."   13. ['brɪmɪŋ] *vt.* 装满

But the lord of men Agamemnon shot back,
"Desert, by all means—if the spirit drives you home!
I will never beg you to stay, not on my account.
Never—others will take my side and do me honor,
Zeus above all, whose wisdom rules the world.
You—I hate you most of all the warlords
loved by the gods. Always dear to your heart,
strife[14], yes, and battles, the bloody **grind**[15] of war.   210   14. [straɪf] *n.* 争斗
What if you are a great soldier? That's just a gift of god.   15. [graɪnd] *n.* 折磨
Go home with your ships and comrades, lord it over
your Myrmidons!

You are nothing to me—you and your **overweening**[1] anger!

But let this be my warning on your way：

since Apollo insists on taking my Chryseis，

I'll send her back in my own ships with my crew.

But I，I will be there in person at your **tents**[2] to take

Briseis in all her beauty，your own prize—so you can

learn just how much greater I am than you and the next

man up may **shrink**[3] from matching words with me，   220

from hoping to **rival**[4] Agamemnon strength for strength！"

He broke off and **anguish**[5] **gripped**[6] Achilles.

The heart in his **rugged**[7] chest was pounding，torn...

Should he draw the long sharp sword **slung**[8] at his hip，

thrust through the ranks and kill Agamemnon now？ —

or **check**[9] his rage and beat his fury down？

As his racing spirit **veered**[10] back and forth，

just as he drew his huge **blade**[11] from its **sheath**[12]，

down from the **vaulting**[13] heavens swept Athena，

the white-armed goddess Hera **sped**[14] her down：   230

Hera loved both men and cared for both alike.

Rearing[15] behind him Pallas seized his fiery hair—

only Achilles saw her，none of the other fighters

struck with wonder he **spun around**[16]，he knew her at once，

Pallas Athena！ the terrible **blazing**[17] of those eyes，

and his winged words went flying："Why，why now？

Child of Zeus with the shield of thunder，why come now？

To witness the **outrage**[18] Agamemnon just committed？

I tell you this，and so help me it's the truth—

he'll soon pay for his **arrogance**[19] with his life！"   240

1. [ˌəʊvəˈwiːnɪŋ] *adj.* 自负的

2. [tent] *n.* 帐篷

3. [ʃrɪŋk] *vi.* 退缩

4. [ˈraɪvl] *vt.* 竞争

5. [ˈæŋgwɪʃ] *n.* 愤怒

6. [grɪp] *vt.* 抓住

7. [ˈrʌgɪd] *adj.* 粗旷

8. [slʌŋ] *vi.* 吊挂

9. [tʃek] *vt.* 控制（愤怒…）

10. [vɪə(r)] *v.* 改变方向

11. [bleɪd] *n.* 叶片

12. [ʃiːθ] *n.* 鞘；套

13. [ˈvɔːltɪŋ] *adj.* 拱形的

14. [sped] *vi.* 急行

15. [rɪə] *vi.* 在后面

16. 旋转；转体

17. [ˈbleɪzɪŋ] *adj.* 闪闪发光的

18. [ˈaʊtreɪdʒ] *n.* 凌辱；暴行

19. [ˈærəgəns] *n.* 傲慢

Achilles quarreled with Agamemnon

Her gray eyes clear，the goddess Athena answered，

"Down from the skies I come to **check**[1] your rage

if only you will **yield**[2]. The white-armed goddess Hera sped me down：

she loves you both，she cares for you both alike.

Stop this fighting，now. Don't lay hand to sword.

Lash[3] him with threats of the price that he will face.

And I tell you this—and I know it is the truth—

one day **glittering**[4] gifts will lie before you，

three times over to pay for all his **outrage**[5].　　　　　250

Hold back now. Obey us both."

So she urged

and the swift runner **complied**[6] at once："I must—

when the two of you hand down commands，Goddess，

a man **submits**[7] though his heart breaks with fury.

Better for him by far. If a man obeys the gods

they're quick to hear his prayers."

And with that

Achilles stayed his **burly**[8] hand on the silver

hilt[9] and slid the huge blade back in its sheath.

He would not fight the orders of Athena.

Soaring[10] home to Olympus，she **rejoined**[11] the gods　　250

aloft[12] in the halls of Zeus whose shield is thunder.

But Achilles **rounded on**[13] Agamemnon once again，

lashing[14] out at him，not relaxing his anger for a moment：

"**Staggering**[15] drunk，with your dog's eyes，your **fawn**[16]'s heart！

Never once did you arm with the troops and go to battle

or risk an **ambush**[17] packed with Achaea's picked men—

you lack the courage，you can see death coming.

Safer by far，you find，to **foray**[18] all through camp，

commandeering[19] the prize of any man who speaks against you.

King who **devours**[20] his people！ Worthless **husks**[21]，the men you

rule-if not，Atrides，this **outrage**[22] would have been your last.

I tell you this，and I swear a mighty oath upon it...

by this，this **scepter**[23]，look，that never again will put

1．[tʃek] *vt*. 控制

2．[jiːld] *vt*. 妥协

3．[læʃ] *vt*. 鞭打

4．['glɪtərɪŋ] *adj*. 闪光的

5．['aʊtreɪdʒ] *n*. 暴行

6．[kəm'plaɪd] *vi*. 合作；顺从

7．[səb'mɪt] *vi*. 服从

8．['bɜːli] *adj*. 粗壮的

9．[hɪlt] *n*. 剑柄

10．['sɔːrɪŋ] *vi*. 高飞

11．[riː'dʒɔɪn] *vt*. 重新加入

12．[ə'lɒft] *adj*. 高高在上的

13．['raʊndɪd] *vi*. 责骂

14．[læʃ] *vi*. 鞭挞

15．['stæɡərɪŋ] *adj*. 摇摇晃晃的

16．[fɔːn] *n*. 小鹿

17．['æmbʊʃ] *n*. 埋伏

18．['fɒreɪ] *vt*. 突然侵袭

19．[ˌkɒmən'dɪə(r)] *vt*. 强占

20．[dɪ'vaʊə(r)] *vt*. 吞吃

21．[hʌsks] *n*. 谷壳

22．['aʊtreɪdʒ] *n*. 暴行

23．['septə] *n*. 王权；权杖

forth crown and branches, now it's left its **stump**[1] on
the mountain ridge forever, nor will it **sprout**[2] new green
again, now the **brazen**[3] **ax**[4] has stripped its **bark**[5] and leaves,
and now the sons of Achaea pass it back and forth as they
hand their judgments down, **upholding**[6] the honored
customs whenever Zeus commands—This scepter will be
the mighty force behind my oath: someday, I swear,   280
a **yearning**[7] for Achilles will strike Achaea's sons and all
your armies! But then, Atrides, **harrowed**[8] as you will
be, nothing you do can save you— not when your **hordes**[9]
of fighters drop and die, cut down by the hands of man-killing
Hector! Then—then you will **tear your heart out**[10], desperate,
raging that you **disgraced**[11] the best of the Achaeans!"

1. [stʌmp] *n*. 树桩

2. [spraut] *vi*. 发芽

3. ['breɪzn] *n*. 坚硬

4. [æks] *n*. 斧头

5. [baːk] *n*. 树皮

6. [ʌp'həʊld] *vt*. 支撑

7. ['jɜːnɪŋ] *n*. 怀念

8. ['hærəʊ] *v*. 被践踏

9. [hɔːd] *n*. 一群群

10. 心碎

11. [dɪs'greɪs] *v*. 侮辱

* * *   * * *   * * *   * * *   * * *   * * *   * * *   * * *

❋**Questions for discussion:**

(6) This section narrated in detail the bitter quarrel between Agamemnon and Achilles. Please retell it in your own words: how and for what reasons the quarrel broke out.

(7) In line 139, Agamemnon says, "Else I alone of the Argives go without my honor. That would be a disgrace." Why did the Greeks take the gift so seriously in your opinion?

(8) Agamemnon's gift was taken away, and he threatened to take away Achilles' gift? Is Agamemnon justified to do so? Please first give a working definition to "justice", and then present your analyses on it.

(9) Achilles was enraged. He would like to kill Agamemnon on the spot. Is his anger justified?

* * *   * * *   * * *   * * *   * * *   * * *   * * *   * * *

Down on the ground

he **dashed**[12] the scepter **studded**[13] bright with golden nails,
then took his seat again. The son of Atreus **smoldered**[14],
glaring across[15] at him, but Nestor rose between   290
them, the man of winning words, the clear speaker of Pylos...
Sweeter than honey from his tongue the voice flowed on and on.
Two generations of mortal men he had seen go down by now,
those who were born and bred with him in the old days,
in Pylos' holy **realm**[16], and now he ruled the third.
He pleaded with both kings, with clear good will,
"No more—or enormous sorrow comes to all Achaea!

12. [dæʃ] *vt*. 掷

13. [stʌd] *vt*. 给…上钉

14. ['sməʊldə] *vi*. 阴燃

15. 瞪眼

16. [reɪlm] *n*. 王国

17. [ɪg'zʌlt] *vi*. 狂喜

How they would **exult**,[17] Priam and Priam's sons
and all the Trojans. Oh they'd **leap**[1] for joy

       300

to hear the two of you battling on this way，
you who excel us all, first in Achaean **councils**[2]，
first in the ways of war.

                     Stop. Please.

Listen to Nestor. You are both younger than I，
and in my time I **struck up with**[3] better men than you，
even you, but never once did they **make light of**[4] me.
I've never seen such men, I never will again...
men like Pirithous, Dryas, that fine captain,
Caeneus and Exadius, and Polyphemus, royal prince，
and Theseus, Aegeus' boy, a match for the immortals.
They were the strongest mortals ever bred on earth，

       310

the strongest, and they fought against the strongest too，
shaggy[5] Centaurs, wild brutes of the mountains—
they **hacked**[6] them down, terrible, deadly work.
And I was in their ranks, fresh out of Pylos，
far away from home-they **enlisted**[7] me themselves
and I fought on my own, **a free lance**[8]，single-handed.
And none of the men who walk the earth these days
could battle with those fighters, none, but they，
they took to heart my **counsels**[9]，marked my words.
So now you listen too. **Yielding**[10] is far better...

       320

Don't seize the girl, Agamemnon, powerful as you are—
leave her, just as the sons of Achaea gave her，
his prize from the very first.
And you, Achilles, never hope to fight it out
with your king, pitting force against his force：
no one can match the honors dealt a king, you know，
a **sceptered**[11] king to whom great Zeus gives glory.
Strong as you are a goddess was your mother-
he has more power because he rules more men.
Atrides, end your anger-look, it's Nestor

       330

I beg you, cool your fury against Achilles.
Here the man stands over all Achaea's armies，
our rugged **bulwark**[12] **braced for**[13] shocks of war."

1．[li:p] *vi*. 跳跃

2．['kaʊs] *n*. 委员会；会议

3．打交道

4．小看

5．['ʃægi] *adj*. 凶猛的

6．[hæk] *vt*. 乱砍

7．[ɪn'lɪst] *vt*. 征召（兵）

8．自由骑士

9．['kaʊnsl] *n*. 建议

10．[ji:ld] *v*. 妥协

11．['septə] *adj*. 有王权的

12．['bʊlwək] *n*. 堡垒

13．[breɪs] *vi*. 支持

But King Agamemnon answered him in haste，
"True，old man—all you say is fit and proper—
but this soldier wants to tower over the armies，
he wants to rule over all，to lord it over all，
give out orders to every man in sight. Well，
there's one，I trust，who will never yield to him!
What if the **everlasting**[1] gods have made a Spearman of him?   340
Have they entitled him to hurl abuse at me?"

1. [ˌevəˈlɑːstɪŋ] *adj*. 永生的

"Yes!"—blazing Achilles broke in quickly—
"What a worthless，burnt-out **coward**[2] I'd be called
if I would **submit**[3] to you and all your orders，
whatever you **blurt out**[4]. **Fling them at**[5] others，
don't give me commands!
Never again，I trust，will Achilles yielded to you.
And I tell you this-take it to heart，I warn you—
my hands will never do battle for that girl，
neither with you，King，nor any man alive.   350
You Achaeans gave her，now you've **snatched**[6] her back.
But all the rest I possess beside my fast black ship—
not one bit of it can you seize against my will，Atrides.
Come，try it! So the men can see，that instant，
your black blood **gush**[7] and **spurt**[8] around my spear!"

2. [ˈkaʊəd] *n*. 懦夫

3. [səbˈmɪt] *vi*. 臣服

4. 脱口而出

5. 对…加以指责

6. [snætʃ] *vt*. 臣服

7. [gʌʃ] *vi*. 喷涌

8. [spɜːt] *vi*. 喷涌

* * *　　* * *　　* * *　　* * *　　* * *　　* * *　　* * *　　* * *

❖**Questions for discussion：**

（10）Greek people were eloquent，and were very impressive in making speeches. Hesiod in *Theogony* demonstrated some wonderful speeches and conversations. Here Homer also presented excellent speeches. Please read the address by Nestor very carefully. Do you think Nestor is an excellent speaker? Do you think that he did a great job in persuasion? What persuasion skills did he use?

（11）Did Nestor succeed in mediating the quarrel between Agamemnon and Achilles? Why?

* * *　　* * *　　* * *　　* * *　　* * *　　* * *　　* * *　　* * *

Once the two had fought it out with words，
battling face-to-face，both sprang to their feet
and broke up the muster beside the Argive **squadrons**[9].
Achilles **strode off**[10] to his trim ships and shelters，
back to his friend Patroclus and their comrades.   360

9. [ˈskwɒdrən] *n*. 有组织群体

10. 大踏步

Agamemnon had a **vessel**[1] **hauled**[2] down to the sea，
he picked out twenty **oarsmen**[3] to man her locks，
put aboard the cattle for sacrifice to the god
and led Chryseis in all her beauty amid ships.
Versatile[4] Odysseus took the **helm**[5] as captain.

All **embarked**[6]，
the party **launched**[7] out on the sea's foaming
lanes[8] while the son of Atreus told his troops to wash，
to purify themselves from the **filth**[9] of plague.
They **scoured**[10] it off，threw scourings in the surf
and sacrificed to Apollo full-grown bulls and goats   370
along the beaten shore of the **fallow**[11] barren sea
and **savory**[12] smoke went **swirling**[13] up the skies.

So the men were engaged throughout the camp.
But King Agamemnon would not stop the quarrel，
the first threat he **hurled**[14] against Achilles.
He called Talthybius and Eurybates **briskly**[15]，
his two **heralds**[16]，ready，willing aides：
"Go to Achilles' **lodge**[17]. Take Briseis at once，
his beauty Briseis by the hand and bring her here.
But if he will not surrender her，I'll go myself，   380
I'll seize her myself，with an army at my back—
and all the worse for him!"

He sent them off
with the strict order ringing in their ears.
Against their will the two men made their way
along the breaking surf of the **barren**[18] salt sea
and reached the Myrmidon shelters and their ships.
They found him beside his lodge and black **hull**[19]，
seated **grimly**[20]—and Achilles took no joy
when he saw the two approaching.
They were afraid，they held the king in **awe**[21]   390
and stood there，silent. Not a word to Achilles，
not a question. But he sensed it all in his heart，
their fear，their charge，and broke the silence for them：
"Welcome，**couriers**[22]! Good heralds of Zeus and men，

1. ['vesl] *n*. 船
2. [hɔːl] *vt*. 拖；拉
3. ['ɔːzmən] *n*. 划手
4. ['vɜːsətaɪl] *adj*. 多才多艺的
5. [helm] *n*. 舵柄
6. [ɪm'bɑːk] *vi*. 启航
7. [lɔːntʃ] *vi*. 出发（发射）
8. [leɪn] *n*. 航线
9. [fɪlθ] *n*. 肮脏
10. ['skaʊə(r)] *vt*. 擦掉
11. ['fæləʊ] *adj*. 贫瘠的
12. ['seɪvəri] *adj*. 香的
13. [swɜːl] *vt*. 旋转
14. [hɜːl] *vi*. 投掷
15. [brɪskli] *adv*. 飞快地
16. ['herəld] *n*. 信使
17. [lɒdʒ] *n*. 房子
18. ['bærən] *adj*. 贫瘠的
19. [hʌl] *n*. 船
20. [grɪmli] *adv*. 严肃
21. [ɔː] *n*. 敬畏
22. ['kʊrɪə(r)] *n*. 送信的

here，come closer. You have done nothing to me.
You are not to blame. No one but Agamemnon—
he is the one who sent you for Briseis.
Go，Patroclus，Prince，bring out the girl
and hand her to them so they can take her back.
But let them both bear **witness**[1] to my loss...   400
in the face of **blissful**[2] gods and mortal men，
in the face of that unbending，**ruthless**[3] king—
if the day should come when the armies need me
to save their ranks from **ignominious**[4]，stark defeat.
The man is **raving**[5]—with all the murderous fury in his heart.
He lacks the sense to see a day behind，a day ahead，
and **safeguard**[6] the Achaeans battling by the ships."

Patroclus obeyed his great friend's command.   408
He led Briseis in all her beauty from the lodge
and handed her over to the men to take away.   410
And the two walked back along the Argive ships
while she **trailed**[7] on behind，**reluctant**[8]，every step.
But Achilles wept，and slipping away from his companions，
far apart，sat down on the beach of the **heaving**[9] gray sea
and scanned the endless ocean. Reaching out his arms，
again and again he prayed to his dear mother：
"Mother! You gave me life，short as that life will be，   418
so at least Olympian Zeus，thundering up on high，
should give me honor-but now he gives me nothing.   420
Atreus' son Agamemnon，for all his far-flung kingdoms—
the man disgraces me，seizes and keeps my prize，
he tears her away himself!"

                    So he wept and prayed
and his noble mother heard him，seated near her father，the
Old Man of the Sea in the salt green depths.
Suddenly up she rose from the **churning**[10] surf like mist and
settling down beside him as he wept，
stroked[11] Achilles gently，whispering his name，"My child—
why in tears? What sorrow has touched your heart?
Tell me，please. Don't **harbor**[12] it deep inside you.

1. ['wɪtnəs] *n*. 见证

2. ['blɪsfl] *adj*. 永乐的

3. ['ruːθləs] *adj*. 无情的

4. [ˌɪgnə'mɪnɪəs] *adj*. 不名誉的

5. ['reɪvɪŋ] *v*. 吼叫

6. ['seɪfgɑːd] *vt*. 保卫

7. [treɪld] *v*. 拖沓而行

8. [rɪ'lʌkt(ə)nt] *adj*. 不情愿的

9. ['hiːvɪŋ] *adj*. 起伏的

10. ['tʃɜːnɪŋ] *n*. 翻腾的海浪

11. [strəʊk] *vt*. 轻抚；轻触

12. ['hɑːbə] *vt*. 心怀

We must share it all."

And now from his depths   430
the proud runner groaned: "You know, you know,
why labor through it all? You know it all so well...
We **raided**[1] Thebe once, Eetion's sacred **citadel**[2],
we **ravaged**[3] the place, hauled all the plunder here
and the armies passed it round, share and share alike,
and they chose the beauty Chryseis for Agamemnon.
But soon her father, the holy priest of Apollo
the **distant deadly Archer**[4], Chryses approached
the fast **trim**[5] ships of the Argives armed in bronze
to win his daughter back, bringing a priceless ransom   440
and bearing high in hand, wound on a golden staff,
the wreaths of the god who strikes from worlds away.
He begged the whole Achaean army but most of all
the two supreme commanders, Atreus' two sons,
and all ranks of Achaeans cried out their assent,
'Respect the priest, accept the shining ransom!'
But it brought no joy to the heart of Agamemnon,
our high and mighty king dismissed the priest
with a brutal order ringing in his ears.
And shattered with anger, the old man withdrew   450
but Apollo heard his prayer—he loved him, deeply—
he loosed his **shaft**[6] at the Argives, withering plague,
and now the troops began to drop and die in **droves**[7],
the arrows of god went showering left and right,
whipping through the Achaeans' vast encampment.
But the old seer who knew the cause full well
revealed the will of the archer god Apollo.
And I was the first, mother, I urged them all,
'**Appease**[8] the god at once!' That's when the fury
gripped the son of Atreus. Agamemnon leapt to his feet   460
and hurled his threat—**his threat's been driven home.**[9]
One girl, Chryseis, the fiery-eyed Achaeans
ferry[10] **out** in a fast trim ship to Chryse Island,
laden[11] **with** presents for the god. The other girl,

1. [reɪd] vt. 攻击
2. ['sɪtədəl] n. 城堡
3. ['rævɪdʒ] vt. 摧毁

4. 致命的远射神
5. [trɪm] adj. 修长的；整洁的

6. [ʃɑːft] n. 箭
7. [drəʊvz] n. 成群

8. [ə'piːz] vt. 平息

9. 说到做到

10. 摆渡

11. ['leɪdn] adj. 满载的

just now, the heralds came and led her away from camp,

Briseus' daughter, the prize the armies gave me.

But you, mother, if you have any power at all,

protect your son! Go to Olympus, plead with Zeus,

if you ever warmed his heart with a word or any action...

     Time and again I heard your claims in father's halls,   470

boasting[1] how you and you alone of all the immortals

rescued Zeus, the lord of the dark storm cloud,

from **ignominious**[2], stark defeat...

That day the Olympians tried to chain him down,

Hera, Poseidon lord of the sea, and Pallas Athena—

you rushed to Zeus, dear Goddess, broke those chains,

quickly ordered the hundred-hander to **steep**[3] Olympus,

that monster whom the immortals call Briareus

but every mortal calls the Sea-god's son, Aegaeon,

though he's stronger than his father. Down he sat,   480

flanking Cronus' son, **gargantuan**[4] in the glory of it all,

and the blessed gods were struck with terror then,

they stopped **shackling**[5] Zeus.

          Remind him of that,

now, go and sit beside him, grasp his knees... persuade

him, somehow, to help the Trojan cause,

to **pin**[6] the Achaeans back against their ships,

trap them round the bay and **mow**[7] them down.

So all can reap the benefits of their king—

so even mighty Atrides can see how mad he was

to disgrace Achilles, the best of the Achaeans!"   490

And Thetis answered, bursting into tears,

"O my son, my sorrow, why did I ever bear you?

All I bore was doom...

Would to god you could **linger**[8] by your ships

without a grief in the world, without a **torment**[9]!

Doomed to a short life, you have so little time.

And not only short, now, but filled with heartbreak too,

more than all other men alive—doomed twice over.

Ah to a cruel fate I bore you in our halls!

1. [bəʊst] *vt.* 自夸

2. [ˌɪɡnə'mɪnɪəs] *adj.* 可耻的

3. [stiːp] *adj.* 陡的

4. [ɡɑː'ɡæntʃuən] *adj.* 巨大的

5. ['ʃækl] *vt.* 捆绑

6. [pɪn] *vt.* 牵制
7. [məu] *vt.* 割;扫射

8. ['lɪŋɡə(r)] *vi.* 逗留,徘徊
9. ['tɔːmənt] *n.* 折磨

Still, I shall go to Olympus crowned with snow   500
and repeat your prayer to Zeus who loves the lightning.
Perhaps he will be persuaded.

Thetis dipped Achilles

But you, my child,
stay here by the fast ships, rage on at the Achaeans,
just keep clear of every **foray**[1] in the fighting.   1. ['fɒrei] *n*. 突袭;冒险
Only yesterday Zeus went off to the Ocean River
to feast with the Aethiopians, loyal, lordly men,
and all the gods went with him. But in twelve days
the Father returns to Olympus. Then, for your sake,
up I go to the bronze floor, the royal house of Zeus—
I'll grasp his knees, I think I'll win him over."

* * *   * * *   * * *   * * *   * * *   * * *   * * *   * * *

❉Questions for discussion:

(12) Read lines 370-372. What beautiful scenes Homer created! Do you agree?

(13) *The Iliad* covers only a few weeks in the final year of the Trojan War. But reading through the whole poem, one will find that *the Iliad* mentions or alludes to many of the Greek legends. Read the dialogues of Achilles with his mother, what stories of Achilles were alluded to? It was said that Achilles would have two fates in his life. What are the two fates?

(14) Achilles was said to be the best man of the Greeks and the greatest fighter in the army. But in his conversations with his mother, we see 'this Achilles' no different from other human beings, like you and me. Do you agree? Give your comments.

(15) Thetis was once the savior of Zeus. Tell the story in your own words.

（16）Achilles asked his mother to go to find Zeus and plead him to "help the Trojan cause, to pin the Achaeans back against their ships, trap them round the bay and mow them down...so even mighty Atrides can see how mad he was to disgrace Achilles, the best of he Achaeans!". It seemed that Achilles was selfish, only caring about his own interests. What are your comments?

* * *　　* * *　　* * *　　* * *　　* * *　　* * *　　* * *　　* * *

With that vow his mother went away and left him there,　510
alone, his heart **inflamed**[1] for the **sashed**[2] and lovely girl
they'd **wrenched**[3] away from him against his will.
Meanwhile Odysseus drew in close to Chryse Island,
bearing the splendid sacrifice in the vessel's hold.
And once they had entered the harbor deep in bays
they **furled**[4] and **stowed**[5] the sail in the black ship,
they lowered the mast by the forestays, smoothly,
quickly let it down on the forked mast-crutch
and rowed her into a **mooring**[6] under oars.　520
Out went the bow-stones—cables fast **astern**[7]—
and the crew themselves **swung**[8] out in the breaking surf,
leading out the sacrifice for the archer god Apollo,
and out of the deep-sea ship Chryseis stepped too.
Then **tactful**[9] Odysseus led her up to the altar,
placing her in her loving father's arms, and said,
"Chryses, the lord of men Agamemnon sent me here　530
to bring your daughter back and perform a sacrifice,
a grand sacrifice to Apollo—for all Achaea's sake—
so we can **appease**[10] the god who's loosed such grief and
torment[11] on the Argives."

With those words he left her in Chryses' arms
and the priest embraced the child he loved, **exultant**[12].
At once the men arranged the sacrifice for Apollo,
making the cattle **ring**[13] his well-built altar,
then they **rinsed** their hands and took up **barley**[14].
Rising among them Chryses stretched his arms to the sky and
prayed in a high **resounding**[15] voice, "Hear me, Apollo!　540
God of the silver bow who strides the walls of Chryse
and Cilla sacrosanct—**lord in power of Tenedos**[16]!
If you honored me last time and heard my prayer

1. [ɪnˈfleɪm] vi. 燃烧
2. [ˈsæʃt] adj. 系腰带的
3. [rentʃ] vt. 扭伤

4. [fɜːl] vt. 收拢
5. [stəʊ] vt. 收藏

6. [ˈmɔːrɪŋ] n. 停泊处
7. [əˈstɜːn] adv. 向后
8. [swʌŋ] vt. (使)摇摆

9. [ˈtæktʃ(ə)] adj. 机智的,机敏的

10. [əˈpiːz] vt. 安抚
11. [ˈtɔːment] n. 折磨

12. [ɪgˈzʌltənt] adj.狂喜的

13. [rɪŋ] vt. 环绕
14. [ˈbɑːli] n. 大麦

15. [rɪˈzaʊndɪŋ] v. 回响

16. 保护神

and rained destruction down on all Achaea's ranks,
now bring my prayer to pass once more. Now, at last,
drive this killing plague from the armies of Achaea!" 544

His prayer went up and Phoebus Apollo heard him.
And soon as the men had prayed and **flung**[1] the barley,
first they lifted back the heads of the victims,
slit[2] their throats, skinned them and carved away
the meat from the **thighbones**[3] and wrapped them in fat,
a double fold sliced clean and topped with strips of flesh. 550
And the old man burned these over dried split wood
and over the quarters poured out **glistening**[4] wine
while young men at his side held **five-pronged**[5] forks.
Once they had burned the bones and tasted the organs
they cut the rest into pieces, pierced them with **spits**[6],
roasted them to a turn and pulled them off the fire.
The work done, the feast laid out, they ate well
and no man's hunger lacked a share of the **banquet**[7].
When they had put aside desire for food and drink,
the young men **brimmed**[8] the mixing bowls with wine 560
and tipping first drops for the god in every cup
they poured full rounds for all. And all day long
they **appeased**[9] the god with song, raising a ringing hymn
to the distant archer god who drives away the plague,
those young Achaean warriors **singing out his power**[10],
and Apollo listened, his great heart warm with joy.

Then when the sun went down and night came on
they made their beds and slept by the **stern-cables**...
When young Dawn with her rose-red fingers shone once more,
they set sail for the main **encampment**[11] of Achaea. 570
The Archer sent them a **bracing**[12] following wind,
they stepped the mast, spread white sails wide,
the wind hit full and the **canvas bellied**[13] out
and a dark blue wave, **foaming**[14] up at the bow,
sang out loud and strong as the ship made way,
skimming the **whitecaps**[15], cutting toward her goal.
And once offshore of Achaea's vast encampment

1. [flʌŋ] vt. 扔

2. [slɪt] vt. 切段
3. ['θaɪbəʊn] n. 大腿骨

4. ['glɪstnɪŋ] adj. 发光的
5. adj. 五叉的
   prong [prɒŋ] 叉
6. [spɪt] n. 噼啪声

7. ['bæŋkwɪt] n. 宴会

8. [brɪm] vt. 充盈

9. [ə'piːz] vt. 安抚、平息

10. 歌唱他的权力

11. [ɪn'kæmpmənt] n. 营地
12. ['breɪsɪŋ] adj. 令人振奋的

13. ['belɪd] vi. 膨胀
14. [fəʊm] vi. 起泡沫

15. ['waɪtkæp] n. 浪端的白泡沫

they eased her in and **hauled**[1] the black ship high,

far up on the sand, and shored her up with **timbers**[2].

Then they scattered, each to his own ship and shelter.　　　　580

1. [hɔːl] *vt*. 拖

2. [ˈtɪmbə] *n*. 木村

＊＊＊　　＊＊＊　　＊＊＊　　＊＊＊　　＊＊＊　　＊＊＊　　＊＊＊　　＊＊＊

�֍ **Questions for discussion:**

(17) Read the lines (527-544) depicting the reunion of Apollo's priest, Chryses, with his dear daughter, Chryseis. Homer presented so wonderful and vivid descriptions of such an occasion. What feelings do you have when you read these words? Read between the lines, does Homer seem to be cursing the cruelty of the war?

(18) Read the line 569, and translate it into Chinese.

＊＊＊　　＊＊＊　　＊＊＊　　＊＊＊　　＊＊＊　　＊＊＊　　＊＊＊　　＊＊＊

But he raged on, grimly camped by his fast fleet,

the royal son of Peleus, the swift runner Achilles.

Now he no longer **haunted**[3] the meeting grounds

where men win glory, now he no longer went to war

3. [hɔːnt] *vt*. 时常出现

but day after day he ground his heart out, waiting there,

yearning[4], always yearning for battle cries and combat.

4. [ˈjɜːnɪŋ] *v*. 渴望

But now as the twelfth dawn after this shone clear

the gods who live forever marched home to Olympus,

all in a long **cortege**[5], and Zeus led their on.

And Thetis did not forget her son's **appeals**[6].　　　590

She broke from a **cresting**[7] wave at first light

and soaring up to the broad sky and Mount Olympus,

found the son of Cronus gazing down on the world,

peaks apart from the other gods and seated high

on the topmost crown of **rugged**[8] ridged Olympus.

And **crouching**[9] down at his feet,

quickly grasping his knees with her left hand,

her right hand holding him underneath the **chin**[10],

she prayed to the lord god Zeus, the son of Cronus:

"Zeus, Father Zeus! If I ever served you well

among the deathless gods with a word or action,

bring this prayer to pass: honor my son Achilles! —

doomed to the shortest life of any man on earth.

And now the lord of men Agamemnon has disgraced him,

seizes and keeps his prize, tears her away himself. But you—

exalt[11] him, Olympian Zeus: your urgings rule the world!

5. [kɔːˈteɪʒ] *n*. 顺从

6. [əˈpiːl] *n*. 请求

7. [ˈkrestɪŋ] *n*. 浪峰

8. [ˈrʌɡɪd] *adj*. 崎岖的

9. [ˈkraʊtʃ] *vi*. 蹲伏

10. [tʃɪn] *n*. 下巴

11. [ɪɡˈzɔːlt] *vt*. 赞扬

Come, grant the Trojans victory after victory
till the Achaean armies pay my dear son back,
building higher the honor he deserves!"

She paused

but Zeus who commands the storm clouds answered nothing. 610

The Father sat there, silent. It seemed an **eternity**[1] ...

1. [ɪˈtɜːnəti] *adj*. 永恒的

But Thetis, **clasping**[2] his knees, held on, **clinging**[3] ,

2. [klɑːsp] *vt*. 抱住

pressing her question once again: "Grant my prayer,

3. [klɪŋ] *vi*. 抓紧

once and for all, Father, bow your head in **assent**[4] !

4. [əˈsent] *n*. 赞同

Or deny me **outright**[5] . What have you to fear?

5. [ˈaʊtraɪt] *adv*. 完全地

So I may know, too well, just how cruelly
I am the most dishonored goddess of them all."

Filled with anger

Zeus who **marshals**[6] the storm clouds answered her at last:

6. [ˈmɑːʃl] *vt*. 集结

"Disaster. You will drive me into war with Hera. 620

She will **provoke**[7] me, she with her shrill abuse.

7. [prəˈvəʊk] *vt*. 触怒

Even now in the face of all the immortal gods
she **harries**[8] me perpetually, Hera charges me

8. [ˈhæri] *vt*. 骚扰;折磨

that I always go to battle for the Trojans.
Away with you now..Hera might catch us here.
I will see to this. I will bring it all to pass.
Look, I will bow my head if that will satisfy you.
That, I remind you, that among the immortal gods
is the strongest, truest sign that I can give.
No word or work of mine-nothing can be **revoked**[9] , 630

9. [rɪˈvəʊk] *vt*. 撤销

there is no **treachery**[10] , nothing left unfinished

10. [ˈtretʃəri] *n*. 背叛

once I bow my head to say it shall be done."

So he **decreed**[11] . And Zeus the son of Cronus bowed 632

11. [dɪˈkriː] *vi*. 命令

his **craggy**[12] dark brows and the deathless locks came pouring

12. [ˈkrægi] *adj*. 陡峭的

down from the thunderhead of the great immortal king
and giant shock waves spread through all Olympus. 635

＊＊＊   ＊＊＊   ＊＊＊   ＊＊＊   ＊＊＊   ＊＊＊   ＊＊＊   ＊＊＊

❀**Questions for discussion**:

(19) How did Zeus respond to Thetis' appeal for his son?

(20) Read the lines 632-635. They gave a vivid description of Zeus' appearance. What

does it look like?

* * *　　* * *　　* * *　　* * *　　* * *　　* * *　　* * *　　* * *

So the two of them made their **pact**[1] and parted.　636　1. [pækt] *n*. 条约

Deep in the sea she dove from **radiant**[2] Mount Olympus.　2. ['reɪdɪənt] *adj*. 照耀的

Zeus went back to his own halls, and all the gods

in full assembly rose from their seats at once

to meet the Father **striding**[3] toward them now　640　3. ['straɪd] *vi*. 大踏步走

None dared remain at rest as Zeus advanced,

they all sprang up to greet him face-to-face

as he took his place before them on his throne.

But Hera knew it all. She had seen how Thetis,

the Old Man of the Sea's daughter, Thetis quick

on her glistening feet was **hatching**[4] plans with Zeus.　4. ['hætʃɪŋ] *vt*. 谋划

And suddenly Hera **taunted**[5] the Father, son of Cronus:　5. [tɔːnt] *vt*. 嘲笑

"So, who of the gods this time, my **treacherous**[6] one,　6. ['tretʃərəs] *adj*. 不忠的

was hatching plans with you?

Always your pleasure, whenever my back is turned,　650

to settle things in your grand **clandestine**[7] way.　7. [klæn'destɪn] *adj*. 秘密的

You never **deign**[8], do you, freely and frankly,　8. [deɪn] *vi*. 屈尊;俯就

to share your plots with me—never, not a word!"

The father of men and gods replied sharply,

"Hera—stop hoping to **fathom**[9] all my thoughts.　9. ['fæðəm] *vt*. 测量

You will find them a **trial**[10], though you are my wife.　10. ['traɪəl] *n*. 困难;磨难

Whatever is right for you to hear, no one, trust me,

will know of it before you, neither god nor man.

Whatever I choose to plan apart from all the gods—no more

of your everlasting questions, **probe and pry**[11] no more."　660　11. 刺探

And Hera the Queen, her dark eyes wide, **exclaimed**[12],　12. [ɪks'kleɪm] *vi*. 惊叫;呼喊;

"Dread majesty, son of Cronus, what are you saying?　大声说

Now surely I've never probed or pried in the past.

Why, you can **scheme**[13] to your heart's content　13. [skiːm] *vi*. 密谋

without a **qualm**[14] in the world for me. But now　14. [kwɑːm] *n*. 不安

I have a terrible fear that she has won you over,

Thetis, the Old Man of the Sea's daughter, Thetis

with her glistening feet. I know it. Just at dawn

she knelt down beside you and grasped your knees

and I suspect you **bowed your head in assent**[1] to her—   670
you granted once and for all to **exalt**[2] Achilles now
and **slaughter**[3] **hordes**[4] of Achaeans pinned against their ships."

And Zeus who marshals the thunderheads returned，
"Maddening one... you and your **eternal**[5] suspicions—
can never escape you. Ah but tell me，Hera，
just what can you do about all this? Nothing.
Only **estrange**[6] yourself from me a little more—
and all the worse for you.
If what you say is true，that must be my pleasure.
Now go sit down. Be quiet now. Obey my orders，   680
for fear the gods，however many Olympus holds，
are powerless to protect you when I come
to **throttle**[7] you with my **irresistible**[8] hands."

                              He **subsided**[9]
but Hera the Queen，her eyes wider，was terrified.
She sat in silence. She **wrenched**[10] her will to his.
And throughout the halls of Zeus the gods of heaven
quaked[11] with fear. Hephaestus the Master Craftsman
rose up first to **harangue**[12] them all，trying now
to bring his loving mother a little comfort，
the white-armed goddess Hera："Oh disaster...   690
that's what it is，and it will be unbearable
if the two of you must come to blows this way，
flinging the gods in chaos just for mortal men.
No more joy for us in the **sumptuous**[13] **feast**[14]
when **riot**[15] rules the day.
I urge you，mother—you know that I am right—
work back into his good graces，so the Father，
our beloved Father will never **wheel on**[16] us again，
send our **banquets**[17] crashing! The Olympian lord of lightning—
what if he would like to blast us from our seats?   700
He is far too strong. Go back to him，mother，
stroke[18] the Father with soft，winning words—
at once the Olympian will turn kind to us again."

1. 低头同意
2. [ɪgˈzɔːlt] vt. 赞扬
3. [ˈslɔːtə] vt. 屠杀
4. [hɔːd] n. 大群
5. [ɪˈtɜːnl] adj. 永久的，永恒的
6. 使…疏远
7. [ˈθrɒtl] vt. 压制
8. 不可抵抗的
9. [səbˈsaɪd] vi. 坐下
10. [rentʃ] vt. 抓紧
11. [kweɪk] vi. 颤抖
12. [həˈræŋ] v. 高谈阔论
13. [ˈsʌmptjʊəs] n. 丰盛的
14. [fiːst] n. 宴会
15. [ˈraɪət] n. 骚乱
16. 发火
17. [ˈbæŋkwɪt] n. 宴会
18. [strəʊk] vt. 安抚

Pleading, springing up with a two-handled cup,
he reached it toward his loving mother's hands
with his own winning words: "Patience, mother!
Grieved[1] as you are, bear up, or dear as you are,
I have to see you beaten right before my eyes.
I would be **shattered**[2]-what could I do to save you?
It's hard to fight the Olympian strength for strength.   710
You remember the last time I rushed to your defense?
He seized my foot, he **hurled**[3] **me off** the tremendous **threshold**[4]
and all day long I dropped, I was dead weight and then,
when the sun went down, down I **plunged**[5] on Lemnos,
little breath left in me. But the mortals there
soon nursed a fallen immortal back to life."

At that the white-armed goddess Hera smiled
and smiling, took the cup from her child's hands.
Then dipping sweet **nectar**[6] up from the mixing bowl
he poured it round to all the immortals, left to right.   720
And uncontrollable laughter broke from the happy gods
as they watched the god of fire breathing hard
and **bustling**[7] through the halls.

                    That hour then
and all day long till the sun went down they **feasted**[8]
and no god's hunger lacked a share of the handsome
banquet[9] or the **gorgeous**[10] lyre Apollo struck or the Muses
singing voice to voice in **choirs**[11], their **vibrant**[12] music rising.

At last, when the sun's **fiery**[13] light had set,
each immortal went to rest in his own house,
the splendid high halls Hephaestus built for each   730
with all his craft and cunning, the famous crippled Smith.
And Olympian Zeus the lord of lightning went to his own
bed where he had always lain when welcome
sleep came on him.
There he climbed and there he slept and by his side
lay Hera the Queen, the goddess of the golden **throne**[14].   735

1. [ɡriːvd] *adj.* 悲伤

2. ['ʃætə(r)] *vt.* 破坏

3. [hɜːl] *vt.* 扔下
4. ['θreʃhəʊld] *n.* 门槛
5. [plʌndʒ] *vt.* 使陷入, 掉入

6. ['nektə(r)] *n.* 仙酒

7. ['bʌsl] *vi.* 喧闹

8. [fiːst] *vi.* 吃大餐

9. ['bæŋkwɪt] *n.* 宴会
10. ['ɡɔːdʒəs] *adj.* 美妙的
11. ['kwaɪə] *n.* 合唱
12. ['vaɪbrənt] *adj.* 响亮的; 充满生气的
13. ['faɪəri] *adj.* 火热的; 激烈的

14. [θrəʊn] *n.* 王座

* * *　　* * *　　* * *　　* * *　　* * *　　* * *　　* * *　　* * *

❖Questions for discussion:

(21) Lines 636-735 present to us a very different world. That's the world for the gods. And this provides very different and contrasting scenes in front of us. For the human world, battles are still going on. Men are dying and suffering. They pray to the gods for their mercy. But for the world of the gods, they are enjoying their sumptuous feasts and gorgeous music by Apollo and the Muses. What are your comments on this contrasting scene?

(22) Greek god of Smith, the "Master Craftsman", looks funny and is ugly in his appearance, but I think he is a brilliant engineer. Do you agree? He told us the story how he got crippled. Can you retell the story in your own words?

(23) Write a summary of Book 1 "The Rage of Achilles". Do you think Achilles' anger is justifiable?

* * *　　* * *　　* * *　　* * *　　* * *　　* * *　　* * *　　* * *

Hector Returns to Troy

（Book 6 of *The Iliad*）

So the **clash**[1] of Achaean and Trojan troops was on its own，
the battle in all its **fury**[2] **veering**[3] **back and forth**，
careering[4] down the plain as they sent their **bronze lances**[5]
hurtling[6] side-to-side between the Simois' banks and Xanthus'
swirling rapids[7].

That Achaean **bulwark**[8] giant Ajax came up first，
broke the Trojan line and brought his men some hope，
spearing the bravest man the **Thracians**[9] fielded，
Acamas tall and **staunch**[10]，Eussorus' son.
The first to hurl，Great Ajax hit the **ridge**[11]　　　　　　　10
of the **helmet's**[12] horsehair crest—the bronze point
stuck in Acamas' forehead pounding through the **skull**[13]
and the dark came **swirling**[14] down to **shroud**[15] his eyes.

A **shattering**[16] war cry! Diomedes killed off Axylus，
Teuthras' son who had lived in rock-built Arisbe，
a man of means and a friend to all mankind，
at his roadside house he'd warm all comers in.
But who of his guests would greet his enemy now，
meet him face-to-face and **ward off**[17] **grisly**[18] death?
Diomedes killed the man and his aide-in-arms at once，　　20
Axylus and Calesius who always drove his team-both
at a stroke[19] he drove beneath the earth.

Euryalus killed Dresus，killed Opheltius，
turned and went for Pedasus and Aesepus，twins
the **nymph**[20] of the spring Abarbarea bore Bucolion...
Bucolion，son himself to the **lofty**[21] King Laomedon，
first of the line，though his mother bore the prince
in secrecy and shadow. Tending his **flocks**[22] one day
Bucolion took the nymph in a strong **surge**[23] of love
and beneath his force she bore him twin sons.　　　　　　30
But now the son of Mecisteus **hacked**[24] the force

1. ［klæʃ］*n*. 战争
2. ［'fjʊəri］*n*. 狂怒；暴怒
3. ［'vɪərɪŋ］*vi*. 改变
4. ［kə'rɪərɪŋ］*v*. 进行
5. ［lɑːns］*n*. 长矛
6. ［'hɜːtl］*v*. 投掷
7. 急流
8. ［'bʊlwək］*n*. 堡垒
9. *n*. 斯拉凯人
10. ［stɔːntʃ］*adj*. 勇敢的
11. ［rɪdʒ］*n*. 背脊
12. ［'helmɪt］*n*. 头盔
13. ［skʌl］*n*. 头骨
14. ［swɜːlɪŋ］*v*. 倾注而下
15. ［ʃraʊd］*vt*. 遮盖
16. ［'ʃætərɪŋ］*adj*. 击碎的

17. 阻挡开
18. ［'grɪsli］*adj*. 可怕的

19. 猛击一下

20. ［nɪmf］*n*. 小女神
21. ［'lɒfti］*adj*. 高贵的

22. ［flɒk］*n*. 羊群
23. ［sɜːdʒ］*n*. 汹涌；大浪

24. ［hæk］*v*. 砍倒

from beneath them both and loosed their gleaming **limbs**[1]
and tore the **armor**[2] off the dead men's shoulders.

Polypoetes **braced for**[3] battle killed Astyalus—
Winging his bronze spear Odysseus **slew**[4] Pidytes
bred[5] in Percote，and Teucer did the same
for the royal Aretaon—

            Ablerus went down too，
under the flashing **lance**[6] of Nestor's son Antilochus，
and Elatus under the lord of men Agamemnon's strength—
Elatus lived by the banks of **rippling**[7] Satniois，   40
in Pedasus **perched**[8] on **cliffs**[9]—

               The hero Leitus
ran Phylacus down to ground at a dead run
and Eurypylus killed Melanthius **outright**[10]—

             But Menelaus
lord of the war cry had caught Adrestus alive.
Rearing，**bolting**[11] in terror down the plain
his horses **snared**[12] themselves **in tamarisk**[13] **branches**，
splintered[14] his curved **chariot**[15] just at the pole's tip
and breaking free they made a dash for the city walls
where battle-teams by the drove **stampeded**[16] back in panic.
But their master hurled from the chariot，**tumbling**[17]
over the wheel and **pitching**[18] facedown in the dust，and above
him now   50
rose Menelaus，his spear's long shadow **looming**[19].
Adrestus **hugged**[20] his knees and begged him，pleading，
"Take me alive，Atrides，take a **ransom**[21] worth my life!
Treasures are piled up in my rich father's house，
bronze and gold and plenty of **well-wrought**[22] iron
father would give you anything，gladly，priceless ransom
if only he learns I'm still alive in Argive ships!"

    His **pleas**[23] were moving the heart in Menelaus，   59
just at the point of handing him to **an aide**[24]   60
to take him back to the fast Achaean ships...
when up rushed Agamemnon，**blocking**[25] his way
and shouting out，"So soft，dear brother，why?

1.［lɪm］n.四肢

2.［'ɑːmə］n.盔甲

3.为…做好准备

4.［sluː］v.砍倒

5.［bred］v.产仔；繁殖

6.［lɑːns］n.尖点

7.［'rɪpl］adj.涟漪

8.［pɜːtʃ］v.俯瞰

9.［klɪf］n.峭壁

10.［'aʊtraɪt］adv./adj.径直

11.［bəʊlt］v.冲出

12.［sneə(r)］vt.捕捉，罗网

13.［'tæmərɪsk］n.柳树

14.［'splɪntə］vt.使裂成碎片

15.［'tʃærɪət］n.战车

16.［stæm'piːd］v.践踏

17.［'tʌmbl］v.跌倒

18.［pɪtʃ］v.抛，扔

19.［luːm］v.迫近

20.［hʌɡ］v.紧抱，拥抱

21.［'rænsəm］n.赎金

22.锻造得好的

23.［pliː］n.请求

24.［eɪd］n.助手

25.［blɒk］v.阻挡

Why such concern for enemies? I suppose you got
such tender loving care at home from the Trojans.
Ah would to god not one of them could escape   66
his sudden **plunging**[1] death beneath our hands!
No baby boy still in his mother's **belly**[2],
not even he escape—all Ilium **blotted**[3] out,
no tears for their lives, no **markers**[4] for their graves!"   70

And the iron warrior **brought** his brother **round**[5]-
rough justice, fitting too. Menelaus **shoved**[6] Adrestus back with
a fist, powerful Agamemnon **stabbed**[7] him in the **flank**[8]
and back on his side the fighter went, faceup.
The son of Atreus **dug a heel**[9] in his heaving chest
and **wrenched**[10] the ash spear out.

1. [plʌndʒ] v. 俯冲
2. ['beli] n. 肚子
3. [blɒt] v. 毁掉
4. ['mɑːkə] n. 标记
5. 说服(某人)
6. [ʃʌv] v. 使猛劲推
7. [stæbd] v. 刺入
8. [flæŋk] n. 侧面
9. 用脚踩住
10. [rentʃ] v. 把长矛拔出

* * *　* * *　* * *　* * *　* * *　* * *　* * *　* * *

✿**Questions for discussion**:

(1) What did you feel like when reading the above lines? I myself felt sorrowful and wanted to show my deepest sympathy to all those who were killed in the battle by the Greek heroes. They were so lovely, kind, and excellent people. They were innocent too, but got killed in the fierce battle field. Though Homer told us what their names were, we, however, would never remember their names. But after a moment of pains came a little bit of happiness! What strange feelings! Where and how did this bit of happiness come from? From Homer's vivid and detailed description! We felt a sense of beauty in Homer's portrait of one's death, or say "seeking poetic beauty in death" (beautiful poem on death). This feeling becomes intense when reading sentences like "the dark came swirling down to shroud his eyes", "at a stroke he drove beneath the earth", and "a man of means and a friend to all mankind". Do you feel like the same? What are your comments on the beginning of book 6?

(2) Besides the cruelty of the war and killings, we also read love stories, and stories of friendship. Please underline lines about these.

(3) When Menelaus was about to kill Adrestus, he begged him for life. What are your comments on Adrestus' pleading? Do you think he is a coward?

(4) Translate lines 66-70 into Chinese.

* * *　* * *　* * *　* * *　* * *　* * *　* * *　* * *

And here came Nestor

with orders ringing down the field: "My comrades—
fighting Danaans, aides of Ares—no **plunder**[11] now!
Don't lag behind, don't **fling**[12] yourself at spoils   80

11. ['plʌndə(r)] n. 抢夺
12. [flɪŋ] v. 抢战利品

just to **haul**[1] the biggest portion back to your ship.
Now's the time for killing! Later, **at leisure**[2],
strip[3] the corpses up and down the plain!"

So he ordered, **spurring**[4] each man's nerve—
and the next moment crowds of Trojans once again
would have **clambered**[5] back inside their city walls,
terror-struck by the Argives **primed**[6] for battle.
But Helenus son of Priam, best of the **seers**[7]
who scan the flight of birds, came **striding**[8] up
to Aeneas and Hector, calling out, "My captains!   90
You bear the **brunt**[9] of Troy's and Lycia's fighting—
you are our bravest men, whatever the enterprise,
pitched battle itself or planning our campaigns,
so stand your ground right here!
Go through the ranks and rally all the troops.
Hold back our **retreating**[10] **mobs**[11] outside the gates
before they throw themselves in their women's arms in fear,
a great joy to our enemies closing for the kill.
And once you've **roused**[12] our lines to the last man,
we'll hold out here and fight the Argives down,   100
hard-hit as we are—necessity drives us on.

But you,

Hector, you go back to the city, tell our mother
to gather all the older noble women together
in gray-eyed Athena's **shrine**[13] on the city's **crest**[14],
unlock the doors of the goddess' **sacred chamber**[15]—
and take a **robe**[16], the largest, loveliest robe
that she can find throughout the royal halls,
a gift that far and away she prizes most herself,
and spread it out across the **sleek-haired**[17] goddess' knees.
Then promise to sacrifice twelve **heifers**[18] in her shrine,   110
yearlings[19] never broken, if only she'll pity Troy,
the Trojan wives and all our helpless children,
if only she'll **hold** Diomedes **back from**[20] the holy city—
that wild spearman, that **invincible**[21] **headlong**[22] terror!
He is the strongest Argive now, I tell you.

1. [hɔːl] *vt.* 拖
2. 闲暇时
3. [strɪp] *vt.* 剥去
4. [spɜː(r)] *v.* 激发
5. [ˈklæmbə(r)] *v.* 攀爬
6. [praɪm] *v.* 使准备好
7. [sɪə(r)] *n.* 预言师
8. [straɪd] *v.* 大踏步
9. [brʌnt] *n.* 进攻
10. [rɪˈtriːt] *v.* 后退的
11. [mɒb] *n.* 大众
12. [raʊz] *v.* 使振奋
13. [ʃraɪn] *n.* 神龛
14. [krest] *n.* 顶部
15. 神圣的房子
16. [rəʊb] *n.* 长袍
17. [sliːk heəd] *adj.* 美发的
18. [ˈhefə(r)] *n.* 小母牛
19. [ˈjɜːlɪŋ] *n.* 牛犊
20. 阻止;阻挡
21. [ɪnˈvɪnsəbl] *adj.* 不可战胜的
22. [ˈhedlɒŋ] *adj.* 急速的;险峻的

Never once did we fear Achilles so,
captain of armies, born of a goddess too,
or so they say. But here's a **maniac**[1] run
amok[2]—no one can match his **fury**[3] man-to-man!"
So he urged
and Hector obeyed his brother start to finish.   120
Down he **leapt**[4] from his chariot fully armed, hit the ground
and **brandishing**[5] two sharp spears went **striding**[6] down his lines,
ranging **flank**[7] to flank, driving his fighters into battle, 9
rousing **grisly**[8] war—and round the Trojans whirled,
bracing[9] to meet the Argives face-to-face.
And the Argives gave way, they quit the **slaughter**[10]—
they thought some god swept down from the starry skies
to back the Trojans now, they wheeled and rallied so.
Hector shouted out to his men in a **piercing**[11] voice,
"**Gallant**[12]-hearted Trojans and far-famed allies!   130
Now be men, my friends, call up your battle-fury!
Till I can return to Troy and tell them all,
the old **counselors**[13], all our wives, to pray to the gods
and vow to offer them many splendid **victims**[14]."

As Hector turned for home his **helmet**[15] flashed
and the long dark hide of his **bossed shield**[16], the **rim**[17]
running the metal edge, **drummed**[18] his neck and ankles.
And now
Glaucus son of Hippolochus and Tydeus' son Diomedes
met in the **no man's land**[19] between both armies,
burning for battle, closing, **squaring**[20] off   140
and the lord of the war cry Diomedes opened up,
"Who are you, my fine friend?—another born to die?
I've never noticed you on the **lines**[21] where we win glory,
not till now. But here you come, **charging out**[22]
in front of all the rest with such **bravado**[23]—
daring to face the flying shadow of my spear.
Pity the ones whose sons stand up to me in war!
But if you are an immortal come from the blue,
I'm not the man to fight the gods of heaven.
Not even Dryas' **indestructibles**[24] on Lycurgus,   150

1. ['meɪnɪæk] n. 疯子
2. [ə'mɒk] adv. 杀气腾腾
3. ['fjʊəri] n. 暴怒
4. [lept] v. 跳
5. ['brændɪʃ] vt. 挥舞
6. [straɪd] vi. 大踏步
7. [flæŋk] n. 侧面
8. ['grɪzli] n. 可怕的
9. [breɪs] n. 准备好
10. ['slɔːtə(r)] n. 屠杀
11. ['pɪəsɪŋ] n. 刺耳的
12. ['gælənt] n. 勇敢的
13. ['kaʊnsələ] n. 参谋
14. ['vɪktɪm] n. 祭祀
15. ['helmɪt] n. 头盔
16. 有浮雕的盾牌
17. [rɪm] n. 边缘
18. [drʌm] vt. 击鼓; 连打
19. 没有人的地方
20. [skweə(r)] n. 准备厮杀
21. n. 阵线
22. [tʃɑːdʒ] n. 攻出来
23. [brə'vɑːdəʊ] n. 虚张声势
24. [ˌɪndɪ'strʌktəbl] n. 不可毁灭的

not even he lived long...that fellow who tried to fight the
deathless gods.

He rushed at the **maenads**[1] once, nurses of wild Dionysus,
scattered them breakneck down the **holy**[2] mountain Nysa.
A rout of them **strewed**[3] their sacred **staves**[4] on the ground,
raked[5] with a cattle **prod**[6] by Lycurgus, **murderous**[7] fool!
And Dionysus was terrified, he dove beneath the **surf**[8]
where the sea-nymph Thetis pressed him to her breast—
Dionysus **numb**[9] with fear: **shivers**[10] racked his body,
thanks to the **raucous**[11] **onslaught**[12] of that man.   160
But the gods who live at ease **lashed**[13] **out** against him—
worse, the son of Cronus struck Lycurgus blind.
Nor did the man live long, not' with the hate.
of all the gods against him.

               No, my friend,
I have no desire to fight the **blithe**[14] immortals.
But if you're a man who eats the crops of the earth,   167
a mortal born for death—here, come closer,
the sooner you will meet your day to die!"   169

    The noble son of Hippolochus answered **staunchly**[15],   170
"High-hearted son of Tydeus, why ask about my birth?
Like the generations of leaves, the lives of mortal men.
Now the wind **scatters**[16] the old leaves across the earth,
now the living **timber**[17] bursts with the new **buds**[18]
and spring comes round again. And so with men:
as one generation comes to life, another dies away.   176
But about my birth, if you'd like to learn it well,
first to last—though many people know it—
here's my story...

              There is a city, Corinth,
deep in a bend of Argos, good **stallion**[19]—country
where Sisyphus used to live, the **wiliest**[20] man alive.   180
Sisyphus, Aeolus' son, who had a son called Glaucus,
and in his day Glaucus **sired**[21] brave Bellerophon,
a man without a fault. The gods gave him beauty
and the fine, **gallant**[22] traits that go with men.
But Proetus **plotted**[23] against him. Far stronger,

1. ['miːnæd] *n.* 狂女
2. ['həʊli] *n.* 神圣的
3. [struː] *n.* 散落
4. [steɪv] *n.* 狭板
5. [reɪk] *v.* 击打
6. [prɒd] *n.* 刺棒
7. ['mɜːd(ə)nrəs] *adj.* 凶残的，
杀人的
8. [sɜːf] *n.* 海浪
9. [nʌm] *n.* 麻木
10. ['ʃɪvə(r)] *n.* 颤抖
11. ['rɔːkəs] *adj.* 粗声的
12. ['ɒnslɔːt] *n.* 猛攻；突击
13. 发怒
14. [blaɪð] *n.* 欢乐的
15. [stɔːntʃli] *adv.* 坚定地
16. ['skætə(r)] *n.* 吹散
17. ['tɪmbə] *n.* 树木
18. [bʌd] *n.* 芽
19. ['stæliən] *n.* 种马
20. ['waɪli] *n.* 最狡猾的
21. ['saɪə(r)] *vt.* 成为…父亲
22. ['gælənt] *n.* 勇敢的
23. [plɒt] *vi.* 谋划

the king in his anger drove him out of Argos,
the kingdom Zeus had brought beneath his **scepter**[1].
Proetus' wife, you see, was mad for Bellerophon,
the lovely Antea **lusted**[2] to couple with him,
all in secret. **Futile**[3]—she could never **seduce**[4]   190
the man's strong will, his seasoned, firm **resolve**[5].
So straight to the king she went, **blurting**[6] out her lies:
'I wish you'd die, Proetus, if you don't kill Bellerophon!
Bellerophon's **bent**[7] on dragging me down with him in **lust**[8]
though I fight him all the way!'

                All of it false
but the king **seethed**[9] when he heard a tale like that.
He **balked**[10] at killing the man—he'd some respect at least
but he quickly sent him off to Lycia, gave him **tokens**[11],
murderous signs, scratched in a folded **tablet**[12],
and many of them too, enough to kill a man.   200
He told him to show them to Antea's father:
that would mean his death.

            So off he went to Lycia,
safe in the **escort**[13] of the gods, and once he reached
the broad highlands cut by the rushing Xanthus,
the king of Lycia gave him a royal welcome.
Nine days he **feasted**[14] him, nine oxen **slaughtered**[15].
When the tenth Dawn shone with her rose-red fingers,
he began to question him, asked to see his **credentials**[16],
whatever he brought him from his in-law, Proetus.
But then, once he received that fatal message   210
sent from his own daughter's husband, first
he ordered Bellerophon to kill the Chimaera-
grim[17] monster sprung of the gods, nothing human,
all lion in front, all snake behind, all goat between,
terrible, **blasting**[18] **lethal**[19] fire at every breath!
But he laid her low, obeying signs from the gods.
Next he fought the Solymi, tribesmen **bent on**[20] glory,
roughest battle of men he ever entered, so he claimed.
Then for a third test he brought the **Amazons**[21] down,
a match for men in war. But as he turned back,   220
his host **spun out**[22] the tightest **trap**[23] of all:

1. ['septə] *n*. 权杖

2. [lʌst] *vi*. 欲望

3. ['fjuːtaɪl] *adj*. 徒劳的

4. [sɪ'djuːs] *n*. 引诱

5. [rɪ'zɒlv] *vt*. 决心

6. [blɜːt] *v*. 脱口而出

7. [bɒnt] *vi*. 决心,决意

8. [lʌst] *n*. 欲望

9. [siːð] *vi*. 强压怒火

10. [bɔːk] *vi*. 对…迟疑不决

11. ['təʊkən] *n*. 记号

12. ['tæblət] *n*. 片状物

13. ['eskɔːt] *n*. 护佑

14. [fiːst] *vt*. 大餐招待

15. ['slɔːtə(r)] *vt*. 屠宰

16. [krə'denʃl] *n*. 信物

17. [grɪm] *adj*. 严酷的;严厉的;冷酷的

18. [blɑːst] *vt*. 喷射出

19. ['liːθl] *adj*. 致命的

20. 下决心

21. 亚马逊女人

22. [spʌn] 编织出

23. [træp] *n*. 陷阱

picking the best men from Lycia far and wide
he set an **ambush**[1] — that never came home again!
Fearless Bellerophon killed them all.

1.［'æmbʊʃ］ *n*. 埋伏

Then，yes，
when the king could see the man's power at last，
a true son of the gods，he **pressed him hard**[2] to stay，
he offered his own daughter's hand in marriage，
he gave him half his royal honors as the king.
And the Lycians **carved**[3] him out a grand estate，
the choicest land in the realm，rich in **vineyards**[4]   230
and good **tilled**[5] fields for him to lord it over.
And his wife bore good Bellerophon three children：
Isander，Hippolochus and Laodamia. Laodamia
lay in the arms of Zeus who rules the world
and she bore the god a son，our great commander，
Sarpedon **helmed**[6] in bronze.
         But the day soon came   236
when even Bellerophon was hated by all the gods.
Across the Alean plain he wandered，all alone，
eating his heart out[7]，a **fugitive**[8] on the run
from the beaten tracks of men. His son Isander?   240
Killed by the War-god，never **sated**[9] — a boy fighting
the Solymi always out for glory. Laodamia? Artemis，
flashing her golden reins，cut her down in anger.
But Hippolochus fathered me，I'm proud to say.
He sent me off to Troy...
and I hear his **urgings**[10] ringing in my ears：
'Always be the best，my boy，the bravest，
and hold your head up high above the others.
Never disgrace the generation of your fathers.
They were the bravest champions born in Corinth，   250
in Lycia far and wide.'
         There you have my **lineage**[11].
That is the blood I claim，my royal birth."

When he heard that，Diomedes' spirits lifted.
Raising his spear，the lord of the war cry **drove it home**[12]，

2. 苦苦请求地

3.［kɑːv］ *v*. 挑选出
4.［'vɪnjəd］ *n*. 葡萄园
5.［tɪl］ *v*. 耕种

6.［helm］ *v*. 戴上头盔

7. 极为悲伤
8.［'fjuːdʒətɪv］ *n*. 亡命天涯
9.［'seɪtɪd］ *adj*. 充分满足的

10.［ɜːdʒɪŋ］ *n*. 敦促

11.［'lɪnɪɪdʒ］ *n*. 直系后代

12. 投掷在地上

planting it deep down in the earth that feeds us all
and with winning words he called out to Glaucus,
the young captain, "Splendid—you are my friend,
my guest from the days of our grandfathers long ago!
Noble Oeneus hosted your brave Bellerophon once,
he held him there in his halls, twenty whole days,   260
and they gave each other handsome gifts of friendship.
My kinsman offered a gleaming sword-belt, rich red,
Bellerophon gave a cup, two-handled, solid gold—
I left it at home when I set out for Troy.
My father, Tydeus, I really don't remember.
I was just a baby when father left me then,
that time an Achaean army went to die at Thebes.
So now I am your host and friend in the heart of Argos,
you are mine in Lycia when I visit in your country.
Come, let us **keep clear of**[1] each other's spears,   270   1. 避开
even there in the thick of battle. Look,
plenty of Trojans there for me to kill,
your famous allies too, any soldier the god
will bring in range or I can run to ground.
And plenty of Argives too—kill them if you can.
But let's **trade**[2] **armor**[3]. The men must know our claim: 2. [treɪd] *v.* 交换
we are sworn friends from our fathers' days till now!"   3. ['ɑːmə] *n.* 盔甲

  Both agreed. Both fighters sprang from their **chariots**[4],   4. ['tʃærɪət] *n.* 战车
clasped each other's hands and traded **pacts**[5] of friendship.   5. [pækt] *n.* 条约
But the son of Cronus, Zeus, stole Glaucus' **wits**[6] away.   280   6. [wɪt] *n.* 智慧
He traded his gold armor for bronze with Diomedes,
the worth of a hundred oxen just for nine.

＊＊＊   ＊＊＊   ＊＊＊   ＊＊＊   ＊＊＊   ＊＊＊   ＊＊＊   ＊＊＊

❀**Questions for discussion:**

(5) This is a very interesting section. Do you think so? The war was going on and killings
    were right there. But we also saw something warm our heart. No killings, no blood,
    or death any more, but faith and friendship. In Ancient Greece, this is seen as a
    sacred oath to Zeus: When a stranger comes to you home, you will receive him with
    hospitality, entertaining him with nice food and wine. Someday in the future, if you
    visit the stranger's home, you will be treated in the same way. What excellent
    customs, do you think so?

（6）Who is Bellerophon? Retell his story in your own words to the whole class? Homer said he is "a man without a fault". Do you agree? Line 236 said, "When even Bellerophon was hated by all the gods". How could this happen for we were told in the prior lines that he was loved by the gods?

（7）Every time when I read lines 170-176, I feel moved. Homer compares lives of mortal men to generations of leaves in the tree. First, translate these several lines into Chinese, and then comment on them.

（8）It can be seen from the above section, Zeus' own son was also fighting in the war. What was his name? If you read the later chapters of *The Iliad*, you will know that he was killed by a Greek hero. Can you guess, how will Zeus respond to the killing and death of his own son?

＊＊＊　　＊＊＊　　＊＊＊　　＊＊＊　　＊＊＊　　＊＊＊　　＊＊＊　　＊＊＊

And now,　　　283

when Hector reached the Scaean Gates and the great **oak**[1],
the wives and daughters of Troy came rushing up around him,
asking about their sons, brothers, friends and husbands.
But Hector told them only, "Pray to the gods"—
all the Trojan women, one after another...
Hard sorrows were hanging over many.

And soon

he came to Priam's palace, that **magnificent**[2] structure
built wide with **porches**[3] and colonnades of **polished**[4] stone.　290
And deep within its walls were fifty sleeping **chambers**[5]
masoned in smooth, lustrous ashlar, linked in a line
where the sons of Priam slept beside their **wedded**[6] wives,
and facing these, opening out across the inner **courtyard**[7],
lay the twelve sleeping chambers of Priam's daughters,
masoned and roofed in lustrous ashlar, linked in a line
where the sons-in-law of Priam slept beside their wives.
And there at the palace Hector's mother met her son,
that warm, goodhearted woman, going in with Laodice,
the loveliest daughter Hecuba ever bred. His mother
clutched[8] his hand and urged him, called his name:　　300
"My child-why have you left the bitter fighting,
why have you come home? Look how they **wear you out**[9],
the sons of Achaea—**curse**[10] them—battling round our walls!
And that's why your spirit brought you back to Troy,
to climb the heights and **stretch**[11] your arms to Zeus.

1. ［əʊk］ *n*. 橡树

2. ［mæg'nɪfɪsnt］ *adj*. 壮丽的，宏伟的

3. ［pɔːtʃ］ *n*. 门廊

4. ［'pɒlɪʃt］ *adj*. 磨光的

5. ［'tʃeɪmbə(r)］ *n*. 房间

6. ［wed］ *adj*. 结婚的

7. ［'kɔːtjɑːd］ *n*. 院子

8. ［klʌtʃ］ *vt*. 抓住；抓紧

9. 累垮

10. ［kɜː(r)s］ *vt*. 诅咒

11. ［stretʃ］ *vt*. 伸展；延伸

But wait, I'll bring you some honeyed, **mellow**[1] wine.
First pour out cups to Father Zeus and the other gods,
then refresh yourself, if you'd like to **quench**[2] your thirst.
When a Man's exhausted, wine will build his strength—   310
battle-**weary**[3] as you are, fighting for your people."

But Hector shook his head, his helmet flashing:
"Don't offer me mellow wine, mother, not now—
you'd **sap**[4] my limbs, I'd lose my nerve for war.
And I'd be ashamed to pour a **glistening**[5] cup to Zeus
with unwashed hands. I'm **splattered**[6] with blood and **filth**[7]—
how could I pray to the lord of storm and lightning?
No, mother, you are the one to pray.
Go to Athena's shrine, the queen of **plunder**[8],
go with offerings, gather the older noble women   320
and take a robe, the largest, loveliest robe
that you can find throughout the royal halls,
a gift that far and away you prize most yourself,
and spread it out across the sleek-haired goddess' knees.
Then promise to sacrifice twelve **heifers**[9] in her shrine,
yearlings[10] never broken, if only she'll pity Troy,
the Trojan wives and all our helpless children,
if only she'll hold Diomedes back from the holy city-
that wild spearman, that **invincible**[11] headlong terror!
Now, mother, go to the queen of plunder's shrine   330
and I'll go hunt for Paris, **summon**[12] him to fight
if the man will hear what I have to say...
Let the earth **gape**[13] and swallow him on the spot!
A great curse Olympian Zeus let live and grow in him,
for Troy and high-hearted Priam and all his sons.
That man—if I could see him bound for the House of Death,
I could say my heart had forgot its **wrenching**[14] grief!"

But his mother simply turned away to the palace.
She gave her servants orders and out they **strode**[15]
to gather the older noble women through the city.   340
Hecuba went down to a storeroom filled with scent
and there they were, **brocaded**[16], beautiful robes...

1. ['meləʊ] *adj.* 甘美多汁的

2. [kwentʃ] *vt.* 解渴

3. ['wɪəri] *adj.* 疲惫的

4. [sæp] *vt.* 消耗
5. ['glɪsn] *v.* 闪闪发光
6. ['splætə(r)] *v.* 溅污
7. [fɪlθ] *n.* 污秽

8. ['plʌndə(r)] *n.* 掠夺

9. ['hefə] *n.* 小母牛
10. ['jɜːlɪŋ; jɜː-] *n.* 一岁家畜

11. [ɪn'vɪnsəbl] *adj.* 无敌的

12. ['sʌmən] *vt.* 传唤,召唤

13. [geɪp] *v.* 裂口张开

14.

15. [strəʊd] *v.* 大踏步

16. [brə'keɪdɪd] *adj.* 织成锦缎的

the work of Sidonian women. Magnificent Paris
brought those women back himself from Sidon,
sailing the open seas on the same long voyage
he swept Helen off, her famous Father's child.
Lifting one from the lot, Hecuba brought it out
for great Athena's gift, the largest, loveliest,
richly worked, and like a star it **glistened**[1],
deep beneath the others. Then she made her way   350
with a file of noble women rushing in her train.

    Once they reached Athena's shrine on the city **crest**[2]
the beauty Theano opened the doors to let them in,
Cisseus' daughter, the horseman Antenor's wife
and Athena's **priestess**[3] chosen by the Trojans. Then
with a **shrill**[4] wail they all stretched their arms to Athena
as Theano, her face **radiant**[5], lifting the robe on high,
spread it out across the sleek-haired goddess' knees
and prayed to the daughter of mighty Father Zeus:
"Queen Athena—**shield**[6] of our city-glory of goddesses!   360
Now shatter the spear of Diomedes! That wild man—
hurl him headlong down before the Scaean Gates!
At once we'll sacrifice twelve heifers in your shrine,
yearlings never broken, if only you'll pity Troy,
the Trojan wives and all our helpless children!"

    But Athena refused to hear Theano's prayers.
And while they prayed to the daughter of mighty Zeus
Hector approached the halls of Paris, **sumptuous**[7] halls
he built himself with the finest **masons**[8] of the day,
master builders famed in the **fertile**[9] land of Troy.   370
They'd raised his sleeping chamber, house and court
adjoining[10] Priam's and Hector's aloft the city heights.
Now Hector, dear to Zeus, **strode**[11] through the gates,
clutching[12] a thrusting-lance eleven forearms long;
the bronze tip of the weapon shone before him,
ringed with a golden **hoop to**[13] grip the shaft.
And there in the bedroom Hector came on Paris
polishing, **fondling**[14] his splendid battle-gear,

1. ['glɪsn] v. 闪光

2. [krest] n. 顶部

3. ['priːstes] n.

4. [ʃrɪl] v. 高声喊叫

5. ['reɪdɪənt] adj.

6. [ʃiːld] n. 保护

7. ['sʌmptʃʊəs] adj. 奢华的

8. ['meɪsn] n. 石匠

9. ['fɜːtaɪl] adj. 富饶的

10. [ə'dʒɔɪnɪŋ] v. 临近

11. [strəʊd] v. 大踏步

12. [klʌtʃ] vt. 抓住

13. [huːp] v. 环

14. ['fɒndl] v. 抚弄

his shield and breastplate, turning over and over

his long curved bow. And there was Helen of Argos,　380

sitting with all the women of the house, directing

the rich **embroidered**[1] work they had in hand.　　1.［ɪmˈbrɔɪdə(r)］v. 绣花

* * *　　* * *　　* * *　　* * *　　* * *　　* * *　　* * *　　* * *

❀**Questions for discussion**:

(9) When Hector returned to Troy, who greeted him at the Gates? What tree grew there
　　at the Gates? How did Hector respond to their questions?

(10) Hector then came to Priam's palace. What did the palace look like? Whom did he
　　first meet in the palace?

(11) Read the dialogue between Hector and his mother. What did his mother offer him?

(12) How did the Trojan women offer sacrifice to Athena? What was Athena's response
　　to their pray?

* * *　　* * *　　* * *　　* * *　　* * *　　* * *　　* * *　　* * *

Seeing Paris,

Hector raked his brother with insults, stinging **taunts**[2]:　　2.［tɔːnt］n. 辱骂

"What on earth are you doing? Oh how wrong it is,

this anger you keep **smoldering**[3] in your heart! Look,　　3.［ˈsməʊldə］v./n. 郁积

your people dying around the city, the steep walls,

dying in arms-and all for you, the battle cries

and the fighting **flaring**[4] up around the **citadel**[5].　　4.［fleɪŋ］

You'd be the first to **lash**[6] out at another—anywhere—　　5.［ˈsɪtədəl］n. 要塞

you saw hanging back from this, this hateful war.　380　6.［læʃ］vi. 猛击

Up with you—

before all Troy is **torched**[7] to a **cinder**[8] here and now!"　　7.［tɔːtʃ］vt. 放火烧

　　　　　　　　　　　　　　　　　　　　　　　　8.［ˈsɪndə(r)］n. 灰烬

And Paris, magnificent as a god, replied,

"Ah Hector, you criticize me fairly, yes,

nothing unfair, beyond what I deserve. And so

I will try to tell you something. Please bear with me,

hear me out. It's not so much from anger or outrage

at our people that I keep to my rooms so long.

I only wanted to plunge myself in **grief**[9].　　9.［griːf］n. 悲痛

But just now my wife was **bringing me round**[10],　　10. 说服我

her winning words urging me back to battle.　400

And it strikes me, even me, as the better way.

Victory shifts, you know, now one man, now another.

So come, wait while I get this war-gear on,

or you go on ahead and I will follow—
I think I can **overtake**[1] you."

        Hector, helmet flashing,
answered nothing. And Helen spoke to him now,
her soft voice **welling up**[2]: "My dear brother,
dear to me, bitch that I am, **vicious**[3], scheming-
horror to freeze the heart! Oh how I wish
that first day my mother brought me into the light   410
some black **whirlwind**[4] had rushed me out to the mountains
or into the surf where the **roaring breakers**[5] crash and drag
and the waves had swept me off before all this had happened!
But since the gods **ordained**[6] it all, these desperate years,
I wish I had been the wife of a better man, someone
alive to **outrage**[7], the withering scorn of men.
This one has no steadiness in his spirit, not now,
he never will... and he's going to reap the fruits of it, I swear.
But come in, rest on this seat with me, dear brother.   420
You are the one hit hardest by the fighting, Hector,
you more than all—and all for me, **whore**[8] that I am,
and this blind mad Paris. Oh the two of us!
Zeus planted a killing doom within us both,
so even for generations still unborn
we will live in song."

        Turning to go,
his helmet flashing, tall Hector answered,
"Don't ask me to sit beside you here, Helen.
Love me as you do, you can't persuade me now.
No time for rest. My heart races to help our Trojans—   430
they long for me, sorely, whenever I am gone.
But **rouse**[9] this fellow, won't you?
And let him hurry himself along as well,
so he can overtake me before I leave the city.
For I must go home to see my people first,
to visit my own dear wife and my baby son.
Who knows if I will ever come back to them again? —
or the deathless gods will strike me down at last
at the hands of Argive fighters."

1. [ˌəʊvəˈteɪk] v. 超过

2. 响起
3. [ˈvɪʃəs] adj. 邪恶的

4. [ˈwɜːlwɪnd] n. 旋风
5. 咆哮的海浪

6. [ɔːˈdeɪn] v. 命令

7. [ˈaʊtreɪdʒ] n. 愤慨

8. [hɔː(r)] n. 婊子

9. [raʊz] v. 唤醒

* * *   * * *   * * *   * * *   * * *   * * *   * * *   * * *

❖**Questions for discussion：**

(13) Who was the second person Hector met when returning home?

(14) Comment on Hector's role as an elder brother.

* * *   * * *   * * *   * * *   * * *   * * *   * * *   * * *

A flash of his helmet

and off he strode and quickly reached his **sturdy**[1]，   440   1.［'stɜːdi］ *adj*. 强壮的
well-built house. But white-armed Andromache-
Hector could not find her in the halls.
She and the boy and a servant finely **gowned**[2]   2.［gaʊn］*vt*. 穿长袍
were standing watch on the tower，sobbing，grieving.
When Hector saw no sign of his loyal wife inside
he went to the doorway，stopped and asked the servants，
"Come，please，tell me the truth now，women.
Where's Andromache gone? To my sisters' house?
To my brothers' wives with their long flowing robes?
Or Athena's shrine where the noble Trojan women   450
gather to win the great grim goddess over?"

A busy，willing servant answered quickly，
"Hector，seeing you want to know the truth，
she hasn't gone to your sisters，brothers' wives
or Athena's shrine where the noble Trojan women
gather to win the great **grim**[3] goddess over.   3.［grɪm］*adj*. 冷酷的
Up to the huge gate-tower of Troy she's gone
because she heard our men are so hard-pressed，
the Achaean fighters coming on in so much force.
She sped to the wall in **panic**[4]，like a mad woman—   460   4.［'pænɪk］*n*. 惊慌
the nurse went with her，carrying your child."

At that，Hector **spun**[5] and rushed from his house，   5.［spʌn］*v*. 转身
back by the same way down the wide，well-paved streets
throughout the city until he reached the Scaean Gates，
the last point he would pass to gain the field of battle.
There his warm，generous wife came **running up to**[6] meet him，   6. 跑到
Andromache' the daughter of **gallant**[7]—hearted Eetion   7.［'gælənt］*adj*. 勇敢的
who had lived below Mount Placos rich with **timber**[8]，   8.［'tɪmbə(r)］*n*. 灌木
in Thebe below the peaks，and ruled Cilicia's people.
His daughter had married Hector **helmed**[9] in bronze.   470   9.［helm］*vt*. 戴上头盔

She joined him now, and following in her steps
a servant holding the boy against her breast,
in the first **flush**[1] of life, only a baby,
Hector's son, the darling of his eyes
and **radiant**[2] as a star...
Hector would always call the boy Scamandrius,
townsmen called him Astyanax, Lord of the City,
since Hector was the lone defense of Troy.
The great man of war breaking into a broad smile,
his gaze fixed on his son, in silence. Andromache,   480
pressing close beside him and weeping freely now,
clung to[3] his hand, urged him, called him: "Reckless one,
my Hector-your own fiery courage will destroy you!
Have you no pity for him, our helpless son? Or me,
and the destiny that weighs me down, your **widow**[4],
now so soon? Yes, soon they will kill you off,
all the Achaean forces massed for **assault**,[5] and then,
bereft of[5] you, better for me to sink beneath the earth.
What other warmth, what comfort's left for me,
once you have met your doom? Nothing but **torment**[7]!   490
I have lost my father. Mother's gone as well.
Father... the brilliant Achilles **laid him low**[8]
when he **stormed**[9] Cilicia's city filled with people,
Thebe with her towering gates. He killed Eetion,
not that he stripped his gear-he'd some respect at least—
for he burned his corpse in all his **blazoned**[10] bronze,
then **heaped**[11] a grave-mound high above the ashes
and nymphs of the mountain planted **elms**[12] around it,
daughters of Zeus whose shield is storm and thunder.
And the seven brothers I had within our halls...   500
all in the same day went down to the House of Death,
the great godlike runner Achilles **butchered**[13] them all,
tending their **shambling**[14] oxen, shining flocks.
                                    And mother,
who ruled under the **timberline**[15] of woody Placos once—
he no sooner **haled**[16] her here with his other **plunder**[17]
than he took a priceless ransom, set her free
and home she went to her father's royal halls
where Artemis, **showering**[18] arrows, shot her down.

1. [flʌʃ] *n.* 奔流
2. ['reidiənt] *adj.* 明亮的
3. 坚持
4. ['widəʊ] *n.* 寡妇
5. [ə'sɔːlt] *n.* 攻击
6. [bɪ'reft] 丧失
7. ['tɔːment] *n.* 折磨
8. 击倒他
9. [stɔːm] *v.* 猛攻
10. ['bleɪzn] *n.* 装饰
11. [hiːp] *v.* 堆起来
12. [elm] *n.* 榆树
13. ['bʊtʃə(r)] *v.* 屠杀
14. ['ʃæmbl] *v.* 蹒跚而行
15. ['tɪmbəlaɪn] *n.* 木林线
16. [heɪl] *v.* 迫使；猛拉
17. ['plʌndə(r)] *v.* 掠夺
18. ['ʃaʊə(r)] *v.* 大量地给予

You，Hector-you are my father now，my noble mother，a
brother too，and you are my husband，young and warm
and strong!   510
Pity me，please! Take your stand on the **rampart**[1] here，
before you orphan your son and make your wife a widow.
Draw your armies up where the wild fig tree stands，
there，where the city lies most open to **assault**[2]，
the walls lower，easily overrun. Three times
they have tried that point，hoping to storm Troy，
their best fighters led by the Great and Little Ajax，
famous Idomeneus，Atreus' sons，**valiant**[3] Diomedes.
Perhaps，a skilled **prophet**[4] revealed the spot—
or their own fury whips them on to attack."   520

    And tall Hector nodded，his helmet flashing：   521
"All this weighs on my mind too，dear woman.   522
But I would die of shame to face the men of Troy
and the Trojan women trailing their long **robes**[5]
if I would **shrink**[6] from battle now，a coward.
Nor does the spirit urge me on that way.
I've learned it all too well. To stand up bravely，
always to fight in the **front ranks**[7] of Trojan soldiers，
winning my father great glory，glory for myself.
For in my heart and soul I also know this well：   530
the day will come when **sacred**[8] Troy must die，
Priam must die and all his people with him，
Priam who **hurls**[9] the strong ash spear...   533
                              Even so，   534
it is less the pain of the Trojans still to come
that weighs me down，not even of Hecuba herself
or King Priam，or the thought that my own brothers
in all their numbers，all their **gallant**[10] courage，
may tumble in the dust，**crushed**[11] by enemies-
That is nothing，nothing beside your **agony**[12]
when some **brazen**[13] Argive **hales**[14] you off in tears， 540
wrenching away[15] your day of light and freedom!

1. ['ræmpɑːt] n. 防御工事
2. [ə'sɔːlt] v. 攻击
3. ['væliənt] adj. 勇敢的
4. ['prɒfit] n. 先知
5. [rəʊb] n. 长袍
6. [ʃrɪŋk] n. 退缩
7. 前排
8. ['seikrid] adj. 神圣的
9. [hɜːl] vt. 猛投
10. ['gælənt] adj. 勇敢的
11. [krʌʃ] vt. 压碎
12. ['ægəni] n. 痛苦
13. ['breizn] adj. 无耻的
14. [heil] 强拉硬拖
15. [rentʃ] v. 扭转

Then far off in the land of Argos you must live,
laboring at a loom, at another woman's **beck and call**[1],
fetching water at some spring, Messeis or Hyperia,
resisting it all the way—
the rough **yoke**[2] of necessity at your neck.
And a man may say, who sees you streaming tears,
'There is the wife of Hector, the bravest fighter
they could field, those **stallion-breaking**[3] Trojans,
long ago when the men fought for Troy.' So he will say 550
and the fresh grief will **swell**[4] your heart once more,
widowed[5], robbed of the one man strong enough
to fight off your day of slavery.

No, no,

let the earth come piling over my dead body
before I hear your cries, I hear you dragged away!"

In the same breath, shining Hector reached
down for his son—but the boy **recoiled**[6],
cringing[7] against his nurse's full breast,
screaming out at the sight of his own father,
terrified by the flashing bronze, the horsehair **crest**[8], 560
the great **ridge**[9] of the helmet nodding, **bristling**[10] terror-
so it struck his eyes. And his loving father laughed,
his mother laughed as well, and glorious Hector,
quickly lifting the helmet from his head,
set it down on the ground, **fiery**[11] in the sunlight,
and raising his son he kissed him, **tossed**[12] him in his arms,
lifting a prayer to Zeus and the other deathless gods:
"Zeus, all you immortals! Grant this boy, my son, may
be like me, first in glory among the Trojans, strong
and brave like me, and rule all Troy in power and 570
one day let them say, 'He is a better man than his father!'—
when he comes home from battle bearing the bloody gear
of the mortal enemy he has killed in war—
a joy to his mother's heart."

So Hector prayed

and placed his son in the arms of his loving wife.
Andromache pressed the child to her **scented**[13] breast,

1. 点头;招手

2. [jəʊk] *n.* 轭

3. ['stælɪən] *n.* 驯马

4. [swel] *v.* 膨胀
5. ['wɪdəʊ] *vt.* 使成寡妇

6. [rɪˈkɔɪl] *v.* 退却
7. [krɪndʒ] *adj.* 畏缩

8. [krest] *n.* 波峰
9. [rɪdʒ] *n.* 脊
10. ['brɪsl] *adj.* 直立的

11. ['faɪəri] *adj.* 火似的
12. [tɒs] *vt.* 抛;掷

13. ['sentɪd] *adj.* 芳香的

smiling through her tears. Her husband noticed，

and filled with pity now，Hector **stroked**[1] her gently，

1.［strəʊk］*vt*. 拍打

trying to **reassure**[2] her，repeating her name："Andromache，

2.［ˌriːəˈʃʊə(r)］*vt*. 使…放心

dear one，why so desperate? Why so much grief for me?   580

No man will hurl me down to Death，against my fate.

And fate? No one alive has ever escaped it，

neither brave man nor coward，I tell you—

it's born with us the day that we are born.

So please go home and tend to your own tasks，

the **distaff**[3] and the **loom**[4]，and keep the women

3.［ˈdɪstɑːf］*n*. 卷线杆

4.［luːm］*n*. 织布机

working hard as well. As for the fighting，

men will **see to**[5] that，all who were born in Troy

5. 负责

but I most of all."

               Hector aflash in arms   589

took up his horsehair-crested helmet once again.   590

And his loving wife went home，turning，glancing

back again and again and weeping live warm tears.

She quickly reached the **sturdy**[6] house of Hector，

6.［ˈstɜːdi］*adj*. 强壮的

man-killing Hector，and found her women gathered there

inside and stirred them all to a high pitch of **mourning**[7].

7.［mɔːn］*n*. 哀悼

So in his house they raised the **dirges**[8] for the dead，

8.［dɜːdʒ］*n*. 挽歌

for Hector still alive，his people were so **convinced**[9]

9.［kənˈvɪnst］*adj*. 坚信的

that never again would he come home from battle，

never escape the Argives' rage and bloody hands.   600

✳ ✳ ✳   ✳ ✳ ✳   ✳ ✳ ✳   ✳ ✳ ✳   ✳ ✳ ✳   ✳ ✳ ✳   ✳ ✳ ✳   ✳ ✳ ✳

❀ Questions for discussion：

(15) Hector did not find his own wife when he returned home. Where was his wife?

(16) Read through the above lines very carefully，especially the dialogues between Hector and his wife. Comment on Hector's role as a husband.

(17) Read lines 521-533. Translate them into Chinese.

(18) "There is the wife of Hector，the bravest fighter they could field，those stallion-breaking Trojans，long ago when the men fought for Troy." Why did Hector say this is what weighs him down most? Comment on it.

(19) In the above lines，Hector interacted with his baby son. Comment on Hector's role as a father.

(20) Plato in his "Republic" portrayed Homer as "first teacher" of the tragedians. Read lines 589-600. Do you agree with Plato's view?

(21)"Fate and free will" is the topic the Greeks often come up with. As an individual， one seems rather free. He could decide what he wants to do as he likes (what to eat at noon, what to do in the afternoon, to go to the library or go to the movie), but can one choose what kind of life he wants? Can a person change his fate? In the later lessons, when you read the story of Oedipus the king, the same feelings might occur to you. Based on your understanding and the materials you can find on the internet, discuss the topic "Free Will and Fate".

＊＊＊　　＊＊＊　　＊＊＊　　＊＊＊　　＊＊＊　　＊＊＊　　＊＊＊　　＊＊＊

Nor did Paris **linger**[1] long in his **vaulted**[2] halls.	601
Soon as he **buckled**[3] on his elegant gleaming bronze	
he rushed through Troy, sure in his racing stride.	
As a **stallion**[4] full-fed at the manger, stalled too long,	
breaking free of his **tether**[5] gallops down the plain,	
out for his favorite **plunge**[6] in a river's cool currents,	
thundering in his pride-his head flung back, his **mane**[7]	
streaming over his shoulders, sure and **sleek**[8] in his glory,	
knees racing him on to the fields and **stallion**[9]—haunts	
he loves—so down from Pergamus heights came Paris, son of	
Priam, **glittering**[10] in his armor like the sun **astride**[11] the	610
skies, **exultant**[12], laughing aloud, his fast feet sped him on.	
Quickly he overtook his brother, noble Hector	
still lingering, slow to turn from the spot	
where he had just **confided**[13] in his wife...	
Magnificent Paris spoke first: "Dear brother,	
look at me, holding you back in all your speed—	
dragging my feet; coming to you so late,	
and you told me to be quick!"	

A flash of his helmet as Hector shot back,	620
"Impossible man! How could anyone fair and just	
underrate[14] your work in battle? You're a good soldier.	
But you hang back of your own accord, refuse to fight.	
And that, that's why the heart inside me aches	
when I hear our Trojans **heap**[15] **contempt**[16] on you,	
the men who bear such struggles all for you.	625

Come,

now for attack! We'll set all this to rights,
someday, if Zeus will ever let us raise
the winebowl of freedom high in our halls,

Vocabulary:

1. ['lɪŋgə(r)] v. 逗留
2. ['vɔːltɪd] adj. 拱形的
3. ['bʌkl] v. 扣紧
4. ['stælɪən] n. 公马
5. ['teðə(r)] v. 束缚
6. [plʌndʒ] n. 跳水
7. [meɪn] n. 鬃毛
8. [sliːk] adj. 圆滑的
9. ['stælɪən] n. 公马生息地
10. ['glɪtərɪŋ] v. 闪闪发光的
11. [ə'straɪd] adv. 跨越
12. [ɪg'zʌltənt] adj. 欢欣鼓舞的
13. [kən'faɪd] v. 吐露;托付
14. [ˌʌndə'reɪt] vt. 低估
15. [hiːp] vt. 堆满
16. [kən'tempt] n. 鄙视

high to the gods of cloud and sky who live forever—　　630
once we drive these Argives **geared**[1] for battle out of Troy!"　　1.[gɪə(r)] *v*. 使适应

Thetis Receiving the Weapons of Achilles from Hephaestus

* * *　　* * *　　* * *　　* * *　　* * *　　* * *　　* * *　　* * *

❉Questions for discussion:

(22) We discussed earlier that Homer is master of metaphors. What metaphor did Homer employ in the above section?

(23) Translate lines 620-625 into Chinese.

(24) Write a summary of Book 6. Some people say Homer's greatness lies in his portrait of a great enemy. What are your comments on this? Compare Achilles and Hector, which one is more true to human being?

* * *　　* * *　　* * *　　* * *　　* * *　　* * *　　* * *　　* * *

Chapter Two   The Persian Wars

Background Knowledge

1. Polis

A polis (plural poleis) is also translated as "city-state". The city-state is seen as one of the greatest political innovations of the ancient Greeks. In the Dark Age, Greek people must have lived in small groups, usually a leader with bands of followers. At that period, Greece experienced material scarcity and also a sharp decline in its population. With the coming of the eighth century BCE, changes had been taking place. The Greek society began to see the increase of prosperity and the expansion of its population. And then another significant change also appeared, that is the emergence of the characteristic unit of Greek social, political, and religious organization. This unit is the rudimentary form of polis. During the latter part of the Dark Age, the essential elements of the Greek city-states were already in place. Polis (the city-state), from which modern terms "political", "politics" and "policy" originated, is a single, self-governing political unit.

Greece in the Archaic Age

The revival of this organized political structure most probably originated from the lack of powerful imperial states ever since the Dark Age. The political collapse of Mycenaean civilization had left a vacuum of power. This then made it possible for small, independent city-states to emerge without being overwhelmed by large states. The gradual emergence of the city-state in the Archaic Age has produced far-reaching influences in Greek and even in human history. It prepared Greece for the path to its economic and political prosperity and is thereof seen as one of the lasting achievements of the Greek Renaissance.

One rather distinctive characteristic of the city-state was **its small size**. Generally, a polis included **an urban center**, often protected by stout walls, which might also take control of the surrounding countryside with its various small settlements. For example, Athens was the urban center of Attica; Thebes of Boeotia; Sparta of the southwestern Peloponnese. The urban center contains an open area and a place for the cult. The open area was called an **AGORA**. An AGORA is the meeting place and market place where members of the polis can interact to conduct trade and to carry out the business of government. With time, the agora was not only a marketplace, but the heart of Greek intellectual life and discourse.

The polis differed from a modern city in two important aspects. The first **was self-governing**. A polis was independent of its neighbors, not subject to the rule of a larger regional or national state. It could decide on its own internal affairs and make its own foreign policies. The second was **the possession and control of a territory**. Though an urban center was usually included in a polis, the possession of a territory was needed for the growth of its agriculturally based economy. The territory might consist of dependent villages and in some cases, there could be no urban center. Sparta, for example, in the early time of the Archaic Age, consisted of only a collection of several villages. These two characteristics of a polis help to explain why a polis is also translated as city-state.

The scale of the polis was indeed small. A modern middle-sized city in China might be as large as or even larger than a Greek polis. The great Greek philosopher Aristotle (384-322 B.C.) discussed the origins of the polis in his book *politics* in the early 4th century B.C. He suggested that "it is necessary for the citizens to be of such a number that they knew each other's personal qualities and thus can elect their officials and judge their fellows in a court of law sensibly". He maintained that the emergence of the polis had been the inevitable result of the forces of nature at work. "Humans", he said, "are beings who by nature live in a polis". Anyone who existed self-sufficiently outside the community of a polis, Aristotle only half-jokingly maintained, "must be either a beast or a god".

The Greek city-state was organized politically on the concept of citizenship. Citizenship as an organizing concept in this period above all carried certain important rights, such as access to courts to resolve disputes, protection against enslavement by kidnapping, and participation in the religious and cultural life of the city-state. It also implied participation in politics, although the extent of participation open to the poorest men varied among different city-states. What's especially remarkable, citizenship ensured the general legal equality provided by the city-state, and this was not absolutely dependent on a citizen's wealth. Citizenship assumed in theory certain basic levels of legal equality, essentially the expectation of equal treatment under the law. For example, in the city-state, even poor men had a vote on political matters.

In any case, the hallmark of the politics of the developed Greek city-states was certainly the practice of the citizen men making decisions communally. **Sparta and Athens** are the two most well-known Greek city-states. Refer to Pericles' *Funeral Oration* in later chapters to know what Athens is like as a city-state.

2. Herodotus

Herodotus (/hɪˈrɒdətəs/; Ancient Greek: Ἡρόδοτος Hēródotos [hɛːródotos]) was a Greek historian who was born in Halicarnassus, Caria (modern-day Bodrum, Turkey) and lived in the fifth century BC (484BC—425BC). It is said Herodotus invented history and thus is often referred to as **"The Father of History"** (first conferred by Cicero). He was said to be the first historian known to collect his materials systematically and critically, and then to arrange them into a historiographic narrative (from Wikipedia).

The *Histories*—his masterpiece and the only work he is known to have produced—is a record of his "inquiry", an investigation of the origins of the Greco-Persian Wars. Herodotus was perhaps one of the most widely traveled persons in the ancient world. At the age of about 30, he began an extensive travel from the north coast of the Black Sea to the south of Egypt, from the eastern lower reaches of Euphrates to the western Italian peninsula and Sicily. Wherever he went, Herodotus would visit the local historical interests, take a survey of the geography, and learn about the local traditions. He preferred to hear the local people relate legends and historic stories, which he recorded by putting them down. Herodotus also traveled through the Persian Empire. Partly for this reason, Herodotus was seen as the first historian known to "collect his materials systematically and test their accuracy to a certain extent."

In the year 445 B.C., Herodotus came to Athens, which was then the political, economic and cultural center of Greece. After the Persian wars, the Athenian politics and economy were prosperous, coupled with the highly developed intellectual life. This was much to Herodotus' excitement, whereby he took an active part in all kinds of gatherings and cultural activities, and soon made friends with famous Athenians like Pericles and Sophocles.

Herodotus marveled at the democracy of Athens, and showed much admiration of the Greek victory over the Persian Empire under the leadership of Athens. He inquired about the war and collected a lot of historic materials. In the spring of 443 B.C., Herodotus settled in one of the Athens' colonies and spent most of his energy writing the book *the Histories*. Unfortunately the book was not finished before he died in the year 425 B.C..

3. The *Histories*

Travelling around and growing up in the Asiatic world, Herodotus could see both sides of the wars. In Herodotus' mind, the generation that fought in the wars was the greatest generation. *The Histories* of Herodotus is the first work of history in Greece. In Greek, the word "historia" means "inquiry" or "research" and therefore "Historia" is the process of finding and gathering together the truth about the past. As Herodotus states in the opening sentence of his work, his purpose was "so that the actions of people shall

She was seen naked

not fade with time" and "so that the great and admirable monuments produced by both Greeks and barbarians shall not go unrenowned" (*The Histories* 1.1, Blanco). Herodotus made it his life's work to travel to all the places that had been involved in the conflict and to create a work that would capture for all time what the wars had been like: *The Histories*.

The work is composed of two sections. The first section records the history, geography, traditions of the Assyrians, Greek city states and the Persian Empire, as well as the cause of the Greco-Persian Wars. The second part is mainly the process and result of the Persian wars, from the Ionian revolt to the year 478 B.C..

Influenced by the traditions of Ionian rationalism, Herodotus had a passionate curiosity about causes and origins. In his book he tried to relate how Darius came to rule the Persian Empire, why the Persians and the Greeks fought with each other, and why the Persians lost the war to the Greeks. Herodotus used the Greek word "historia" to show his understanding and explanation of the way things worked out. Because of this, the word *history* came to mean the investigation and analysis of the past. He accounted for the cause of the Greek victory over the Persian Empire as the victory of democracy over the tyrannical monarchy.

Herodotus was not only interested in the historical events, but also in what history revealed about human nature. What he learned from his study of history was that the mighty seldom think over their condition with enough judiciousness and reflection and jump headlong to their own doom. This could be illustrated in his imaginative reconstruction of a conversation between Solon and Croesus, the king of Lydia. After giving the law to Athens, Solon had resigned and traveled around. Once, Solon came to Croesus' palace. Croesus asked him to name who in the world was the most fortunate person, expecting in his conceitedness that Solon would answer it was he himself, the king of Lydia, who was most fortunate. Yet Solon gave two examples of little known people who had died with much honor. Croesus was indignant that Solon should consider such people as fortunate, upon which Solon answered,

"To me, it is obvious that you have great wealth and that you rule over many people, but it will be impossible for me to answer your question until I learn that you have happily ended your allotted life. After all, the rich man is not really happier than the man who lives from day to day unless good fortune stays with him and he dies painlessly, and in possession of all the good things life has to offer.... You have to consider how everything ends—how it turns out. For god gives many a glimpse of happiness and then withers them at their very roots."

(The Histories 1.32, Blanco)

Croesus, however, did not listen. He just listened to what he wanted to hear. Later he misinterpreted a series of oracles, and as we mention before, he finally lost his empire and eventually recognized Solon's wisdom.

Also in the case of the Persian king Xerxes, Herodotus believed Xerxes' fault lay in his "hybris". Brought up in a situation that everybody else was slave to the king, the Persian king exaggerated his own importance, related himself to the god, and did everything at his will. In a sense, the Persian king was the Persian Empire. In contrast, the Greek people had the free institutions, the rule of law, and the respect for gods. Eventually, the Persian king Xerxes was defeated by the Greeks who considered themselves a free people.

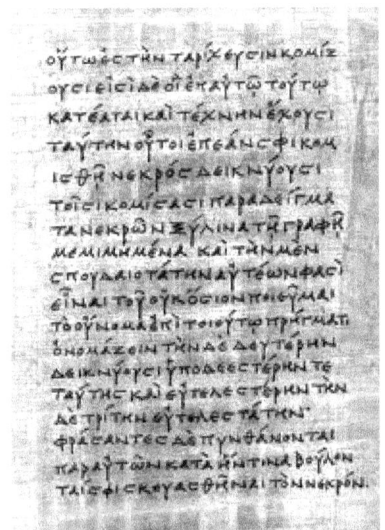

Herodotus Papyrus

In his book Herodotus also tried to undermine the assumptions of the Greeks that non-Greek cultures were inferior and women had low intellect. He thought the Greeks needed to think longer and harder about their place in the world. He included in his work several stories of intelligent queens. Besides, he related the achievements of the Egyptians, stressed the greater antiquity of Egyptian culture in relation to the Greeks and suggested Egyptian origins for the Greek gods.

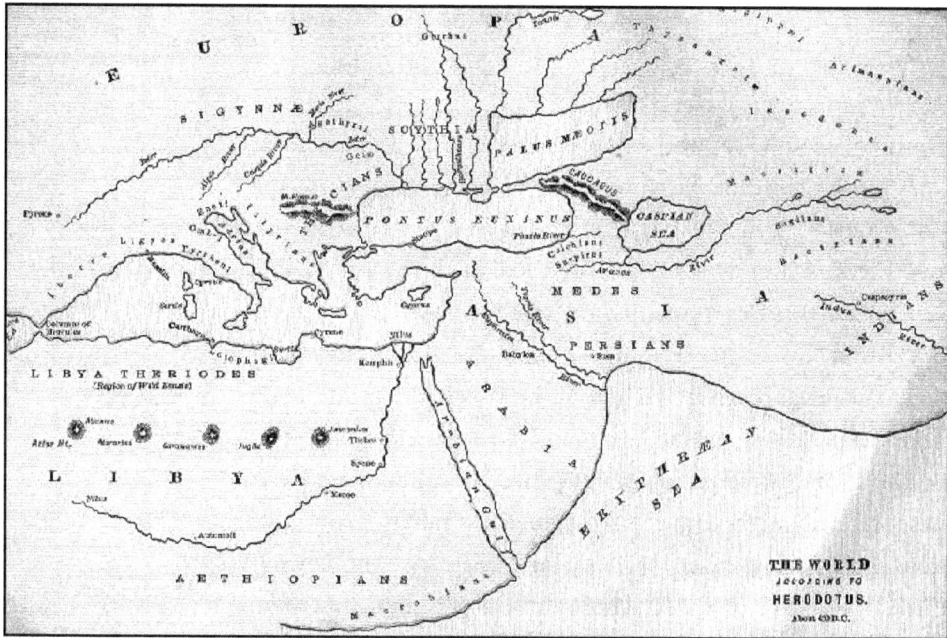

The World according to Herodotus

Herodotus read his history before the entire Assembly of the Athenian citizens near 445 B.C.. The Athenian citizens were so pleased and moved to his history that they gave Herodotus ten talents as a reward, one talent was enough to build the warship, so this made him wealthy forever. He now set off to Italy, lived out his life, but left behind the history, which was read on a regular basis, at the Olympic Games. In history, Herodotus searched for moral truth, and for him that was the ultimate purpose of history, just as it was for Plutarch, that the reader will be instructed and made better, better as an individual, better as a citizen.

It stands as one of the first accounts of the rise of the Persian Empire, the events of, and causes for, the Greco-Persian Wars between the Achaemenid Empire and the Greek city-states in the 5th century BC. Herodotus portrays the conflict as one between the forces of slavery (the Persians) on the one hand, and freedom (the Athenians and the confederacy of Greek city-states which united against the invaders) on the other.

The *Histories* was at some point divided into the nine books of modern editions, conventionally named after the Muses.

Solon's View of Happiness

By Herodotus

On this account，as well as to see the world，Solon set out upon his travels，in the course of which he went to Egypt to the court of **Amasis**[1]，and also came on a visit to Croesus at Sardis. Croesus received him as his guest，and **lodged**[2] him in the royal palace. On the third or fourth day after，he **bade**[3] his servants conduct Solon over his treasuries，and show him all their greatness and **magnificence**[4]. When he had seen them all，and，so far as time allowed，inspected them，Croesus **addressed**[5] this question to him. "Stranger of Athens，we have heard much of **thy**[6] wisdom and of thy travels through many lands，from love of knowledge and a wish to see the world. I am curious therefore to **inquire**[7] of thee，whom，of all the men that thou has seen，thou deemest the most happy?" This he asked because he thought himself the happiest of mortals：but Solon answered him without **flattery**[8]，according to his true **sentiments**[9]，"Tellus of Athens，**sire**[10]." Full of **astonishment**[11] at what he heard，Croesus demanded sharply，"And wherefore dost thou deem Tellus happiest?" To which the other replied，"First，because his country was **flourishing**[12] in his days，and he himself had sons both beautiful and good，and he lived to see children born to each of them，and these children all grew up；and further because，after a life spent in what our people look upon as comfort，his end was **surpassingly**[13] **glorious**[14]. In a battle between the Athenians and their neighbours near Eleusis，he came to the assistance of his countrymen，**routed**[15] the **foe**[16]，and died upon the field most **gallantly**[17]. The Athenians gave him a public **funeral**[18] on the spot where he fell，and paid him the highest honours."

Thus did Solon **admonish**[19] Croesus by the example of Tellus，**enumerating**[20] the manifold particulars of his happiness. When he had ended，Croesus **inquired**[21] a second time，who after Tellus seemed to him the happiest，expecting that **at any rate**[22]，he would be given the second place. "Cleobis and Bito,"

1. 阿玛西斯(国王)
2. ［lɒdʒ］ *vt*. 提供住宿
3. ［beɪd］ *v*. 叮嘱
4. ［mæɡ'nɪfɪsns］ *n*. 华丽
5. ［ə'drest］ *v*. 提出
6. ［ðai］ *n*.（旧式用法）你的
7. ［ɪn'kwaɪə(r)］ *v*. 询问
8. ［'flætəri］ *n*. 奉承
9. ［'sentɪmənt］ *n*. 感情
10. ［saɪə(r)］ *n*. 陛下；大人
11. ［ə'stɒnɪʃmənt］ *n*. 吃惊
12. ［'flʌrɪʃ］ *n*. 繁荣
13. ［sə'pɑːsɪŋli］ *adv*. 卓越地
14. ［'ɡlɔːrɪəs］ *adj*. 光荣的
15. ［raut］ *vt*. 打垮
16. ［fəʊ］ *n*. 敌人
17. ［'ɡæləntli］ *adv*. 勇敢地
18. ［'fjuːnərəl］ *n*. 葬礼
19. ［əd'mɒnɪʃ］ *vt*. 训诫
20. ［ɪ'njuːməreɪt］ *vt*. 列举
21. ［ɪn'kwaɪə(r)］ *vt*. 询
22. 无论如何

Solon answered; "they were of Argive race; their **fortune**[1] was enough for their wants, and they were besides **endowed**[2] with so much bodily strength that they had both gained prizes at the Games. Also this tale is told of them: There was a great festival in honour of the goddess **Juno at Argos**[3], to which their mother must needs be taken in a car. Now the **oxen**[4] did not come home from the field in time; so the youths, fearful of being too late, put the **yoke**[5] on their own necks, and themselves drew the car in which their mother rode. Five and forty **furlongs**[6] did they draw her, and stopped before the temple. This deed of theirs was witnessed by the whole **assembly**[7] of worshippers, and then their life closed in the best possible way. Herein, too, God showed forth most evidently, how much better a thing for man death is than life. For the Argive men, who stood around the car, **extolled**[8] the vast strength of the youths; and the Argive women extolled the mother who was **blessed**[9] with such a pair of sons; and the mother herself, **overjoyed**[10] at the deed and at the praises it had won, standing straight before the image, **besought**[11] the goddess to **bestow**[12] on Cleobis and Bito, the sons who had so mightily honoured her, the highest blessing to which mortals can attain. Her prayer ended, they offered sacrifice and partook of the holy **banquet**[13], after which the two youths fell asleep in the temple. They never woke more, but so passed from the earth. The Argives, looking on them as among the best of men, caused **statues**[14] of them to be made, which they gave to the **shrine**[15] at Delphi."

When Solon had thus assigned these youths the second place, Croesus broke in angrily, "What, stranger of Athens, is my happiness, then, so **utterly set at nought**[16] by thee, that thou dost not even put me on a level with private men?"

"Oh! Croesus," replied the other, "thou askedst a question **concerning**[17] the condition of man, of one who knows that the power above us is full of jealousy, and fond of troubling our lot. A long life gives one to witness much, and experience much oneself, that one would not choose. Seventy years I regard as the limit of the life of man. In these seventy years are contained, without reckoning **intercalary months**[18], twenty-five thousand and two hundred days. Add an intercalary month to

1. ['fɔːtʃuːn] *n.* 财富
2. [ɪn'dau] *vt.* 被赋予
3. 天后赫拉（Hera）
4. ['ɒksn] *n.* 牛
5. [jəuk] *n.* 牛轭
6. ['fɜːlɒŋ] *n.* 0 长度单位
7. [ə'sembli] *n.* 聚集
8. [ɪk'stəul] *vt.* 称颂
9. [bles] *vi.* 赐福
10. [ˌəuvə'dʒɔɪ] *vt.* 使大喜
11. [bɪ'sɔːt] *vt.* 请求；赠给
12. [bɪ'stəu] *vt.* 授予
13. ['bæŋkwɪt] *n.* 宴会
14. ['stætʃuː] *n.* 雕像
15. [ʃraɪn] *n.* 神龛
16. 完全无视
17. [kən'sɜːn] *prep.* 论及
18. 闰月

every other year, that the seasons may come round at the right time, and there will be, besides the seventy years, thirty-five such months, making an addition of one thousand and fifty days. The whole number of the days contained in the seventy years will thus be twenty-six thousand two hundred and fifty, whereof not one but will produce events unlike the rest. Hence man is wholly accident. For **thyself**[1], oh! Croesus, I see that thou art wonderfully rich, and art the lord of many nations; but **with respect to**[2] that whereon thou questionest me, I have no answer to give, until I hear that thou hast closed thy life happily. For **assuredly**[3] he who possesses great store of riches is no nearer happiness than he who has what **suffices**[4] for his daily needs, unless it so **hap**[5] that luck attend upon him, and so he continue in the enjoyment of all his good things to the end of life. For many of the wealthiest men have been unfavoured of fortune, and many whose means were **moderate**[6] have had excellent luck. Men of the former class **excel**[7] those of the latter but in two respects; these last excel the former in many. The wealthy man is better able to content his desires, and to bear up against a sudden **buffet**[8] of **calamity**[9]. The other has less ability to **withstand**[10] these evils (from which, however, his good luck keeps him clear), but he enjoys all these following blessings: he is whole of **limb**[11], a stranger to disease, free from misfortune, happy in his children, and **comely**[12] to look upon. If, in addition to all this, he end his life well, he is of a truth the man of whom thou art in search, the man who may rightly be **termed**[13] happy. Call him, however, until he die, not happy but fortunate. Scarcely, indeed, can any man unite all these advantages: as there is no country which contains within it all that it needs, but each, while it possesses some things, lacks others, and the best country is that which contains the most; so no single human being is complete in every respect- something is always lacking. He who unites the greatest number of advantages, and **retaining**[14] them to the day of his death, then dies peaceably, that man alone, sire, is, in my judgment, **entitled**[15] to bear the name of 'happy'. But in every matter it **behoves**[16] us to mark well the end: for often times God gives men a **gleam**[17] of happiness, and then plunges them into ruin."

1. [ðaɪˈself] n. 你自己（古体）

2. 关于

3. [əˈʃʊəd] adv. 确实地

4. [səˈfaɪs] vi. 足够；运气

5. [hæp] n. 运气

6. [ˈmɒdərət] vt. 中等的

7. [ɪkˈsel] n. 超越；优秀

8. [ˈbʊfeɪ] n. 打击

9. [kəˈlæməti] n. 灾难

10. [wɪðˈstænd] vt. 抵挡

11. [lɪm] n. 四肢

12. [ˈkʌmli] adj. 合适的

13. [tɜːm] vt. 称作

14. [rɪˈteɪn] vt. 维持，保留

15. [ɪnˈtaɪtl] vt. 使有资格

16. [bɪˈhəʊv] vt. 理应

17. [gliːm] n. 瞥一眼

Such was the speech which Solon addressed to Croesus, a speech which brought him neither largess nor honour. The king saw him **depart**[1] with much indifference, since he thought that a man must be an **arrant**[2] fool who made no account of present good, but **bade**[3] men always wait and mark the end.

After Solon had gone away a dreadful **vengeance**[4], sent of God, came upon Croesus, to punish him, it is likely, for deeming himself the happiest of men. First he had a dream in the night, which **foreshowed**[5] him truly the evils that were about to befall him in the person of his son. For Croesus had two sons, one blasted by a natural defect, being deaf and dumb; the other, distinguished far above all his co-mates in every pursuit. The name of the last was Atys. It was this son concerning whom he dreamt a dream that he would die by the blow of an iron weapon. When he woke, he considered earnestly with himself, and, greatly alarmed at the dream, instantly made his son take a wife, and whereas in former years the youth **had been wont to**[6] command the Lydian forces in the field, he now would not suffer him to accompany them. All the spears and javelins, and weapons used in the wars, he removed out of the male apartments, and laid them in heaps in the chambers of the women, fearing lest perhaps one of the weapons that hung against the wall might fall and strike him.

1. [dɪˈpɑːt] n. 离开,打发
2. [ˈærənt] n. 彻头彻尾
3. [beɪd] vt. 叮嘱;嘱咐
4. [ˈvendʒəns] n. 报复

5. [fɔːˈʃəʊ] vt. 预示,预告

6. 表示曾经习惯的事

* * *   * * *   * * *   * * *   * * *   * * *   * * *   * * *

❀**Questions for discussion:**

(1) Summarize the main points of Solon's view of happiness in your own words.

(2) Let's review "the manifold particulars of Tellus' happiness". Why did Solon deem Tellus the happiest man in the world? Are people like Tellus hard to find around us? Or Tellus is just like you and me and his happiness is not hard to acquire?

(3) What are so special about the Cleobis and Bito that Solon deemed them the second happiest in the world?

(4) In what aspects is the wealthiest man more advantageous than the man with moderate means? Why did Solon think the moderate man is more advantageous than the wealthiest man?

(5) Do you find a link of Solon's view of happiness with Apollo's Delphic oracle "Know thyself" and "Nothing in Excess"?

(6) Come up with a definition of happiness of your own and then write an essay to discuss Solon's view of happiness.

* * *   * * *   * * *   * * *   * * *   * * *   * * *   * * *

Story of Candaules and His Wife

By Herodotus

For two and twenty generations of men, a space of five hundred and five years; during the whole of which period, from Agron to Candaules, the crown descended in the direct line from father to son.

Now it happened that this Candaules was in love with his own wife; and not only so, but thought her the **fairest**[1] woman in the whole world. This fancy had strange consequences. There was in his bodyguard a man whom he specially favoured, Gyges, the son of Dascylus. All affairs of greatest moment were **entrusted**[2] by Candaules to this person, and him he was **wont**[3] to **extol**[4] the surpassing beauty of his wife. So matters went on for a while. At length, one day, Candaules, who was **fated**[5] to end ill, thus addressed his follower: "I see thou dost not **credit**[6] what I tell thee of my lady's loveliness; but come now, since men's ears are less credulous than their eyes, **contrive**[7] some means whereby thou mayst behold her naked." At this the other loudly **exclaimed**[8], saying, "What most unwise speech is this, master, which thou hast **uttered**?[9] Wouldst thou have me behold my **mistress**[10] when she is naked? Bethink thee that a woman, with her clothes, puts off her **bashfulness**[11]. Our fathers, in time past, distinguished right and wrong plainly enough, and it is our wisdom to **submit**[12] to be taught by them. There is an old saying, 'Let each look on his own.' I hold thy wife for the fairest of all womankind. Only, I **beseech**[13] thee, ask me not to do **wickedly**[14]."

Gyges thus **endeavored**[15] to decline the king's proposal, trembling lest some dreadful evil should befall him through it. But the king **replied**[16] to him, "Courage, friend; suspect me not of the design to prove thee by this discourse; nor dread thy mistress, lest **mischief**[17] be. thee at her hands. Be sure I will so manage that she shall not even know that thou hast looked upon her. I will place thee behind the open door of the **chamber**[18] in which we sleep. When I enter to go to rest she will follow me. There stands a chair close to the entrance, on which

1. [feə(r)] n. 最美丽的

2. [ɪn'trʌst] vt. 委托;托付
3. [wəʊnt] adj. 习惯的;称颂的
4. [ɪk'stəʊl] vt. 吹捧
5. [feɪt] vt. 命中注定
6. ['kredɪt] vt. 可信的

7. [kən'traɪv] vt. 构想
8. [ɪk'skleɪm] vi. 喊叫
9. ['ʌtə(r)] n. 说出
10. ['mɪstrəs] n. 女主人
11. ['bæʃflnəs] n. 羞耻

12. [səb'mɪt] vt. 呈送

13. [bɪ'siːtʃ] vt. 恳求
14. ['wɪkɪdlɪ] n. 邪恶
15. [ɪn'devə(r)] n. 努力

16. [rɪ'plaɪ] n. 回复

17. ['mɪstʃɪf] n. 不幸

18. ['tʃeɪmbə(r)] n. 房间

she will lay her clothes one by one as she takes them off. Thou wilt be able thus at thy leisure to **peruse**[1] her person. Then, when she is moving from the chair toward the bed, and her back is turned on thee, be it thy care that she see thee not as thou passest through the doorway."

Gyges, unable to escape, could but declare his readiness. Then Candaules, when bedtime came, led Gyges into his **sleeping-chamber**[2], and a moment after the queen followed. She entered, and laid her **garments**[3] on the chair, and Gyges gazed on her. After a while she moved toward the bed, and her back being then turned, he **glided**[4] **stealthily**[5] from the apartment. As he was passing out, however, she saw him, and instantly **divining**[6] what had happened, she neither screamed as her shame **impelled**[7] her, nor even appeared to have noticed aught, purposing to take vengeance upon the husband who had so **affronted**[8] her. For among the Lydians, and indeed among the **barbarians**[9] generally, it is **reckoned**[10] a deep disgrace, even to a man, to be seen naked.

No sound or sign of intelligence escaped her at the time. But in the morning, as soon as day broke, she **hastened**[11] to choose from among her **retinue**[12] such as she knew to be most faithful to her, and preparing them for what was to **ensue**[13], summoned Gyges into her presence. Now it had often happened before that the queen had desired to **confer**[14] with him, and he was **accustomed**[15] to come to her at her call. He therefore obeyed the **summons**[16], not suspecting that she knew aught of what had occurred. Then she addressed these words to him: "Take thy choice, Gyges, of two courses which are open to thee. Slay Candaules, and thereby become my lord, and obtain the Lydian **throne**[17], or die this moment in his room. So wilt thou not again, obeying all **behests**[18] of thy master, **behold**[19] what is not lawful for thee. It must needs be that either he perish by whose counsel this thing was done, or thou, who sawest me naked, and so **didst break our usages**[20]." At these words Gyges stood awhile in mute **astonishment**[21]; recovering after a time, he earnestly besought the queen that she would not **compel**[22] him to so hard a choice. But finding he **implored**[23] in vain, and that necessity was indeed laid on him to kill or to

1. [pə'ru:z] vt. 仔细地看
2. ['tʃeimbə] n. 卧室
3. ['gɑ:mənt] vt. 外套
4. [glaɪd] vi. 滑
5. ['stelθɪli] adv. 偷偷地
6. [dɪ'vaɪnɪŋ] vt. 明白
7. [ɪm'peld] vt. 迫使
8. [əf'rʌntɪd] vt. 冒犯
9. [bɑ:'beəriən] n. 野蛮人
10. ['rekən] vi. 认为
11. ['heɪsn] vi. 急忙
12. ['retɪnju:] n. 仆从
13. [ɪn'sju:] vi. 接踵发生
14. [kən'fɜ:] vi. 商议
15. [ə'kʌstəm] adj. 习惯的
16. ['sʌmənz] n. 传唤
17. [θrəʊn] n. 王位
18. [bɪ'hest] n. 命令
19. [bɪ'həʊld] n. 看到;根据他的主意
20. 破坏了我们的惯例
21. [ə'stɒnɪʃmənt] n. 震惊
22. [kəm'pel] vt. 迫使
23. [ɪm'plɔ:(r)] vi. 请求

be killed, he made choice of life for himself, and replied by this inquiry: "If it must be so, and thou compellest me against my will to put my lord to death, come, let me hear how thou wilt have me set on him." "Let him be attacked", she answered, "on the spot where I was by him shown naked to you, and let the **assault**¹ be made when he is asleep."

All was then prepared for the attack, and when night fell, Gyges, seeing that he had no **retreat**² or escape, but must absolutely either slay Candaules, or himself be **slain**³, followed his mistress into the sleeping-room. She placed a **dagger**⁴ in his hand and hid him carefully behind the self-same door. Then Gyges, when the king was fallen asleep, entered **privily**⁵ into the chamber and struck him dead. Thus did the wife and kingdom of Candaules pass into the possession of Gyges, of whom Archilochus the Parian, who lived about the same time, made mention in a poem written in iambic trimeter verse.

1. [ə'sɔːlt] *n*. 攻击

2. [rɪ'triːt] *n*. 退却

3. [sleɪn] *vt*. 杀

4. ['dægə(r)] *n*. 匕首

5. ['prɪvɪli] *adv*. 秘密地

* * *　　* * *　　* * *　　* * *　　* * *　　* * *　　* * *　　* * *

❋Questions for discussion:

(1) Retell the story in your own words.

(2) Why was it so serious to be seen in naked is lydia?

(3) Comment on the three story characters, candaules, his wife, and his bodyguard Gyges.

* * *　　* * *　　* * *　　* * *　　* * *　　* * *　　* * *　　* * *

Story of A Thief

By Herodotus

When Proteus died, **Rhampsinitus**[1], the priests informed me, succeeded to the **throne**[2]. His monuments were the western **gateway**[3] of the temple of Vulcan, and the two **statues**[4] which stand in front of this gateway, called by the Egyptians, the one Summer, the other Winter, each twenty-five cubits in height. The statue of Summer, which is the northernmost of the two, is worshipped by the natives, and has offerings made to it; that of Winter, which stands towards the south, is treated in exactly the contrary way. King Rhampsinitus was possessed, they said, of great riches in silver- indeed to such an amount, that none of the princes, his successors, **surpassed**[5] or even equalled his wealth.

For the better **custody**[6] of this money, he proposed to build a vast **chamber**[7] of hewn stone, one side of which was to form a part of the outer wall of his palace. The builder, therefore, having designs upon the treasures, **contrived**[8], as he was making the building, to insert in this wall a stone, which could easily be removed from its place by two men, or even by one. So the chamber was finished, and the king's money stored away in it. Time passed, and the builder fell sick, when finding his end approaching, he called for his two sons, and **related**[9] to them the **contrivance**[10] he had made in the king's treasure-chamber; telling them it was **for their sakes**[11] he had done it, that so they might always live in **affluence**[12]. Then he gave them clear directions concerning the **mode**[13] of removing the stone, and communicated the measurements, **bidding**[14] them carefully keep the secret, whereby they would be Comptrollers of the Royal Exchequer so long as they lived.

Then the father died, and the sons were not slow in setting to work: they went by night to the palace, found the stone in the wall of the building, and having removed it with ease, **plundered**[15] the treasury of a round sum.

When the king next paid a visit to the apartment, he was astonished to see that the money was sunk in some of the

1. 西尼德斯
2. [θrəʊn] n . 王位
3. ['ɡeɪtweɪ] n . 门
4. [s'tætʃuːz] n . 雕像

5. [sə'pɑːs] v . 超过

6. ['kʌstədi] n . 监管
7. ['tʃeɪmbə(r)] n . 卧室

8. [kən'traɪvd] n . 构想

9. [rɪ'leɪtɪd] v . 讲述
10. [kən'traɪvəns] v . 发明
11. 为了他们
12. ['æfluəns] n . 富裕
13. [məʊd] n . 方式
14. ['bɪdɪŋ] v . 命令

15. ['plʌndə(r)] v . 掠夺

vessels[1] wherein it was stored away. Whom to accuse, however, he knew not, as the **seals**[2] were all perfect, and the fastenings of the room **secure**[3]. Still each time that he repeated his visits, he found that more money was gone. The thieves in truth never stopped, but plundered the treasury ever more and more. At last the king determined to have some **traps**[4] made, and set near the vessels which contained his wealth. This was done, and when the thieves came, as usual, to the treasure-chamber, and one of them entering through the **aperture**[5], made straight for the jars, suddenly he found himself caught in one of the traps. **Perceiving**[6] that he was lost, he instantly called his brother and telling him what had happened, entreated him to enter as quickly as possible and cut off his head, that when his body should be discovered it might not be recognized, which would have the **effect**[7] of bringing ruin upon both. The other thief thought the advice good, and was persuaded to follow it then, fitting the stone into its place, he went home, taking with him his brother's head.

When day **dawned**[8], the king came into the room, and **marvelled**[9] greatly to see the body of the thief in the trap without a head, while the building was still whole, and neither entrance nor exit was to be seen anywhere. In this **perplexity**[10] he commanded the body of the dead man to be hung up outside the palace wall, and set a guard to watch it, with orders that if any persons were seen weeping or **lamenting**[11] near the place, they should be seized and brought before him. When the mother heard of this exposure of the **corpse**[12] of her son, she took it sorely to heart, and spoke to her surviving child, **bidding**[13] him devise some plan or other to get back the body, and threatening, that if he did not **exert**[14] himself, she would go herself to the king, and **denounce**[15] him as the robber.

The son said all he could to persuade her to let the matter rest, but in vain; she still continued to trouble him, until at last he **yielded**[16] to her importunity, and contrived as follows: Filling some **skins**[17] with wine, he loaded them on donkeys, which he drove before him till he came to the place where the guards were watching the dead body, when pulling two or three of the

1. ['vesl] *n.* 船
2. [si:l] *n.* 封条
3. [sɪ'kjʊə(r)] *adj.* 安全的

4. [træp] *n.* 圈套

5. ['æpətʃə(r)] *n.* 孔,洞

6. [pə'si:vɪŋ] 感知到

7. [ɪ'fekt] *n.* 后果

8. [dɔːn] *vi.* 天亮
9. ['maːvl] *vi.* 吃惊

10. [pə'pleksəti] *n.* 困惑

11. [lə'ment] *vi.* 悲叹

12. [kɔːps] *n.* 尸体
13. ['bɪdɪŋ] *v.* 叮嘱

14. [ɪg'zɜːt] *vt.* 用(力)
15. [dɪ'naʊns] *v.* 指控

16. [ji:ld] *v.* 让步
17. [skɪn] *n.* 皮囊

skins towards him, he untied some of the necks which **dangled**[1] by the asses' sides. The wine poured freely out, whereupon he began to beat his head, and shout with all his might, seeming not to know which of the donkeys he should turn to first. When the guards saw the wine running, delighted to profit by the occasion, they rushed one and all into the road, each with some **vessel**[2] or other, and caught the liquor as it was spilling. The driver pretended anger, and loaded them with **abuse**[3]; whereon they did their best to **pacify**[4] him, until at last he appeared to soften, and recover his good humour, drove his asses aside out of the road, and set to work to rearrange their **burthens**[5]; meanwhile, as he talked and chatted with the guards, one of them began to **rally**[6] him, and make him laugh, whereupon he gave them one of the skins as a gift. They now made up their minds to sit down and have a drinking-bout where they were, so they begged him to remain and drink with them. Then the man let himself be persuaded, and stayed. As the drinking went on, they grew very friendly together, so presently he gave them another skin, upon which they drank so **copiously**[7] that they were all overcome with the liquor, and growing **drowsy**[8] lay down, and fell asleep on the spot. The thief waited till it was the dead of the night, and then took down the body of his brother; after which, in **mockery**[9], he shaved off the right side of all the soldiers' beards, and so left them. Laying his brother's body upon the asses, he carried it home to his mother, having thus accomplished the thing that she had required of him.

When it came to the king's ears that the thief's body was stolen away, he was sorely **vexed**[10]. Wishing, therefore, whatever it might cost, to catch the man who had contrived the trick, he had **recourse**[11] (the priests said) to an **expedient**[12], which I can scarcely credit. He sent his own daughter to the **common stews**[13], with orders to **admit**[14] all comers, but to require every man to tell her what was the cleverest and **wickedest**[15] thing he had done in the whole course of his life.

If any one in reply told her the story of the thief, she was to **lay hold of**[16] him and not allow him to get away. The daughter

1. ['dæŋgl] v. 摇摆不定

2. ['vesl] n. 容器
3. [ə'bjuːs] n. 辱骂
4. ['pæsifai] v. 抚慰；安静

5. [bɜːðən] n. 负荷，重荷
6. ['ræli] vt. 使…振作

7. ['kəupiəsli] adv. 充裕地
8. ['drauzi] adj. 昏昏欲睡的

9. ['mɒkəri] n. 嘲笑

10. [veks] v. 使烦恼；使苦恼

11. [ri'kɔːs] n. 依赖；求援
12. [ik'spiːdiənt] n. 方便的
13. 窑子
14. [əd'mit] vt. 接待
15. ['wikid] adj. 最邪恶的

16. 抓住 控制

did as her father willed, whereon the thief, who was well aware of the king's **motive**[1], felt a desire to outdo him in craft and cunning. Accordingly he contrived the following plan: — He **procured**[2] the corpse of a man lately dead, and cutting off one of the arms at the shoulder, put it under his dress, and so went to the king's daughter. When she put the question to him as she had done to all the rest, he replied that the wickedest thing he had ever done was cutting off the head of his brother when he was caught in a trap in the king's treasury, and the cleverest was making the guards drunk and carrying off the body. As he spoke, the princess caught at him, but the thief took advantage of the darkness to hold out to her the hand of the **corpse**[3]. Imagining it to be his own hand, she seized and **held it fast**[4]; while the thief, leaving it in her grasp, made his escape by the door.

1. ['məʊtɪv] n. 动机

2. [prə'kjʊə(r)] n. 获得

3. [kɔːps] n. 尸体
4. 紧紧抓住

The king, when word was brought him of this fresh success, amazed at the **sagacity**[5] and **boldness**[6] of the man, sent messengers to all the towns in his **dominions**[7] to proclaim a free pardon for the thief, and to promise him a rich reward, if he came and made himself known. The thief took the king at his word, and came **boldly**[8] into his presence; whereupon Rhampsinitus, greatly admiring him, and looking on him as the most knowing of men, gave him his daughter in marriage. "The Egyptians," he said, "excelled all the rest of the world in wisdom, and this man excelled all other Egyptians."

5. [sə'ɡæsəti] n. 机智
6. ['bəʊldnɪs] n. 大胆
7. [də'mɪnɪən] n. 统治地盘

8. ['bəʊldli] n. 大胆地

* * *　* * *　* * *　* * *　* * *　* * *　* * *　* * *

✱Questions for discussion

(1) It can be seen that the father mentioned in the text should be a wonderful engineer, a great craftsman. Do you agree? Is he also a great father?

(2) When one of the two brothers was caught in one of the traps, what did they do in order not to be discovered by the king? Is it the best solution to the problem?

(3) We have read many wonderful stories by the Greeks. It seems that the Greeks are very good at telling stories, Hesiod, Homer, and Herodotus among many others. An aim of this book is to help readers develop their narrative abilities. Can you retell the whole story in your own words? Have you ever read similar stories in Chinese?

(4) Translate the last sentence of the passage into Chinese.

* * *　* * *　* * *　* * *　* * *　* * *　* * *　* * *

Three Forms of Government

By Herodotus

And now when five days were gone, and the **hubbub**[1] had settled down, the **conspirators**[2] met together to consult about the situation of affairs. At this meeting speeches were made, to which many of the Hellenes **give no credence**[3], but they were made nevertheless. Otanes recommended that the management of public affairs should **be entrusted to**[4] the whole nation. "To me," he said, "it seems advisable, that we should no longer have a single man to rule over us—the rule of one is neither good nor pleasant. You cannot have forgotten to what lengths Cambyses went in his **haughty**[5] **tyranny**[6], and the haughtiness of the Magi you have yourselves experienced. How indeed is it possible that **monarchy**[7] should be a well-adjusted thing, when it allows a man to do as he likes without being answerable? Such licence is enough to stir strange and **unwonted**[8] thoughts in the heart of the worthiest of men. Give a person this power, and straightway his manifold good things **puff**[9] him up with pride, while **envy**[10] is so natural to human kind that it cannot but arise in him. But pride and envy together include all wickedness—both of them leading on to deeds of **savage**[11] violence.

True it is that kings, possessing as they do all that heart can desire, ought to **be void of**[12] envy; but the contrary is seen in their conduct towards the citizens. They are **jealous**[13] of the most **virtuous**[14] among their **subjects**[15], and wish their death; while they take delight in the meanest and basest, being ever ready to listen to the tales of **slanderers**[16]. A king, besides, is beyond all other men **inconsistent**[17] with himself. Pay him **court**[18] in **moderation**[19], and he is angry because you do not show him more **profound**[20] respect—show him profound respect, and he is offended again, because (as he says) you **fawn**[21] on him. But the worst of all is, that he sets aside the laws of the land, puts men to death without trial, and subjects women to violence. The rule of the many, on the other hand, has, in the first place, the fairest of names, to wit, **isonomy**[22]; and further it is

1. ['hʌbʌb] n. 骚动
2. [kən'spɪrətə(r)] n. 共谋者
3. 不相信
4. 交给;委托给
5. ['hɔːtɪ] adj. 傲慢的
6. ['tɪrəni] n. 专横
7. ['mɒnəki] n. 君主政治
8. [ʌn'wəʊntɪd] adj. 异常的
9. [pʌf] vt. 吹捧
10. ['envi] n. 嫉妒
11. ['sævɪdʒ] adj. 野蛮的
12. 缺乏;没有
13. ['dʒeləs] adj. 嫉妒的
14. ['vɜːtʃʊəs] adj. 善良的
15. ['sʌbdʒɪkt] n. 臣民
16. ['slɑːndərə] n. 中伤者
17. [ˌɪnkən'sɪstənt] adj. 不一致
18. [kɔːt] n. 向…献殷勤
19. [ˌmɒdə'reɪʃən] n. 适度
20. [prə'faʊnd] n. 深度的
21. [fɔːn] vi. 摇尾乞怜
22. [aɪ'sɒnəmi] n. 法律面前人人平等

free from all those **outrages**[1] which a king is wont to commit. There, places are given by lot, the **magistrate**[2] is answerable for what he does, and measures rest with the **commonalty**[3]. I vote, therefore, that we do away with **monarchy**[4], and raise the people to power. For the people are all in all."

1. ['aʊtreɪdʒ] n . 暴行

2. ['mædʒɪstreɪt] n . 法官

3. ['kɒmənlti] n . 平民大众

4. ['mɒnəki] n . 专制

✱ ✱ ✱   ✱ ✱ ✱   ✱ ✱ ✱   ✱ ✱ ✱   ✱ ✱ ✱   ✱ ✱ ✱   ✱ ✱ ✱   ✱ ✱ ✱

✿Questions for discussion:

(1) Based on Otanes' analysis, what is bad for "rule of one"? Do you agree with Otanes' comments on monarchy?

(2) According to Otanes, what are the advantages of "rule of the many"? Why is it better than "rule of one" (or monarchy)?

✱ ✱ ✱   ✱ ✱ ✱   ✱ ✱ ✱   ✱ ✱ ✱   ✱ ✱ ✱   ✱ ✱ ✱   ✱ ✱ ✱   ✱ ✱ ✱

Such were the **sentiments**[5] of Otanes. Megabyzus spoke next, and advised the setting up of an **oligarchy**[6]: "In all that Otanes has said to persuade you to put down monarchy," he observed, "I fully **concur**[7]; but his recommendation that we should call the people to power seems to me not the best advice. For there is nothing so **void**[8] of understanding, nothing so full of **wantonness**[9], as the **unwieldy**[10] **rabble**[11]. It were **folly**[12] not to be borne, for men, while seeking to escape the wantonness of a tyrant, to give themselves up to the wantonness of a rude **unbridled**[13] mob. The tyrant, in all his doings, at least knows what is he about, but a mob is altogether **devoid**[14] of knowledge; for how should there be any knowledge in a **rabble**[15], untaught, and with no natural sense of what is right and fit? It rushes wildly into state affairs with all the fury of a stream swollen in the winter, and confuses everything. Let the enemies of the Persians be ruled by **democracies**[16]; but let us choose out from the citizens a certain number of the worthiest, and put the government into their hands. For thus both ourselves shall be among the governors, and power being entrusted to the best men, it is likely that the best **counsels**[17] will **prevail**[18] in the state."

5. ['sentɪmənts] n . 想法

6. ['ɒlɪgɑːki] n . 寡头；精英统治

7. [kən'kɜː(r)] vi . 同意

8. [vɒɪd] adj . 缺乏的；缺少的

9. ['wɒntən] n . 放荡

10. [ʌn'wiːldi] adj . 笨拙的

11. [ræb(ə)l] n . 乌合之处

12. ['fɒlɪ] n . 蠢事

13. [ʌn'braɪdld] n . 不受约的

14. [dɪ'vɒɪd] adj . 缺乏的

15. ['ræbl] n . 乌合之众

16. [dɪ'mɒkrəsi] n . 民主

17. ['kaʊnsəl] n . 忠告 劝告

18. [prɪ'veɪl] vi . 占上风

✱ ✱ ✱   ✱ ✱ ✱   ✱ ✱ ✱   ✱ ✱ ✱   ✱ ✱ ✱   ✱ ✱ ✱   ✱ ✱ ✱   ✱ ✱ ✱

✿Questions for discussion:

(3) On what grounds did Megabyzus not favor the rule of the many?

(4) On what points did Megabyzus think oligarchy or rule of the best is better than the

other two (monarchy and democracy)?

* * *　　* * *　　* * *　　* * *　　* * *　　* * *　　* * *　　* * *

This was the advice which Megabyzus gave, and after him Darius came forward, and spoke as follows: "All that Megabyzus said against democracy was well said, I think; but about **oligarchy**[1] he did not speak **advisedly**[2]; for take these three forms of government—democracy, oligarchy, and monarchy—and let them each be at their best, I **maintain**[3] that monarchy far **surpasses**[4] the other two. What government can possibly be better than that of the very best man in the whole state? The **counsels**[5] of such a man are like himself, and so he **governs**[6] the mass of the people to their heart's **content**[7]; while at the same time his measures against evil-doers are kept more secret than in other states. **Contrariwise**[8], in oligarchies, where men vie with each other in the service of the **commonwealth**[9], fierce enmities are apt to arise between man and man, each wishing to be leader, and to carry his own measures; whence **violent**[10] quarrels come, which lead to open **strife**[11], often ending in **bloodshed**[12]. Then monarchy is sure to follow; and this too shows how far that rule **surpasses**[13] all others.

Again, in a democracy, it is impossible but that there will be malpractices: these **malpractices**[14], however, do not lead to **enmities**[15], but to close friendships, which are formed among those engaged in them, who must hold well together to carry on their **villainies**[16]. And so things go on until a man stands forth as **champion**[17] of the commonalty, and puts down the evil-doers. Straightway the author of so great a service is admired by all, and from being admired soon comes to be appointed king; so that here too it is plain that monarchy is the best government. Lastly, to sum up all in a word, whence, I ask, was it that we got the freedom which we enjoy? Did democracy give it us, or oligarchy, or a monarch? As a single man recovered our freedom for us, my **sentence**[18] is that we keep to the rule of one. Even apart from this, we ought not to change the laws of our forefathers when they work fairly; for to do so is not well."

1. ['ɒlɪgɑːki] n. 精英统治
2. [əd'vaɪzədli] adv. 明智地
3. [meɪn'teɪn] vt. 认为
4. [sə'pɑːs] vt. 超过
5. ['kaʊnsl] n. 计划
6. ['gʌvn] vt. 统治
7. [kən'tent] n. 满足；满意
8. [kən'treərɪwaɪz] adv. 相反
9. ['kɒmənwelθ] n. 联邦
10. ['vaɪələnt] adj. 暴力的
11. [straɪf] n. 冲突
12. ['blʌdʃed] n. 流血
13. [sə'pɑːs] vt. 超过
14. [ˌmæl'præktɪs] n. 弊端
15. ['enməti] n. 敌意
16. ['vɪlən] n. 恶行
17. ['tʃæmpɪən] n. 冠军
18. ['sentəns] n. 裁决；vt. 坚持

Such were the three opinions brought forward at this meeting; the four other Persians voted in favor of the last. Otanes, who wished to give his countrymen a democracy, when he found the decision against him, arose a second time, and spoke thus before the assembly: "Brother conspirators, it is plain that the king who is to be chosen will be one of ourselves, whether we make the choice by **casting lots**[1] for the prize, or by letting the people decide which of us they will have to rule over them, in or any other way. Now, as I have neither a mind to rule nor to be ruled, I shall not enter the lists with you in this matter. I withdraw, however, on one condition—none of you shall claim to exercise rule over me or my seed for ever." The six agreed to these terms, and Otanes withdraw and stood **aloof**[2] from the contest. And still to this day the family of Otanes continues to be the only free family in Persia; those who belong to it submit to the rule of the king only so far as they themselves choose; they are bound, however, to **observe the laws**[3] of the land like the other Persians.

1. 抓阄

2. [ə'luːf] *adj*. 远离

3. 遵守法律

After this the six took counsel together, as to the fairest way of setting up a king: and first, with respect to Otanes, they resolved, that if any of their own number got the kingdom, Otanes and his seed after him should receive year by year, as a mark of special honor, a Median robe, and all such other gifts as are accounted the most honorable in Persia. And these they resolved to give him, because he was the man who first planned the outbreak, and who brought the seven together. These privileges, therefore, were assigned specially to Otanes. The following were made common to them all: It was to be free to each, whenever he pleased, to enter the palace unannounced, unless the king were in the company of one of his wives; and the king was to be bound to marry into no family excepting those of the conspirators. Concerning the appointment of a king, the resolve to which they came was the following: They would ride out together next morning into the skirts of the city, and he whose steed first **neighed**[4] after the sun was up should have the kingdom. (To be conitued)

4. [nei] *vi*. 马嘶声

* * *   * * *   * * *   * * *   * * *   * * *   * * *   * * *

❈Questions for discussion:

(5) Darius favored the rule of one. He thought rule of one is more advantageous than rule of the many (democracy) and rule of the best (oligarchy). What are the good points he listed for rule of one? What is bad for democracy and oligarchy?

(6) Darius seemed very eloquent and good at debating skills. Are there any logic problems when he puts forward his ideas that rule of one is the best form of government?

(7) Comment on the three forms of government based on your analyses. Please refer to some books and discussions by scholars.

* * *   * * *   * * *   * * *   * * *   * * *   * * *   * * *

Chapter Three　Greek Tragedy

Background Knowledge

1. Introduction

It is said that almost all the western drama owes a debt to Greek tragedy which has had far reaching influences, not only on the theatrical stage, but also on the development of western literature. The time and place for the origin of Greek tragedy is Athens in the fifth century B.C. Athens in the fifth century B.C., especially after the establishment of the Delian League, had grown into a major sea power. This provided protection to the development of its trade criss crossing the Aegean and Mediterranean seas. Greek colonies from the Black Sea in the north to Southern Italy, the South of France, and Spain all had trade links with Athens. Athenians olives, and also its pottery among other resources at Attica were exported to all over the Greek world. Athens, with her three excellent harbors at Piraeus, was thus turned into a cultural sponge, taking in influences from all over. As is often the case, "trade and money flowed, art flourished, and new ideas spread".

On the other hand, Athenian political system encourages creativity and competition. The presentations of the plays became political events, were financed by the state, and were part of a huge national holiday. The Theatre of Dionysus was constructed by Athenian government and there each year a drama competition was held. Tragedy, in some sense, could be seen as the characteristic culture statement of the Athenian democracy.

In sum, both economic and political activities turned Athens in the fifth century B. C. into a great breeding ground for the origin and flourishing of Greek tragedy.

2. Tragedy Defined

In his *Poetics*, Aristotle defined what tragedy is: Tragedy "is an **imitation** of an action that is serious, complete, and of a certain magnitude; in language **embellished** with each kind of artistic **ornament** ...; in the form of action, not of narrative; with incidents arousing pity and fear...."Tragedy always deals with noble themes, like about god, or a great king.

The word "tragedy" itself derives from the Greek word meaning "goat song", as it is composed of tragos = "goat" and aeidein = "to sing". It is guessed that in the beginning a goat may have been used as the prize in a competition of singing or dancing, or that a goat may have been sacrificed preceded by a choral dancing.

Aristotle in his work *Poetics* said that the Greek Tragedy originated from the improvisations of dithyrambs(酒神的赞美歌,狂热的诗) sung in praise of the Dionysus. Dionysus is the son of Zeus and a major figure of Greek mythology

Dionysus, god of wine

and is included as one of the twelve Olympians. In Greek myths he is the god of wine and also the god of "nothing in excess". Known as the Liberator, he frees one from one's normal self, by madness, ecstasy or wine. Dionysus is also the patron deity of agriculture and the theater. His divine mission is to mingle the music and to put an end to care and worry. In honor of Dionysus, in every march the Athenians would have a festival, with the name Dionysia. Approximately in the year 534, Thespis, a winner of the drama contest, was said to be the first one to transmit the dithyramb into the tragedy. Originally sung by a narrative chorus, the dithyramb was now performed on the stage. Because of this, a performer was later referred to as a "thespian".

As dramatic performances were held each year, more performers were known to have taken part in the competition besides Thespis: Choerilus, Pratinas, and Phrynichus. Each of them had contributed more innovations to the field of tragedy. The tragedy competition was held among three playwrights. Each playwright would prepare a trilogy of tragedies usually featuring linked stories, and a satyr play, which was an unrelated comic piece. The performances of a trilogy and the satyr play probably lasted most of the day. All citizens, probably including women, were admitted to view the performances.

The theatre was built in the open air, mostly on the side of a hill, as it had to be able to create acoustics so that the actors' voice could be heard throughout the theater. For instance, the Theatre of Dionysus was a major theatre in Athens, built at the foot of the Acropolis. It was dedicated to Dionysus, the god of wine and fertility, and it hosted the City Dionysia festival. Among those to have competed at the theater were the renowned dramatists of that time, such as Aeschylus, Sophocles, Euripides, and Aristophanes the comedian. The theater probably held between 14,000 and 17,000 spectators.

During the performances, a chorus danced as well as sang. The chorus sang all of the choral parts, to the accompaniment of the flute, and some of the actors' answers as well. Originally there was only one actor to perform with the singing of the chorus. Aristotle claimed that Aeschylus added the second actor, and Sophocles added the third, all of them being male. These few actors would play the various roles of the play. All actors

Mask of Dionysus stored at the Louvre

wore masks, which were shaped like helmets, covering the entire face and head, with holes for the eyes and the mouth. The masks had intensely over-exaggerated facial features and expressions. Thus the audience was able to see the characters' face more clearly in a large open-air theater, like the theater of Dionysus. Different masks enabled an actor to appear and reappear in different roles and enabled the audience to recognize each of them and to distinguish sex, gender and social status. Also, the mask could serve as a resonator for the head and enhanced vocal acoustics.

In *Poetics*, Aristotle said that tragedy is characterized by seriousness and dignity and involves a great person who experiences a reversal of fortune, preferably from good to bad. In response to the suffering of the characters in the tragedy, the audience experienced a kind of catharsis, or purgation in their emotions as the tragedy evoked in the spectators pity and fear.

We now possess the writings of three great tragedians, Aeschylus, Euripides, and Sophocles. Each of them is an Athenian Citizen with Aeschylus the oldest one.

3. Sophocles

Sophocles(496—406B.C.)

Sophocles, the second great tragedian, was born in 496 B.C. in Athens. When he was young, he received good education and was influenced by his father, who was good at music and dance. In 480 B.C., young Sophocles was selected as a chorus boy for celebrating Athenian victory over the Persians. Later Sophocles entered into politics. In 443 B.C. he was Financial Chief for the Delian League headed by Athens, and was later elected twice as strategoi. He was appointed as one of ten advisers to handle Athens's crisis after the defeat of her Sicilian expedition in 413 B.C. which we will come back to in chapter 13.

Sophocles' plays differ greatly from Aeschylus's (the first Athenian tragedian). He had learned the style of tragedy from Aeschylus, but soon had his own unique style. Sophocles introduced into the play the third actor, to demonstrate the conflicts of the characters even more sufficiently. In his tragedy, the importance of chorus was much lowered, while the importance of actions and dialogues was increased. What's more, Sophocles concentrates more attention on the individual, "typically characterized by a kind of heroic or splendid isolation". As the great critic Bernard Knox summed up, Sophocles invented the "tragic hero."

In 468 B.C. Sophocles participated in the drama competition in Athens at the City Dionysia for the first time and won Aeschylus. In his lifetime, Sophocles won at least twenty victories and perhaps more.

When Sophocles passed away in 406 B.C., the Athenians and the Spartans were fighting with each other. Because of the war, his body was not able to be sent back to his hometown for burial. When the Spartan general heard of this, he ordered to have a truce so that the Athenians could bury Sophocles. During his long life, Sophocles had been high in position and leading a happy life.

Sophocles wrote altogether 123 plays. Unfortunately, only seven of then have survived. These seven plays were *Antigone*, *Oedipus the King*, *Ajax*, *Trachinian Women*, *Electra*, *Piloctetes*, *Aedipus at Colonus*. The most famous tragedies of Sophocles feature Oedipus and also Antigone: they are generally known as the Theban plays, although each play was actually a part of a different tetralogy, the other members of which are now lost.

4. Oedipus the King: An Introduction

Sophocles' *Oedipus the King* is the most famous of all Greek tragedies and also probably the most often performed Greek tragedy. Aristotle, in his *Poetics*, claimed that *Oedipus the King* was a peerless example of tragedy:

Fear and pity may be aroused by spectacular means: but they may also result from the inner structure of the piece, which is the better way, and indicates a superior poet. For the plot ought to be so constructed that, even without the aid of the eye, he who hears the tale told will thrill with horror and met to pity at what takes place. This is the impression we should receive from hearing the story of Oedipus.

—Aristotle, Poetics, line 1453 b

(Trans, S.H. Butcher, Quoted from Professor Peter Meineck)

In the twentieth century, Freud, in his book *Interpretation of Dreams*, adopted Sophocles' *Oedipus the King* as evidence for his theory of infant sexuality and psychological development. The name of his "Oedipus complex" is taken from it. In Freud' assumption, the play represents unconscious desires, and as a kind of "wish-fulfillment fantasy", it attracts modern audiences, as it did to ancient ones, *Oedipus the King* was performed in 429 B.C.. In the play, Thebes, the prosperous city, was suddenly suffering from a plague and the whole city was full of anguished moans. The devastating effect of such a pestilence was not alien to everyone in the audience at that time. A plague, in 429 B.C., was also ravaging Athens when she was still involved in the Peloponnesian War with Sparta. Taking this historical context into consideration, some scholars hold that Sophocles who produced this play dealing with the city of Thebes was, in fact, putting Pericles on blame. It was Pericles who had led the Athenians into this endless war in his absolute conviction that the Athenians would win. Pericles, like Oedipus the ruler of Thebes, believes that reason can solve everything and puts very little credit in the Gods. The sufferings of Oedipus as shown in the later stories, then, serve as a warning both to

Dionysus surrounded by satyrs

Pericles and to the Athenian people. Seen from this perspective, Sophocles was right for, at the very end of his life, he witnessed the collapse of the Athenian fleets in Sicily, seeing Athens brought to the brinks of utter defeat in the Peloponnesian War.

Oedipus the King reflected a common theme in Sophocles' plays, that is the conflict between fate and free will. Oedipus, a king who has been considered the most unhappy man that ever lived, meant to be good, yet was forced by fate to sin the most terrible crime, and finally died of grief.

Oedipus the King

By Sophocles

(Translated by Robert Fagles)

GUIDE FOR READING:

A terrible plague has struck the city of Thebes. Plants, animals, and people are dying in great numbers. The **priests**[1] *of the city seek help from Oedipus, their king.*

TIME AND SCENE: *The royal house of Thebes. Double doors dominate the* **façade**[2]; *a stone* **altar**[3] *stands at the center of the stage.*

Many years have passed since Oedipus solved the **riddle**[4] *of the* **Sphinx**[5] *and* **ascended the throne**[6] *of Thebes, and now a plague has struck the city. A procession of priests enters;* **suppliants**[7], *broken and* **despondent**[8], *they carry branches wound in wool and lay them on the altar.*

The doors open. Guards **assemble**[9]. *Oedipus comes forward, majestic but for a* **telltale**[10] **limp**[11], *and slowly views the condition of his people.*

1. [priːst] *n.* 牧师

2. [fəˈsɑːd] *n.* 建筑物的正面

3. [ˈɔːltə(r)] 圣坛

4. [ˈrɪdl] *n.* 谜

5. [sfɪŋks] *n.* 斯芬克斯

6. 登基

7. [ˈsʌplɪənt] *n.* 恳求者

8. [dɪˈspɒndənt] *adj.* 沮丧的

9. [əˈsembl] *vi.* 聚集

10. [ˈtelteɪl] *adj.* 泄露秘密的

11. [lɪmp] *n.* 瘸腿

Oedipus. Oh my children, the new blood of ancient Thebes, why are you here? **Huddling**[12] at my altar, praying before me, your branches wound in wool. Our city **reeks**[13] with the smoke of burning **incense**[14], rings with cries for the Healer and **wailing**[15] for the dead. I thought it wrong, my children, to hear the truth from others, messengers. Here I am myself—you all know me, the world knows my fame:
I am Oedipus.

(*Helping a Priest to his feet*)

12. [ˈhʌdl] *vi.* 聚集

13. [riːk] *n.* 发出恶臭

14. [ˈɪnsens] *n.* 香

15. [weɪl] *vi.* 哀嚎

Speak up, old man. Your years,
your **dignity**[16]—you should speak for the others.   10
Why here and kneeling, what **preys**[17] upon you so?
Some sudden fear? Some strong desire?
You can trust me. I am ready to help,
I'll do anything. I would be blind to misery
not to pity my people kneeling at my feet.   15

16. [ˈdɪgnəti] *n.* 尊严

17. [preɪ] *vi.* 折磨

Priest y. Oh Oedipus, king of the land, our greatest power!
You see us before you now, men of all ages
clinging[1] to your altars. Here are boys,
still too weak to fly from the **nest**[2],
and here the old, bowed down with the years,   20
the holy ones—a priest of Zeus myself—and here
the picked, unmarried men, the young hope of Thebes.
And all the rest, your great family gathers now,
branches **wreathed**[3], massing in the squares,
kneeling before the two temples of queen Athena   25
or the river-shrine where the **embers**[4] glow and die
and Apollo sees the future in the ashes.

Our city—

look around you, see with your own eyes—
our ship **pitches**[5] wildly, cannot lift her head
from the depths, the red waves of death...   30
Thebes is dying. A **blight**[6] on the fresh crops
and the rich **pastures**[7], cattle sicken and die,
and the women die in **labor**[8], children **stillborn**[9],
and the plague, the **fiery**[10] god of fever hurls down
on the city, his lightning **slashing**[11] through us—   35
raging plague in all its vengeance, **devastating**[12]
the house of Cadmus! And black Death **luxuriates**[13]
in the raw, **wailing**[14] miseries of Thebes.

Now we pray to you. You cannot equal the gods,
your children know that, bending at your **altar**[15].   40
But we do rate you first of men,
both in the common crises of our lives
and face-to-face **encounters**[16] with the gods.
You freed us from the Sphinx, you came to Thebes
and cut us loose from the bloody **tribute**[17] we had paid   45
that harsh, brutal singer. We taught you nothing,
no skill, no extra knowledge, still you **triumphed.**[18]
A god was with you, so they say, and we believe it—
you lifted up our lives.

1. [klɪŋ] *vi.* 紧紧抓住
2. [nest] *n.* 巢穴
3. [ri:ð] *v.* 被环绕
4. ['embə(r)] *n.* 余烬
5. [pɪtʃ] *n.* 向前跌或冲
6. [blaɪt] *n.* 凋萎
7. ['pɑ:stʃə(r)] *n.* 牧场
8. ['leɪbə(r)] *n.* 分娩
9. ['stɪlbɔ:n] *vi.* 夭折
10. ['faɪəri] *adj.* 易怒的
11. [slæʃ] *v.* 劈
12. ['devəsteɪtɪŋ] *adj.* 毁灭性的
13. [lʌɡ'ʒʊərɪeɪt] *vi.* 茂盛的生长
14. [weɪl] *v.* 哭
15. ['ɔ:ltə(r)] *n.* 圣坛
16. [ɪn'kaʊntə(r)] *n.* 遭遇
17. ['trɪbju:t] *n.* 贡品;摆脱
18. ['traɪʌmf] *vi.* 获胜

So now again，

Oedipus，king，we bend to you，your power—   50
we **implore**[1] you，all of us on our knees：   1. ［ɪmˈplɔː(r)］ vt. 恳求
find us strength，rescue! Perhaps you've heard
the voice of a god or something from other men，
Oedipus... what do you know?
The man of experience—you see it every day—   55
his plans will work in a **crisis**[2]，his first of all.   2. ［ˈkraɪsɪs］ n. 危机

Act now—we beg you，best of men，raise up our city!
Act，defend yourself，your former glory!
Your country calls you **savior**[3] now   3. ［ˈseɪvjə］ n. 救星
for your **zeal**[4]，your action years ago.   60   4. ［ziːl］ n. 热情
Never let us remember of your **reign**[5]：   5. ［reɪn］ n. 统治
you helped us stand，only to fall once more.
Oh raise up our city，set us on our feet.
The **omens**[6] were good that day you brought us joy—   6. ［ˈəʊmən］ n. 征兆
be the same man today!   65
Rule our land，you know you have the power，
but rule a land of the living，not a wasteland.
Ship and towered city are nothing，**stripped of**[7] men   7. 被…剥夺
alive within it，living all as one.
Oedipus.   My children，
I pity you. I see—how could I fail to see   70
what longings bring you here? Well I know
you are sick to death，all of you，
but sick as you are，not one is sick as I.
Your pain strikes each of you alone，each
in the **confines**[8] of himself，no other. But my spirit   75   8. ［kənˈfaɪn］ n. 限制
grieves[9] for the city，for myself and all of you.   9. ［griːv］ vi. 悲痛
I wasn't asleep，dreaming. You haven't wakened me—
I have wept through the nights，you must know that，
groping[10]，laboring over many paths of thought.   10. ［grəʊp］ vi. 摸索
After a painful search I found one **cure**[11]：   80   11. ［kjʊə(r)］ n. 治疗
I acted at once. I sent Creon，
my wife's own brother，to Delphi—
Apollo the Prophet's oracle—to learn
what I might do or say to save our city.

Today's the day. When I count the days gone by   85
it **torments**[1] me... what is he doing?   1. ['tɔ:ment] *vt.* 折磨
Strange, he's late, he's gone too long.
But once he returns, then, I'll be a **traitor**[2]   2. ['treɪtə(r)] *n.* 叛徒
if I do not do all the god makes clear.
Priest. Timely words. The men over there   90
are signaling—Creon's just arriving.

✳ ✳ ✳   ✳ ✳ ✳   ✳ ✳ ✳   ✳ ✳ ✳   ✳ ✳ ✳   ✳ ✳ ✳   ✳ ✳ ✳   ✳ ✳ ✳

✽Questions for Discussion

(1) What is the riddle of Sphinx? How did Oedipus ascend the throne of Thebes?

(2) A terrible plague has struck the city of Thebes. Based on your reading of the beginning of Homer's *Iliad*, what is usually the cause of a plague in ancient Greece?

(3) Reading through this section (the conversations), what are your impressions of Oedipus as a king of Thebes?

✳ ✳ ✳   ✳ ✳ ✳   ✳ ✳ ✳   ✳ ✳ ✳   ✳ ✳ ✳   ✳ ✳ ✳   ✳ ✳ ✳   ✳ ✳ ✳

Oedipus. (*sighting Creon, then turning to the altar*)
Lord Apollo, let him come with a lucky word of rescue,
shining like his eyes!
Priest. Welcome news, I think—he's crowned, look,
and the **laurel**[3] wreath is bright with berries.   3. ['lɒrəl] *n.* 桂冠

Oedipus. We'll soon see. He's close enough to hear—
(*Enter Creon from the side; his face is shaded with a
wreath.*)
Creon, prince, my **kinsman**[4], what do you bring us?   4. ['kɪnzmən] *n.* 亲人
What message from the god?
Creon.   Good news.
I tell you even the hardest things to bear,
if they should turn out well, all would be well.
Oedipus. Of course, but what were the god's words? There's
no hope and nothing to fear in what you've said so far.
Creon. If you want my report **in the presence of**[5] these   5. 当着…的面
people...
(*pointing to the priests while drawing Oedipus toward the
palace*)
I'm ready now, or we might go inside.
Oedipus.   Speak out,
speak to us all. I **grieve for**[6] these, my people,   6. 为…悲痛

• 134 •

far more than I fear for my own life.

Creon .   Very well，

I will tell you what I heard from the god.

Apollo commands us—he was quite clear—

"Drive the corruption from the land，

don't **harbor**¹ it any longer, past all cure，

don't nurse it in your soil—root it out!"

Oedipus . How can we **cleanse**² ourselves—what rites?

What's the source of the trouble?

Creon . **Banish**³ the man, or pay back blood with blood.

Murder sets the plague-storm on the city.

Oedipus .   Whose murder?

Whose fate does Apollo bring to light?

Creon .   Our leader，

my lord, was once a man named Laius，

before you came and put us straight on course.

Oedipus .   I know—

or so I've heard. I never saw the man myself.

Creon . Well, he was killed, and Apollo commands us now—

he could not be more clear，

"Pay the killers back—whoever is responsible."

Oedipus . Where on earth are they? Where to find it now，

the **trail**⁴ of the ancient **guilt**⁵ so hard to **trace**⁶?

Creon . "Here in Thebes," he said.

Whatever is sought for can be caught, you know，

whatever is neglected slips away.

Oedipus . But where，

in the palace, the fields or foreign soil，

where did Laius meet his bloody death?

Creon . He went to consult an **oracle**⁷, Apollo said，

and he set out and never came home again.

Oedipus . No messenger, no fellow-traveler saw what

happened?

Someone to cross-examine?

1. ['hɑːbə] *vt* . 藏

2. [klenz] *n* . 清洗

3. ['bænɪʃ] *n* . 驱逐

4. [treɪl] *n* . 追踪

5. [ɡɪlt] *n* . 有罪，犯罪行为，罪恶

6. [treɪs] *v* . 找寻，追查

7. ['ɒrəkl] *n* . 神谕

Creon .   No,
they were all killed but one. He escaped,
terrified, he could tell us nothing clearly,
nothing of what he saw—just one thing.

Oedipus .   What's that?
One thing could hold the key to it all,
a small beginning give us grounds for hope.

Creon . He said thieves attacked them—**a whole band**[1],   1. 一群
not single-handed, cut King Laius down.

Oedipus .   A thief,
so daring, so wild, he'd kill a king? Impossible,
unless **conspirators**[2] paid him off in Thebes.   2. [kən'spɪrətə(r)] *n.* 共谋

Creon . We suspected as much. But with Laius dead
no leader appeared to help us in our troubles.

Oedipus . Trouble? Your king was murdered—royal blood!
What stopped you from **tracking down**[3] the killer   3. [træk] *v.* 追捕
then and there?

Creon .   The singing, riddling Sphinx.
She... persuaded us to let the mystery go
and concentrate on what lay at our feet.

Oedipus .   No,
I'll start again—I'll bring it all to light myself!
Apollo is right, and so are you, Creon,
to turn our attention back to the murdered man.
Now you have me to fight for you, you'll see:
I am the land's **avenger**[4] by all rights,   4. [ə'vendʒə(r)] *n.* 复仇者
and Apollo's champion too.

But not to assist some distant **kinsman**[5], no,   5. ['kɪnzmən] *n.* 亲人
for my own sake I'll rid us of this corruption.
Whoever killed the king may decide to kill me too,
with the same **violent**[6] hand—by **avenging**[7] Laius   6. ['vaɪələnt] *adj.* 暴力的
I defend myself.   160   7. [ə'vendʒ] *v.* 报仇
(*to the priests*)
                      Quickly, my children.
Up from the steps, take up your branches now.
(*to the guards*)
One of you **summon**[8] the city here before us,   8. ['sʌmən] *vt.* 号召

tell them I'll do everything. God help us，

we will see our **triumph**[1]—or our fall.   1.［'traɪʌmf］*n*.成功

（*Oedipus and Creon enter the palace，followed by the guards*.）

Priest. Rise，my sons. The kindness we came for   165

Oedipus volunteers himself.

Apollo has sent his word，his oracle—

Come down，Apollo，save us，stop the plague.

（The priests rise，remove their branches and exit to the side.）

✳ ✳ ✳　　✳ ✳ ✳　　✳ ✳ ✳　　✳ ✳ ✳　　✳ ✳ ✳　　✳ ✳ ✳　　✳ ✳ ✳　　✳ ✳ ✳

❖**Questions for Discussion**

（4）Why didn't Creon report Apollo's words in the presence of all other people?

（5）According to Apollo's oracle，what is the cause of the plague in Thebes? Translate Apollo's words into Chinese.

（6）Tell the story in your own words how King Laius was murdered.

✳ ✳ ✳　　✳ ✳ ✳　　✳ ✳ ✳　　✳ ✳ ✳　　✳ ✳ ✳　　✳ ✳ ✳　　✳ ✳ ✳　　✳ ✳ ✳

（*Enter a **Chorus**[2]，the citizens of Thebes，who have not*   2.［'kɔːrəs］*n*.歌队

heard the news that Creon brings. They march around the

*altar，**chanting**[3].*）   3.［tʃɑːnt］*n*.吟唱

Chorus.   Zeus！

Great welcome voice of Zeus，what do you bring?

What word from the gold vaults of Delphi   170

comes to brilliant Thebes? **Racked**[4] with terror—   4.［ræk］*vt*.使痛苦

　　　　　　　　　　terror shakes my heart

and I cry your wild cries，Apollo，**Healer**[5] of Delos   5.［'hiːlə(r)］*n*.治愈者

I worship you in dread... what now，what is your price?

some new sacrifice? some ancient **rite**[6] from the past   175   6.［raɪt］*n*.祭祀仪式

come round again each spring? —

　　　　　　　　what will you bring to birth?

Tell me，child of golden Hope

　　　　　　　warm voice that never dies!

You are the first I call，daughter of Zeus

deathless Athena—I call your sister Artemis，

heart of the market place **enthroned**[7] in glory，   7.［ɪn'θrəʊn］*v*.使登基

　　　　　　　　guardian of our earth—

I call Apollo，**Archer**[8] astride the thunderheads of heaven—   8.［'ɑːtʃə］*n*.弓箭手

O triple **shield**[9] against death，shine before me now!   9.［ʃiːld］*n*.保护

If ever，once in the past，you stopped some **ruin**[10]   10.［'ruːɪn］*n*.毁灭

launched against our walls

     you **hurled**[1] the flame of pain

far，far from Thebes—you gods

come now，come down once more!

       No，no

the **miseries**[2] numberless，grief on grief，no end—

too much to bear，we are all dying

O my people...

     Thebes like a great army dying

and there is no **sword**[3] of thought to save us，no

and the fruits of our famous earth，they will not **ripen**[4]

no and the women cannot scream their pangs to birth—

screams for the Healer，children dead in the **womb**[5]

     and life on life goes down

    you can watch them go 200

like seabirds winging west，**outracing**[6] the day's fire

down the horizon，**irresistibly**[7]

   streaking[8] on to the shores of Evening

       Death

so many deaths，numberless deaths on deaths，no end—

Thebes is dying，look，her children 205

stripped[9] of pity...

  generations **strewn**[10] on the ground

unburied，unwept，the dead spreading death

and the young wives and gray-haired mothers with them

cling[11] **to** the altars，**trailing**[12] in from all over the city— 210

Thebes，city of death，one long **cortege**[13]

    and the suffering rises

    wails[14] for mercy rise

  and the wild hymn for the Healer **blazes out**[15]

clashing[16] with our sobs our cries of mourning— 215

  O golden daughter of god，send rescue

radiant[17] as the kindness in your eyes!

Drive him back! —the fever，the god of death

     that raging god of war

not **armored**[18] in bronze，not shielded now，he burns me， 220

battle cries in the **onslaught**[19] burning on—

1．[hɜːl] vt．用力投掷

2．[ˈmɪzəri] n．痛苦

3．[sɔːd] n．剑

4．[ˈraɪpən] vi．成熟

5．[wuːm] n．子宫

6．[aʊˈreɪs] vt．赛跑胜过

7．[ˌɪrɪˈzɪstəbli] adv．不可抗拒地

8．[striːk] vi．闪现

9．[strɪpt] vt．被剥夺了

10．[struːn] vt．散落

11．靠近，坚持

12．[treɪl] v．缓慢行走

13．[kɔːˈteʒ] n．送葬行列

14．[weɪl] n．哀嚎

15．爆发出来

16．[klæʃ] vi．冲突

17．[ˈreɪdɪənt] adj．发光的

18．[ˈɑːməd] vt．武装

19．[ˈɒnslɔːt] n．猛攻

O **rout**[1] him from our borders!

Sail him，blast him out to the Sea-queen's chamber

                the black Atlantic gulfs

       or the northern harbor，death to all   225

where the Thracian surf comes crashing.

Now what the night spares he comes by day and kills—

the god of death.

           O lord of the storm cloud，

you who **twirl**[2] the lightning，Zeus，Father，

thunder Death to nothing!   230

Apollo，lord of the light，I beg you—

whip[3] your longbow's golden cord

showering arrows on our enemies—**shafts**[4] of power

champions strong before us rushing on!

Artemis，Huntress，**torches**[5] flaring over the eastern ridges—

           ride Death down in pain!

God of the **headdress**[6] gleaming gold，I cry to you—

your name and ours are one，Dionysus—

      come with your face aflame with wine

      your **raving**[7] women's cries

      your army on the march! Come with the lightning，

come with torches blazing，eyes **ablaze**[8] with glory!

Burn that god of death that all gods hate!

1. ［raʊt］ vt . 攻击

2. ［twɜːl］ vt . 快速转动

3. ［wɪp］ vt . 抽打
4. ［ʃɑːft］ n . 箭

5. ［tɔːtʃ］ n . 火炬

6. ［ˈheddres］ n . 头饰

7. ［ˈreɪvɪŋ］ adj . 胡说的

8. ［əbˈleɪz］ adj . 明亮的

* * *　　* * *　　* * *　　* * *　　* * *　　* * *　　* * *　　* * *

❋**Questions for Discussion**

（7）A chorus，in the context of Ancient Greek tragedy，had important functions in the drama performance. How did the chorus function in the above section of this play?

（8）Thebes was conceived of as "a city of death" by details presented in the play. What are these details?

* * *　　* * *　　* * *　　* * *　　* * *　　* * *　　* * *

（*Oedipus enters from the palace to address the Chorus，as if addressing the entire city of Thebes*.）

Oedipus. You pray to the gods? Let me grant your prayers.

Come，listen to me—do what the plague demands：you'll find **relief**[9] and lift your head from the depths.

9. ［rɪˈliːf］ n . 宽慰，轻松

I will speak out now as a stranger to the story，

a stranger to the crime. If I'd been present then，

there would have been no mystery，no long hunt
without a clue in hand. So now，counted
a native Theban years after the murder，
to all of Thebes I make this **proclamation**[1]：

1.［ˌprɒkləˈmeɪʃn］*n*.宣称

if any one of you knows who murdered Laius，
the son of Labdacus，I order him to **reveal**[2]

2.［rɪˈviːl］*vt*.揭露

the whole truth to me. Nothing to fear，
even if he must **denounce**[3] himself，

3.［dɪˈnaʊns］*vt*.指责

let him speak up
and so escape the **brunt**[4] of the **charge**[5]—

4.［brʌnt］*n*.冲击

he will suffer no unbearable punishment，

5.［tʃɑːdʒ］*vt*.指控

nothing worse than **exile**[6]，totally unharmed.

6.［ˈeksaɪl］*n*.流放

(*Oedipus pauses，waiting for a reply*.)

                                        Next，

if anyone knows the murderer is a stranger，
a man from **alien**[7] soil，come，speak up.

7.［ˈeɪliən］*adj*.外国的

I will give him a handsome reward，and lay up
gratitude[8] in my heart for him besides.

265   8.［ˈɡrætɪtjuːd］*n*.感激

(*silence again，no reply*)
But if you keep silent，if anyone **panicking**[9]，

9.［ˈpænɪkɪ］*adj*.感到惊慌的

trying to **shield**[10] himself or friend or **kin**[11]，

10.［ʃiːld］*vt*.藏起来

rejects my offer，then hear what I will do.

11.［kɪn］*n*.亲戚

I order you，every citizen of the state
where I hold **throne**[12] and power：**banish**[13] this man—

270   12.［θrəʊn］*n*.王位

whoever he may be—never **shelter**[14] him，never

13.［ˈbænɪʃ］*vt*.驱赶

speak a word to him，never make him partner

14.［ˈʃeltə(r)］*vt*.提供藏身

to your prayers，your victims burned to the gods.

之地

Never let the **holy water**[15] touch his hands.

15.*n*.圣水

Drive him out，each of you，from every home.

275

He is the plague，the heart of our corruption，
as Apollo's oracle has just revealed to me.
So I honor my **obligations**[16]：

16.［ˌɒblɪˈɡeɪʃən］*n*.义务；责任

I fight for the god and for the murdered man.

Now my **curse on**[17] the murderer. Whoever he is，

280   17.［kɜːs］*n*.诅咒

a lone man unknown in his crime
or one among many，let that man **drag out**[18]

18.把…拖出；(使)拖延

his life in **agony**[1]，step by painful step—
I curse myself as well... if by any chance
he proves to be an **intimate**[2] of our house，
here at my **hearth**[3]，with my full knowledge，
may the curse I just called down on him strike me!

These are your orders：perform them to the last.
I command you, for my sake, for Apollo's, for this country
blasted[4] root and branch by the angry heavens.
Even if god had never urged you on to act，
how could you leave the crime **uncleansed**[5] so long?
A man so noble—your king, brought down in blood—
you should have searched. But I am the king now，
I hold the **throne**[6] that he held then, possess his bed
and a wife who shares our seed... why, our seed
might be the same, children born of the same mother
might have created blood-**bonds**[7] between us
if his hope of **offspring**[8] had not met disaster—

but fate **swooped**[9] at his head and cut him short.
So I will fight for him as if he were my father，
stop at nothing, search the world
to lay my hands on the man who **shed**[10] his blood，
the son of Labdacus **descended**[11] of Polydorus，
Cadmus of old and **Agenor**[12]，founder of the line：
their power and mine are one.

                           Oh dear gods，
my curse on those who disobey these orders!
Let no crops grow out of the earth for them—
Shrivel[13] their women, kill their sons，
burn them to nothing in this plague
that hits us now, or something even worse.
But you, loyal men of Thebes who approve my actions，
may our champion, Justice, may all the gods
be with us, fight beside us to the end!
Leader. In the **grip**[14] of your curse, my king, I swear
I'm not the murderer, I cannot point him out.

285

290

295

300

305

310

315

1.［'ægəni］*n*.痛苦
2.［'ɪntɪmət］*n*.至交；密友
3.［hɑ:θ］*n*.灶台；家庭
4.［'blɑ:stɪd］*adj*.枯萎的
5.［ˌʌn'kli:nst］*vt*.没被清洗
6.［θrəʊn］*n*.王位
7.［'bɒnds］*n*.纽带
8.［'ɒf'sprɪŋ］*n*.后代
9.［swu:p］*vt*.突然袭击
10.［ʃed］*vt*.流（出）
11.［dɪ'sendɪd］*vt*.继承；下来
12.（a son of Pleuron and Xanthippe）阿革诺耳
13.［'ʃrɪvəl］*vt*.（使）干枯；（使）枯萎

As for the search, Apollo **pressed**[1] it on us—
he should name the killer.

Oedipus.   Quite right,
but to force the gods to act against their will—
no man has the power.   320

Leader.   Then if I might mention
the next best thing...

Oedipus.   The third best too—
don't hold back, say it.

Leader.   I still believe...
Lord Tiresias[2] sees with the eyes of Lord Apollo.
Anyone searching for the truth, my king,
might learn it from the **prophet**[3], clear as day.   325

Oedipus. I've not been slow with that. On Creon's **cue**[4]
I sent the **escorts**[5], twice, within the hour.
I'm surprised he isn't here.

Leader.   We need him—
without him we have nothing but old, useless **rumors**[6].

Oedipus. Which rumors? I'll search out every word.   330

Leader. Laius was killed, they say, by certain travelers.

Oedipus. I know—but no one can find the murderer.

Leader. If the man has a **trace**[7] of fear in him
                      he won't stay silent long,
not with your curses ringing in his ears.   335

Oedipus. He didn't **flinch**[8] at murder,
he'll never flinch at words.

✳ ✳ ✳   ✳ ✳ ✳   ✳ ✳ ✳   ✳ ✳ ✳   ✳ ✳ ✳   ✳ ✳ ✳   ✳ ✳ ✳   ✳ ✳ ✳

❖ Questions for Discussion

(9) Read his speeches to his people, what does Oedipus intend to do to the killer of Laius?

(10) What curses does Oedipus put on the killer of Laius? Translate these cursing words into Chinese.

✳ ✳ ✳   ✳ ✳ ✳   ✳ ✳ ✳   ✳ ✳ ✳   ✳ ✳ ✳   ✳ ✳ ✳   ✳ ✳ ✳   ✳ ✳ ✳

(*Enter Tiresias, the blind prophet, led by a boy with escorts*[9]
in attendance. He remains at a distance.)

Leader. Here is the one who will **convict**[10] him, look,
they bring him on at last, the **seer**[11], the man of god.
The truth lives inside him, him alone.   340

1. ['pres] *vt.* 坚持,用力压

2. (古希腊神话里的)预言大师

3. ['prɔfɪt] *n.* 预言家
4. [kju:] *n.* 提示
5. ['eskɔːt] *n.* 护卫

6. ['ruːmə] *n.* 流言

7. [treɪs] *n.* 痕迹

8. ['flɪntʃ] *vt.* 畏缩;退缩

9. ['eskɔːt] *n.* 护送

10. [kən'vɪkt] *vt.* 指控;宣判有罪

11. ['siːə(r)] *n.* 预言师

Tiresias appears to Odysseus

Oedipus.   O Tiresias，

master of all the mysteries of our life，

all you teach and all you dare not tell，

signs in the heavens，signs that walk the earth!

Blind as you are，you can feel all the more

what sickness **haunts**[1] our city. You，my lord，   345   1. ［hɔːnt］ *vt*. 常至；萦绕于

are the one **shield**[2]，the one **savior**[3] we can find.   2. ［ʃiːld］ *n*. 保护

                                                                   3. ［'seɪvjə(r)］ *n*. 拯救者

We asked Apollo—perhaps the **messengers**[4]   4. ［'mesɪndʒə(r)］ *n*. 信使

haven't told you—he sent his answer back：

"**Relief**[5] from the plague can only come one way.   5. ［rɪ'liːf］ *n*. 缓解

Uncover the murderers of Laius，   350

put them to death or drive them into **exile**[6]．"   6. ［'eksaɪl］ *n*. 流亡，流放

So I beg you，**grudge**[7] us nothing now，no voice，   7. ［grʌdʒ］ *vt*. 吝惜；不愿

no message **plucked**[8] from the birds，the **embers**[9]   8. ［plʌk］ *vt*. 摘；拔

or the other **mantic**[10] ways within your grasp.   9. ［'embə］ *n*. 余烬

Rescue yourself，your city，rescue me—   355   10. ［ʊ'mæntɪk］ *adj*. 预言的，预

rescue everything **infected**[11] by the dead.   言性的

We are in your hands. For a man to help others   11. ［ɪn'fektɪd］ *vt*. 被感染的

with all his gifts and native strength：

that is the noblest work.

Tiresias.   How terrible—to see the truth

when the truth is only pain to him who sees!   360

I knew it well，but I put it from my mind，

else I never would have come.

Oedipus. What's this? Why so **grim**[1], so **dire**?[2]

Tiresias. Just send me home. You bear your burdens，

I'll bear mine. It's better that way，   365

please believe me.

Oedipus.   strange response... unlawful，

unfriendly too to the state that **bred and reared**[3] you—

you **withhold**[4] the word of god.

Tiresias.   I fail to see

that your own words are so well-timed.

I'd rather not have the same thing said of me...   370

Oedipus. For the love of god，don't turn away，

not if you know something. We beg you，

all of us on our knees.

Tiresias.   None of you knows—

and I will never **reveal**[5] my dreadful secrets，

not to say your own.   375

Oedipus. What? You know and you won't tell?

You're **bent on**[6] betraying us，destroying Thebes?

Tiresias. I'd rather not cause pain for you or me.

So why this... useless **interrogation**?[7]

380 You'll get nothing from me.

Oedipus.   Nothing! You，

You **scum**[8] of the earth，you'd **enrage**[9] a heart of stone!

You won't talk? Nothing moves you?

Out with it[10]，once and for all!

Tiresias. You criticize my **temper**[11]... unaware

385 of the one you live with，you **revile**[12] me.

Oedipus. Who could **restrain**[13] his anger hearing you?

What outrage—you **spurn**[14] the city!

Tiresias. What will come will come.

Even if I **shroud**[15] it all in silence.

Oedipus. What will come? You're **bound to**[16] tell me that.   390

Tiresias. I will say no more. Do as you like，build your

anger to whatever **pitch**[17] you please，rage your worst—

Oedipus. Oh I'll **let loose**[18]，I have such fury in me—

now I see it all. You helped **hatch**[19] the plot，

you did the work，yes，short of killing him   395

1. ［grɪm］ *adj*. 冷酷的

2. ［ˈdaɪə(r)］ *adj*. 可怕的；悲惨的

3. 养育

4. ［wɪðˈhəʊld］ *vt*. 坚持（不说）

5. ［rɪˈviːl］ *vt*. 揭露

6. 下决心

7. ［ˌɪnterəʊˈɡeɪʃən］ *n*. 质询

8. ［skʌm］ *n*. 渣滓

9. ［ɪnˈreɪdʒ］ *vt*. 让…愤怒

10. 说出来

11. ［ˈtempə(r)］ *n*. 性情，脾气

12. ［rɪˈvaɪl］ *vt*. 辱骂，痛斥

13. ［rɪˈstreɪn］ *vt*. 制止；抑制

14. ［spɜːn］ *vt*. 蔑视；侮辱

15. ［ʃraʊd］ *vt*. 遮盖

16. 必须

17. ［pɪtʃ］ *n*. 音高

18. ［luːs］ *vi*. 放松，放任

19. ［hætʃ］ *vt*. 孵化；策划

with your own hands—and given eyes I'd say

you did the killing single-handed!

Tiresias.   Is that so!

I charge you, then, submit to that **decree**¹   1.［dɪˈkriː］*n*.命令

you just laid down：from this day onward

speak to no one，not these citizens，not myself.   400

You are the curse，the corruption of the land！

Oedipus. You，shameless—

aren't you **appalled**² to start up such a story?   2.［əˈpɔːl］*vi*.恐惧；害怕

You think you can get away with this?

Tiresias.   I have already.

The truth with all its power lives inside me.   405

Oedipus. Who **primed**³ you for this? Not your prophet's   3.［praɪm］*vt*.事先指导

trade.

Tiresias. You did，you forced me，**twisted**⁴ it out of me.   4.［twɪst］*v*.扭，缠绕

Oedipus. What? Say it again—I'll understand it better.

Tiresias. Didn't you understand，just now?

Or are you tempting me to talk?   410

Oedipus. No，I can't say I **grasped**⁵ your meaning.   5.［ɡrɑːsp］*v*.理解

Out with it，again!

Tiresias. I say you are the murderer you hunt.

Oedipus. That **obscenity**⁶，twice—by god，you'll pay.   6.［əbˈsenɪti］*n*.猥亵下流

Tiresias. Shall I say more，so you can really rage?   415

Oedipus. Much as you want. Your words are nothing—

futile⁷.   7.［ˈfjuːtaɪl］*adj*.无用的

Tiresias. You cannot imagine... I tell you，

you and your loved ones live together in **infamy**⁸，   8.［ˈɪnfəmi］*n*.羞辱地

you cannot see how far you've gone in **guilt**⁹.   9.［ɡɪlt］*n*.罪恶

Oedipus. You think you can keep this up and never suffer?   420

Tiresias. Indeed，if the truth has any power.

Oedipus.   It does

but not for you，old man. You've lost your power，

stone-blind，stone-deaf—senses，eyes blind as stone！

Tiresias. I pity you，**flinging at**¹⁰ me the very **insults**¹¹   10.［flɪŋ］激动地说出

each man here will fling at you so soon.   425   11.［ɪnˈsʌlt］*n*.侮辱

Oedipus.   Blind，

lost in the night，endless night that nursed you！

You can't hurt me or anyone else who sees the light—you can

never touch me.

Tiresias.   True, it is not your fate

to fall at my hands. Apollo is quite enough,

and he will take some pains to work this out.   430

Oedipus. Creon! Is this **conspiracy**[1] his or yours?

1. [kən'spɪrəsi] *n*. 共谋;计谋

Tiresias. Creon is not your downfall, no, you are your own.

Oedipus.   O power—

wealth and empire, skill **outstripping**[2] skill

2. [ˌaʊt'strɪpɪŋ] *vt*. 超过,越过

in the **heady**[3] rivalries of life,

3. ['hedi] *adj*. 兴奋的

what envy **lurks**[4] inside you! Just for this,   435

4. [lɜːk] *vi*. 潜伏;潜藏

the crown the city gave me—I never sought it,

they laid it in my hands—for this alone, Creon,

the soul of trust, my loyal friend from the start

steals against me... so hungry to **overthrow**[5] me

5. [ˌəʊvə'θrəʊ] *vt*. 推翻

he sets this **wizard**[6] on me, this **scheming quack**[7],   440

6. ['wɪzəd] *n*. 魔咒

this fortune-teller **peddling**[8] lies, eyes **peeled**[9]

7. [kwæk] *n*. 江湖医生

for his own profit—seer blind in his craft!

8. ['pedl] *vt*. 兜售

9. [piːl] *vt*. 剥落;剥皮

Come here, you pious **fraud**[10]. Tell me,

10. [frɔːd] *n*. 欺骗

when did you ever prove yourself a **prophet**?[11]

11. ['prɒfɪt] *n*. 预言家

When the Sphinx, that **chanting**[12] Fury kept her death-   445

12. ['tʃɑːntɪŋ] *adj*. 歌唱的

watch here,

why silent then, not a word to set our people free?

There was a riddle, not for some passer-by to solve—

it cried out for a prophet. Where were you?

Did you rise to the crisis? Not a word,

you and your birds, your gods—nothing.   450

No, but I came by, Oedipus the **ignorant**[13],

13. ['ɪgnərənt] *adj*. 无知的

I stopped the Sphinx! With no help from the birds,

the **flight**[14] of my own intelligence hit the mark.

14. [flaɪt] *n*. 飞翔

And this is the man you'd try to **overthrow**[15]?

15. [ˌəʊvə'θrəʊ] *vt*. 推翻

You think you'll stand by Creon when he's king?   455

You and the great **mastermind**[16]—

16. ['mɑːstəmaɪnd] *n*. 策划者, 智多星

you'll pay in tears, I promise you, for this,

this witch-hunt. If you didn't look so **senile**[17]

17. ['siːnaɪl] *adj*. 衰老的;高龄的

the lash would teach you what your **scheming**[18] means!

18. ['skiːmɪŋ] *n*. 阴谋

Leader. I would suggest his words were spoken in anger，　460
Oedipus... yours too，and it isn't what we need.
The best solution to the oracle，the riddle
posed by god—we should look for that.

Tiresias. You are the king no doubt，but in one respect，
at least，I am your equal：the right to reply.　465
I claim that **privilege**¹ too.

1. ['prɪvɪlɪdʒ] *n*. 特权，特免

I am not your slave. I serve Apollo.
I don't need Creon to speak for me in public.

So，

You **mock**² my blindness? Let me tell you this.

2. [mɒk] *vt*. 取笑

You with your precious eyes，　470
you're blind to the corruption of your life，
to the house you live in，those you live with—

who are your parents? Do you know? All unknowing
you are the **scourge**³ of your own flesh and blood，

3. [skɜːdʒ] *n*. 灾难

the dead below the earth and the living here above，　475
and the double **lash**⁴ of your mother and your father's

4. [læʃ] *n*. 鞭挞，鞭子

curse
will whip you from this land one day，their footfall
treading⁵ you down in terror，**darkness shrouding**⁶

5. [tred] *vt*. 踩
6. 黑暗笼罩

your eyes that now can see the light!

Soon，soon
you'll scream aloud—what **haven**⁷ won't **reverberate**?⁸　480

7. ['heɪv(ə)n] *n*. 避难所
8. [rɪ'vɜːbəreɪt] 回响

What rock of **Cithaeron**⁹ won't scream back in echo?

9. 西塞隆山

That day you learn the truth about your marriage，　481
the wedding-march that sang you into your halls，
the **lusty**¹⁰ voyage home to the fatal harbor!

10. ['lʌsti] *adj*. 健壮的

And a crowd of other horrors you'd never dream　485
will level you with yourself and all your children.

There. Now **smear**¹¹ us with insults—Creon，myself

11. [smɪə(r)] *vt*. 弄脏；诽谤

and every word I've said. No man will ever
be rooted from the earth as brutally as you.
Oedipus. Enough! Such **filth**¹² from him? Insufferable—　490

12. [fɪlθ] *n*. 肮脏

what，still alive? Get out—
faster，back where you came from—**vanish**¹³!

13. ['vænɪʃ] *vi*. 消失吧

Tiresias. I would never have come if you hadn't called me
here.

Oedipus. If I thought you would **blurt out such absurdities**¹,
you'd have died waiting before I'd had you summoned.   495

1. 说出荒唐之事

Tiresias. Absurd，am I! To you，not to your parents：
the ones who bore you found me sane enough.

Oedipus. Parents—who? Wait... who is my father?

Tiresias. This day will bring your birth and your destruction.

Oedipus. Riddles—all you can say are riddles，**murk**² and   500
darkness.

2. [mɜːk] *n.* 黑暗

Tiresias. Ah，but aren't you the best man alive at solving
riddles?

Oedipus. **Mock**³ me for that，go on，and you'll reveal my
greatness.

3. [mɒk] *vt.* 嘲笑

Tiresias. Your great good fortune，true，it was your **ruin**⁴.

4. ['ruːɪn] *n.* 垮台，破产

Oedipus. Not if I saved the city—what do I care?

Tiresias. Well then，I'll be going.   505

(*To his attendant*)

                    Take me home，boy.

Oedipus. Yes，take him away. You're a **nuisance**⁵ here.
Out of the way，the **irritation**⁶ 's gone.

5. ['njuːsns] *n.* 讨厌的东西

6. [ˌɪrɪ'teɪʃn] *n.* 可憎的、讨厌
的人

(turning his back on Tiresias，moving toward the palace)

Tiresias.   I will go，
once I have said what I came here to say.
I will never **shrink from**⁷ the anger in your eyes—
you can't destroy me. Listen to me closely：   510

7. [ʃrɪŋk] *vi.* 退缩

the man you've **sought**⁸ so long，proclaiming，
cursing up and down，the murderer of Laius—
he is here. A stranger，

8. [sɔːt] *v.* 寻找

you may think，who lives among you，
he soon will be revealed a native Theban   515
but he will take no joy in the **revelation**⁹.

9. [ˌrevə'leɪʃn] *n.* 揭露

Blind who now has eyes，beggar who now is rich，
he will **grope**¹⁰ his way toward a foreign soil，
a stick tapping before him step by step.

10. [grəʊp] *v.* 摸索

(*OEDIPUS enters the palace.*)

Revealed at last，brother and father both   520

to the children he **embraces**[1]，to his mother

son and husband both—he **sowed**[2] the loins

his father sowed，he spilled his father's blood！

1.［ɪm'breɪs］v.拥抱

2.［'səʊə］v.播（种）

Go in and reflect on that，solve that.

And if you find I've lied   525

from this day onward call the prophet blind.

(Tiresias and the boy exit to the side.)

＊＊＊   ＊＊＊   ＊＊＊   ＊＊＊   ＊＊＊   ＊＊＊   ＊＊＊   ＊＊＊

❖Questions for Discussion

(11) Tiresias was a well-known prophet in ancient Greek mythology.He was depicted as a blind prophet. Search more information about him，and find out how he was blinded.

(12) For what reasons did Oedipus quarrel bitterly with the prophet Tiresias?

(13) Translate lines 469-489 into Chinese. Comment on what Tiresias said here.

(14) Based on what Tiresias said，who was，in fact，the murderer of Laius?

＊＊＊   ＊＊＊   ＊＊＊   ＊＊＊   ＊＊＊   ＊＊＊   ＊＊＊   ＊＊＊

Chorus.   Who—

who is the man the voice of god **denounces**[3]

resounding[4] out of the rocky **gorge**[5] of Delphi?

The horror too dark to tell，

whose **ruthless**[6] bloody hands have done the work?   530

His time has come to fly

to **outrace**[7] the **stallions**[8] of the storm

                        his feet a streak of speed—

Cased in armor，Apollo son of the Father

lunges[9] on him，lightning-bolts afire！   535

And the grim **unerring**[10] **Furies**[11]

                        closing for the kill.

                                Look，

the word of god has just come blazing

flashing off **Parnassus'**[12] snowy heights！

That man who left no trace—   540

after him，hunt him down with all our strength！

Now under **bristling timber**[13]

up through rocks and caves he **stalks**[14]

                        like the wild mountain bull—

cut off from men，each step an agony，frenzied，racing   545

blind but he cannot outrace the dread voices of

3.［dɪ'naʊns］vt.指摘

4.［rɪ'zaʊndɪŋ］v.回响

5.［gɔːdʒ］n.峡谷

6.［'ruːθlɪs］adj.无情的

7.［ˌaʊt'reɪs］vt.超越

8.［'stæliən］n.种马

9.［lʌndʒ］vi.刺；踢

10.［ˌʌn'ɜːrɪŋ］adj.准确

11.［'fjʊəri］n.复仇女神

12.帕纳塞斯山

13.［'brɪslɪŋ］［'tɪmbə］竖立的灌木

14.［stɔːk］vi.高视阔步地走

Delphi ringing out of the heart of Earth,
the dark wings beating around him **shrieking**[1] doom

       the doom that never dies, the terror—The skilled
prophet scans the birds and **shatters**[2] me with terror!   550
I can't accept him, can't deny him, don't know what to
say, I'm lost, and the wings of dark **foreboding**[3]
beating—I cannot see what's come, what's still to come...
and what could breed a blood **feud**[4] between
Laius' house and **the son of Polybus**?[5]   555
I know of nothing, not in the past and not now,
no charge to bring against our king, no cause
to attack his fame that rings throughout Thebes—
not without proof—not for the **ghost**[6] of Laius,
not to avenge a murder gone without a **trace**[7].   560

Zeus and Apollo know, they know, the great masters
       of all the dark and depth of human life.
But whether a mere man can know the truth,
whether a **seer**[8] can **fathom**[9] more than I—
there is no test, no certain proof
       though matching skill for skill
a man can **outstrip**[10] a rival. No, not till I see
these charges proved will I **side with**[11] his accusers.
We saw him then, when the **she-hawk**[12] swept against him,
saw with our own eyes his skill, his brilliant **triumph**[13]—   570
       there was the test—he was the joy of Thebes!
      Never will I **convict**[14] my king, never in my heart.

1. [ʃriːkɪŋ] *vi.* 尖叫

2. ['ʃætə] *v.* 粉碎

3. ['fɔːbəʊdɪŋ] *adj.* 预感的,预知的

4. [fjuːd] *adj.* 不和,世仇

5. 柯林斯国王

6. [gəʊst] *n.* 鬼魂

7. [treɪs] *n.* 痕迹

8. ['siːə(r)] *n.* 预言师

9. ['fæðəm] *vi.* 理解

10. [ˌaʊt'strɪp] *vt.* 超过;胜过

11. [saɪd] *v.* 支持

12. 狮身人面像

13. ['traɪəmf] *n.* 胜利

14. [kən'vɪkt] 指控…有罪

The Chorus

＊＊＊   ＊＊＊   ＊＊＊   ＊＊＊   ＊＊＊   ＊＊＊   ＊＊＊   ＊＊＊

❄ Questions for Discussion

(15) How did the chorus function at this point in the play?

(16) According to Schlegel，the Chorus is "the ideal spectator"，and conveys to the actual spectator "a lyrical and musical expression of his own emotions，and elevates him to the region of contemplation." (Refer to Wikipedia). In many of Greek plays，the chorus expressed to the audience what the main characters could not say，such as their hidden fears or secrets. What emotions does the chorus describe of Oedipus?

＊＊＊   ＊＊＊   ＊＊＊   ＊＊＊   ＊＊＊   ＊＊＊   ＊＊＊   ＊＊＊

(*Enter Creon from the side*.)

Creon. My fellow-citizens，I hear King Oedipus

levels[1] terrible charges at me. I had to come.

I **resent**[2] it deeply. If，in the present crisis，   575

he thinks he suffers any **abuse**[3] from me，

anything I've done or said that offers him

the slightest injury，why，I've no desire

to **linger out**[4] this life，my **reputation**[5] in ruins.

The damage I'd face from such an **accusation**[6]   580

is nothing simple. No，there's nothing worse：

branded[7] a traitor in the city，a traitor

to all of you and my good friends.

Leader.   True，

but a **slur**[8] might have been forced out of him，

by anger perhaps，not any firm conviction.   585

Creon. The charge was made in public，wasn't it?

I put the prophet up to spreading lies?

Leader. such things were said...

I don't know with what **intent**[9]，if any.

Creon. Was his glance steady，his mind right   590

when the charge was brought against me?

Leader. I really couldn't say. I never look

to judge the ones in power.

(*The doors open*. Oedipus enters.)

Wait，

here's Oedipus now.

Oedipus.   You—here? You have the **gall**[10]

to show your face before the palace gates?   595

You，**plotting**[11] to kill me，kill the king—

1. ['levl] *v*. 推测；夷平
2. [rɪ'zent] *vt*. 不满
3. [ə'bjuːs] *n*. 侮辱；恶言

4. [lɪngə] *vi*. 逗留；磨蹭
5. [ˌrepjʊ'teɪʃən] *n*. 名声
6. [ˌækjuː'zeɪʃən] *n*. 指控
7. [brænd] *vt*. 侮辱；铭刻于

8. [slɜː(r)] *n*. 诽谤

9. [ɪn'tent] *n*. 意图

10. [gɔːl] *n*. 大胆

11. ['plɒtɪŋ] *v*. 谋划

I see it all, the **marauding**[1] thief himself
scheming[2] to steal my crown and power!

                                    Tell me,

in god's name, what did you take me for,
coward[3] or fool, when you **spun out your plot**?[4]   600
Your **treachery**[5]—you think I'd never detect it
creeping[6] against me in the dark? Or sensing it,
not defend myself? Aren't you the fool,
you and your high adventure. Lacking numbers,
powerful friends, out for the big game of empire—   605
you need riches, armies to bring that **quarry**[7] down!
Creon. Are you quite finished? It's your turn to listen
for just as long as you've... instructed me.
Hear me out, then judge me on the facts.
Oedipus. You've a wicked way with words, Creon,   610
but I'll be slow to learn—from you.
I find you a **menace**[8], a great burden to me.
Creon. Just one thing, hear me out in this.
Oedipus.   Just one thing,
don't tell me you're not the enemy, the **traitor**[9].
Creon. Look, if you think crude, mindless **stubbornness**[10]   615
such a gift, you've lost your sense of balance.
Oedipus. If you think you can abuse a **kinsman**[11],
then escape the penalty, you're **insane**[12].
Creon. Fair enough, I grant you. But this injury
you say I've done you, what is it?   620
Oedipus. Did you induce me, yes or no,
to send for that **sanctimonious**[13] prophet?
Creon. I did. And I'd do the same again.
Oedipus. All right then, tell me, how long is it now
since Laius...   625
Creon.   Laius—what did he do?
Oedipus.   **Vanished**[14],
swept from sight, murdered in his tracks.
Creon. The count of the years would run you far back...
Oedipus. And that far back, was the prophet at his trade?
Creon. skilled as he is today, and just as honored.
Oedipus. Did he ever refer to me then, at that time?   630

1. [məˈrɔːd] v. 抢劫;掠夺
2. vi. 计谋
3. [ˈkaʊəd] n. 懦夫
4. [plɒt] vt. 思考出你的阴谋
5. [ˈtretʃərɪ] n. 背叛
6. [ˈkriːpɪŋ] vi. 偷偷地
7. [ˈkwɒrɪ] n. 猎物
8. [ˈmenəs] n. 威胁
9. [ˈtreɪtə(r)] n. 叛徒
10. [ˈstʌbənnɪs] n. 顽固不化
11. [ˈkɪnzmən] n. 亲戚
12. [ɪnˈseɪn] adj. 失去了理智;疯了
13. [ˌsæŋktɪˈməʊnɪəs] 伪善的
14. [ˈvænɪʃ] vi. 消失

Creon.   No，
never，at least，when I was in his presence.

Oedipus. But you did investigate the murder，didn't you?

Creon. We did our best，of course，discovered nothing.

Oedipus. But the great **seer**¹ never accused me then—why
not?

1. ['siːə(r)] *n.* 语言师

Creon. I don't know. And when I don't，I keep quiet.   635

Oedipus. You do know this，you'd tell it too—
if you had **a shred of**² **decency**³.

2. 少许

3. ['diːsənsɪ] *n.* 正派；体面

Creon.   What?
If I know，I won't hold back.

Oedipus.   Simply this：
if the two of you had never put heads together，
we would never have heard about my killing Laius.   640

Creon. If that's what he says... well，you know best.
But now I have a right to learn from you
as you just learned from me.

Oedipus.   Learn your fill，
you never will **convict**⁴ me **of** the murder.

4. [kən'vɪkt] *vt.* 指控…有罪

Creon. Tell me，you're married to my sister，aren't you?   645

Oedipus. A genuine discovery—there's no denying that.

Creon. And you rule the land with her，with equal power?

Oedipus. she receives from me whatever she desires.

Creon. And I am the third，all of us are equals?

Oedipus. Yes，and it's there you show your **stripes**⁵—   650
you betray a kinsman.

5. [straɪp] *n.* 条纹；种类

Creon.   Not at all.

Not if you see things calmly，rationally，
as I do. Look at it this way first：
who in his right mind would rather rule
and live in anxiety than sleep in peace?   655
Particularly if he enjoys the same authority.
Not I，I'm not the man to **yearn**⁶ for **kingship**⁷，
not with a king's power in my hands. Who would?
No one with any sense of self-control.
Now，as it is，you offer me all I need，   660
not a fear in the world. But if I wore the crown...
there'd be many painful duties to perform，

6. [jɜːn] *vi.* 渴望

7. ['kɪŋʃɪp] *n.* 王位

hardly to my taste.

How could kingship

please me more than influence, power
without a **qualm**?[1] I'm not that **deluded**[2] yet,   665
to reach for anything but privilege outright,
profit free and clear.
Now all men sing my praises, all salute me,
now all who request your favors **curry**[3] mine.
I am their best hope: success rests in me.   670
Why give up that, I ask you, and borrow trouble?
A man of sense, someone who sees things clearly
would never **resort**[4] to **treason**[5].
No, I have no lust for **conspiracy**[6] in me,   674
nor could I ever suffer one who does.   675

Do you want proof? Go to Delphi yourself,
examine the oracle and see if I've reported
the message word-for-word. This too:
if you detect that I and the **clairvoyant**[7]
have plotted anything in common, arrest me,   680
execute me. Not on the strength of one vote,
two in this case, mine as well as yours.
But don't convict me on sheer **unverified**[8] surmise.
How wrong it is to take the good for bad,
purely **at random**[9], or take the bad for good.   685
But reject a friend, a kinsman? I would as soon
tear out the life within us, priceless life itself.
You'll learn this well, without fail, in time.
Time alone can bring the just man to light—
the criminal you can spot in one short day.   690
Leader.   Good advice,
my lord, for anyone who wants to avoid disaster.
Those who jump to conclusions may go wrong.
Oedipus. When my enemy moves against me quickly,
plots in secret, I move quickly too, I must,
I plot and pay him back. Relax my guard a moment,   695
waiting his next move—he wins his objective,
I lose mine.

1. [kwɑːm] n. 疑虑；紧张不安
2. [dɪˈluːd] vt. 被蛊惑
3. [ˈkʌrɪ] vt. 讨好
4. [rɪˈzɔːt] vt. 采用；诉诸
5. [ˈtriːzən] n. 背叛
6. [kənˈspɪrəsɪ] n. 阴谋
7. [kleəˈvɔɪənt] n. 声称能设见未来的人
8. [ʌnˈverɪfaɪd] adj. 未经证实的
9. 随意

Creon.   What do you want?
You want me banished?

Oedipus.   No，I want you dead.

Creon. Just to show how ugly a **grudge**¹ can...   1.［grʌdʒ］*n*.怨恨；恶意

Oedipus.   So，
still stubborn? you don't think I'm serious?   700

Creon. I think you're insane.

Oedipus.   Quite sane—in my behalf.

Creon. Not just as much in mine?

Oedipus.   You—my mortal enemy?

Creon. What if you're wholly wrong?

Oedipus.   No matter—I must rule.

Creon. Not if you rule unjustly.

Oedipus.   Hear him，Thebes，my city!

Creon. My city too，not yours alone!   705

Leader. Please，my lords.

（*Enter Jocasta from the palace*.）

                    Look，Jocasta's coming，
and just in time too. With her help
you must put this fighting of yours to rest.

Jocasta. Have you no sense? Poor misguided men，
such shouting—why this public **outburst**?²   710   2.［'aʊtbɜːst］*n*.爆发
Aren't you ashamed，with the land so sick，
to **stir up**³ private quarrels?   3.［stɜː］*vt*.搅起

（*To Oedipus*）

Into the palace now. And Creon，you go home.
Why make such a **furor**⁴ over nothing?   4.［fjuːˈrɔːrɪ］*n*.激怒；骚乱

Creon. My sister，it's dreadful... Oedipus，your husband，   715
he's bent on a choice of punishments for me，
banishment from the fatherland or death.

Oedipus. Precisely. I caught him in the act，Jocasta，
plotting，about to **stab me in the back**⁵.   5.背后捅刀子

Creon. Never—curse me，let me die and be damned   720
if I've done you any wrong you charge me with.

Jocasta. Oh god，believe it，Oedipus，
honor the solemn oath⁶ he swears to heaven.   6.庄严的誓言

Do it for me，for the sake of all your people.

(*The Chorus begins to chant*.)

Chorus. Believe it, be sensible   725

give way, my king, I beg you!

Oedipus. What do you want from me, **concessions**?[1]   1. [kən'seʃən] *n*. 特许权

Chorus. Respect him—he's been no fool in the past

and now he's strong with the oath he swears to god.

Oedipus. You know what you're asking?   730

Chorus.   I do.

Oedipus.   Then out with it!

Chorus. The man's your friend, your kin, he's under oath—

don't cast him out, disgraced

branded with guilt on the strength of hearsay only.

Oedipus. Know full well, if that is what you want

you want me dead or banished from the land.   735

Chorus.   Never—

no, by the blazing Sun, first god of the heavens!

Stripped of the gods, stripped of loved ones,

let me die by inches if that ever crossed my mind.

But the heart inside me sickens, dies as the land dies

and now on top of the old griefs you pile this,   740

your fury—both of you!

Oedipus.   Then let him go,

even if it does lead to my ruin, my death

or my disgrace, driven from Thebes for life.

It's you, not him I pity—your words move me.

He, wherever he goes, my hate goes with him.   745

Creon. Look at you, **sullen**[2] in yielding, brutal in your rage—   2. ['sʌlən] *adj*. 愠怒的; 阴沉

you will go too far. It's perfect justice: 的; 闷闷不乐的

natures like yours are hardest on themselves.

Oedipus. Then leave me alone—get out!

Creon. I'm going.

You're wrong, so wrong. These men know I'm right.   750

(Exit to the side.)

✳✳✳   ✳✳✳   ✳✳✳   ✳✳✳   ✳✳✳   ✳✳✳   ✳✳✳   ✳✳✳

❖Questions for Discussion

(17) Oedipus and Creon were also involved in a bitter quarrel. Why does Oedipus turn against Creon?

✳✳✳   ✳✳✳   ✳✳✳   ✳✳✳   ✳✳✳   ✳✳✳   ✳✳✳   ✳✳✳

（*The Chorus turns to Jocasta*.）

Chorus. Why do you hesitate，my lady

why not help him in？

Jocasta. Tell me what's happened first.

Chorus. Loose，**ignorant**[1] talk started dark suspicions

and a sense of injustice cut deeply too.   755

1. [ˈɪɡnərənt] *adj*. 无知的，愚昧的

Jocasta. On both sides？

Chorus.   Oh yes.

Jocasta.   What did they say？

Chorus. Enough，please，enough！The land's so **racked**[2] already

or so it seems to me...

2. [rækt] *adj*. 使…痛苦

End the trouble here，just where they left it.

Oedipus. You see what comes of your good intentions now？   760

And all because you tried to **blunt**[3] my anger.

3. [blʌnt] *vt*. 减弱

Chorus.   My king，

I've said it once，I'll say it time and again—

I'd be insane，you know it，

senseless，ever to turn my back on you.

You who set our beloved land—storm-tossed，   765

shattered—

straight on course. Now again，good helmsman，

steer us through the storm！

（The Chorus draws away，leaving Oedipus and Jocasta side

by side.）

Jocasta.   For the love of god，

Oedipus，tell me too，what is it？

Why this rage？You're so unbending.

Oedipus. I will tell you. I respect you，Jocasta，   770

much more than these men here...

（glancing at the Chorus）

Creon's to blame，Creon schemes against me.

Jocasta. Tell me clearly，how did the quarrel start？

Oedipus. He says I murdered Laius—I am guilty.

Jocasta. How does he know？Some secret knowledge   775

or simple hearsay？

Oedipus.   Oh，he sent his prophet in

to do his dirty work. You know Creon，

Creon keeps his own lips clean.

Jocasta.   A prophet?

Well then，free yourself of every charge！

Listen to me and learn some peace of mind： 780

no skill in the world，

nothing human can **penetrate**[1] the future.   1．［'penɪtreɪt］*vt*．刺入；刺进

Here is proof，quick and to the point.

An oracle came to Laius one fine day

(I won't say from Apollo himself   785

but his underlings，his priests）and it declared

that doom would strike him down at the hands of a son，

our son，to be born of our own flesh and blood. But Laius，

so the report goes at least，was killed by strangers，

thieves，at a place where three roads meet... my son—   790

he wasn't three days old and the boy's father

fastened his ankles，had a **henchman**[2] **fling**[3] him away   2．［'hentʃmən］*n*．亲信

on a **barren**[4]，**trackless**[5] mountain.   793   3．［flɪŋ］*vt*．扔掉

                                      There，you see？   4．［'bærən］*adj*．贫瘠的

Apollo brought neither thing to pass. My baby   5．［'træklɪs］*adj*．没有路的

no more murdered his father than Laius suffered—   795

his wildest fear—death at his own son's hands.

That's how the seers and all their revelations

mapped out the future. Brush them from your mind.

Whatever the god needs and seeks

he'll bring to light himself，with ease.   800

Oedipus.   Strange，

hearing you just now... my mind wandered，

my thoughts racing back and forth.

Jocasta. What do you mean? Why so anxious，**startled**?[6]   6．［'stɑːtl］*vt*．吃惊；惊慌

Oedipus. I thought I heard you say that Laius

was cut down at a place where three roads meet.   805

Jocasta. That was the story. It hasn't died out yet.

Oedipus. Where did this thing happen? Be precise.

Jocasta. A place called **Phocis**[7]，where two branching roads，   7．福基斯(希腊中部古地名)

one from Daulia，one from Delphi，

come together—a crossroads.   810

Oedipus. When? How long ago?

Jocasta. The **heralds**[8] no sooner reported Laius dead   8．［'herəld］*n*．使者；传令官

than you appeared and they **hailed**[1] you king of Thebes.

Oedipus. My god，my god—what have you planned to do

to me?

Jocasta. What，Oedipus? What **haunts**[2] you so?   815

Oedipus.   Not yet.

Laius—how did he look? Describe him.

Had he reached his **prime**?[3]

Jocasta.   He was **swarthy**[4]，

and the gray had just begun to **streak**[5] his **temples**[6]，

and his build... wasn't far from yours.

Oedipus.   Oh no no，

I think I've just called down a dreadful curse   820

upon myself—I simply didn't know!

Jocasta. What are you saying? I **shudder**[7] to look at you.

Oedipus. I have a terrible fear the blind seer can see.

I'll know in a moment. One thing more—

Jocasta.   Anything，

afraid as I am—ask，I'll answer，all I can.   825

Oedipus. Did he go with a light or heavy **escort**[8]，

several men-at-arms，like a lord，a king?

Jocasta. There were five in the party，a herald among them，

and a single **wagon**[9] carrying Laius.

Oedipus.   Ai—

now I can see it all，clear as day.   830

Who told you all this at the time，Jocasta?

Jocasta. A servant who reached home，the lone survivor.

Oedipus. So，could he still be in the palace—even now?

Jocasta. No indeed. Soon as he returned from the scene

and saw you on the throne with Laius dead and gone，   835

a region of central Greece，between Delphi and Thebes.

he knelt and **clutched**[10] my hand，pleading with me

to send him into the hinterlands，to **pasture**[11]，

far as possible，out of sight of Thebes.

I sent him away. Slave though he was，

he'd earned that favor—and much more.   840

Oedipus. Can we bring him back，quickly?

Jocasta. Easily. Why do you want him so?

Oedipus.   I am afraid，

1. [heɪl] *vt*. 欢呼

2. [hɔːnt] *vt*. 受到困扰

3. [praɪm] *n*. 壮年
4. ['swɔːði] *adj*. 黑黝黝的
5. [striːk] *vt*. 条痕
6. ['templ] *n*. 太阳穴

7. ['ʃʌdə(r)] *vt*. 颤抖；吃惊

8. ['eskɔːt] *n*. 护送

9. ['wægən] *n*. 马车

10. [klʌtʃ] *vt*. 抓住
11. ['pɑːstʃə(r)] *n*. 牧场

Jocasta, I have said too much already.

That man—I've got to see him.

Jocasta.   Then he'll come.

But even I have a right, I'd like to think,   845

to know what's **torturing**[1] you, my lord.

Oedipus. And so you shall—I can hold nothing back from

you,

now I've reached this pitch of dark **foreboding**[2].

Who means more to me than you? Tell me,

whom would I turn toward but you   850

as I go through all this?

My father was Polybus, king of Corinth.

My mother, a **Dorian**[3], Merope. And I was held

the prince of the realm among the people there,

till something struck me out of nowhere,   855

something strange... worth remarking perhaps,

hardly worth the anxiety I gave it.

Some man at a banquet who had drunk too much

shouted out—he was far gone, mind you—

that I am not my father's son. Fighting words!   860

I barely **restrained**[4] myself that day

but early the next I went to mother and father,

questioned them closely, and they were **enraged**[5]

at the **accusation**[6] and the fool who **let it fly**[7].

So as for my parents I was satisfied,   865

but still this thing kept **gnawing**[8] at me,

the **slander**[9] spread—I had to make my move.

                                        And so,

unknown to mother and father I set out for Delphi,

and the god Apollo **spurned**[10] me, sent me away

denied the facts I came for,   870

but first he flashed before my eyes a future

great with pain, terror, disaster—I can hear him cry,

"You are fated to couple with your mother, you will

bring a breed of children into the light no man can bear to

see—you will kill your father, the one who gave you life!" 875

I heard all that and ran. I abandoned Corinth,

1. ['tɔːtʃə(r)] *vt*. 折磨

2. ['fɔːbəʊdɪŋ] *n*. 不祥的预感

3. *n*. 多里安人

4. [rɪ'streɪnd] *vt*. 控制

5. [ɪn'reɪdʒd] *vt*. 愤怒

6. [ˌækjuː'zeɪʃən] *n*. 指控

7. 说出来

8. [nɔː] *vi*. 折磨

9. ['slɑːndə(r)] *n*. 诽谤

10. *vt*. 唾弃

from that day on I **gauged**[1] its landfall only

by the stars, running, always running

toward some place where I would never see

the shame of all those oracles come true.　　　　880

And as I fled I reached that very spot

where the great king, you say, met his death.

Now, Jocasta, I will tell you all.

Making my way toward this **triple**[2] crossroad

I began to see a herald, then **a brace of colts**[3]　　　885

drawing a wagon, and mounted on the bench... a man,

just as you've described him, coming face-to-face,

and the one in the lead and the old man himself

were about to thrust me off the road—brute force—

and the one shouldering me aside, the driver,　　　890

I strike him in anger! —and the old man, watching me

coming up along his wheels—he brings down

his **prod**[4], two prongs **straight at**[5] my head!

I paid him back with interest!

Short work, by god—with one blow of the staff　　　895

in this right hand I knock him out of his high seat,

roll him out of the wagon, **sprawling headlong**[6]—

I killed them all—every mother's son!

Oh, but if there is any blood-tie

between Laius and this stranger...　　　　　　900

what man alive more miserable than I?

More hated by the gods? I am the man

no alien, no citizen welcomes to his house,

law forbids it—not a word to me in public,

driven out of every **hearth and home**[7].　　　905

And all these curses I—no one but I

brought down these piling curses on myself!

And you, his wife, I've touched your body with these,

the hands that killed your husband cover you with

blood.

Wasn't I born for **torment**?[8] Look me in the eyes!　　910

1. [ɡeɪdʒ] *vt*. 估计;判断;测量

2. [ˈtrɪpl] *adj*. 三岔路

3. 一车队

4. [prɒd] *n*. 刺棒

5. 刺

6. 头朝前地摊开

7. 家

8. [ˈtɔːmənt] *n*. 折磨

I am **abomination**[1]—heart and soul!

I must be exiled, and even in exile

never see my parents, never set foot

on native ground again. Else I am doomed

to couple with my mother and cut my father down...　　915

Polybus who reared me, gave me life.

　　　　　　　　　　　　　But why, why?

Wouldn't a man of judgment say—and wouldn't he be

　　right—

some **savage**[2] power has brought this down upon my

head?

Oh no, not that, you pure and awesome gods,

never let me see that day! Let me slip　　920

from the world of men, vanish without a trace

before I see myself **stained**[3] with such corruption,

stained to the heart.

Leader. My lord, you fill our hearts with fear.

But at least until you question the witness,　　925

do take hope.

Oedipus.　　　　　　　Exactly. He is my last hope—

I am waiting for the shepherd. He is crucial.

Jocasta. And once he appears, what then? Why so urgent?

Oedipus. I will tell you. If it turns out that his story

matches yours, I've escaped the worst.　　930

Jocasta. What did I say? What struck you so?

Oedipus.　　　　　　You said thieves—

he told you a whole band of them murdered Laius.

So, if he still holds to the same number,

I cannot be the killer. One can't equal many.

But if he refers to one man, one alone,　　935

clearly the scales come down on me:

I am guilty.

Jocasta.　　　　　　Impossible. Trust me,

I told you precisely what he said,

and he can't **retract**[4] it now;

the whole city heard it, not just I.　　940

And even if he should vary his first report

by one man more or less, still, my lord,

1. [ˌæbɒmɪ'neɪʃən] *n*. 极令人厌恶的人(事)

2. ['sævɪdʒ] *adj*. 野蛮的

3. [steɪnd] *v*. 沾染

4. [rɪ'trækt] *vt*. 收回

he could never make the murder of Laius
truly fit the prophecy. Apollo was **explicit**[1]:
my son was doomed to kill my husband... my son,   945
poor defenseless thing, he never had a chance
to kill his father. They destroyed him first.
So much for prophecy. It's neither here nor there.
From this day on, I wouldn't look right or left.
Oedipus. True, true. Still, that shepherd,   950
someone fetch him—now!
Jocasta. I'll send at once. But do let's go inside.
I'd never displease you, least of all in this.
(*Oedipus and Jocasta enter the palace*.)

1. [ɪksˈplɪsɪt] *adj*. 清楚的；明
白的

* * * * * * * * * * * * * * * * * * * * * * * *

❋Questions for Discussion

(18) As a young boy, how did Oedipus get the words that he was fated to kill his father
and marry his mother? How did he respond to the prophecy? Tell the story.

(19) When Jocasta told him that Laius was killed at "a place where three roads meet",
Oedipus became fearful. Why? He said, "He is my last hope". Who does "He" refer
to here? Why did Oedipus say he was his last hope?

* * * * * * * * * * * * * * * * * * * * * * * *

Chorus. **Destiny**[2] guide me always
Destiny find me filled with **reverence**[3]   955
pure in word and deed.
Great laws tower above us, reared on high
born for the brilliant **vault**[4] of heaven—
Olympian Sky their only father,
nothing mortal, no man gave them birth,   960
their memory deathless, never lost in sleep:
within them lives a mighty god, the god does not
grow old.

2. [ˈdestɪni] *n*. 命运
3. [ˈrevərəns] *n*. 敬畏

4. [vɔːlt] *n*. 穹，拱顶

Pride **breeds**[5] the **tyrant**[6]
violent pride, **gorging**[7], crammed to bursting
with all that is overripe and rich with ruin—   965
clawing up to the heights, headlong pride
crashes down the abyss—sheer doom!
No footing helps, all foothold lost and gone.
But the healthy strife that makes the city strong—

5. [briːd] *v*. 哺育
6. [ˈtaɪrənt] *n*. 独裁者
7. 暴食；狼吞虎咽

I pray that god will never end that **wrestling**[1]:   970   1.['resəl] n.角斗;角力
god, my champion, I will never let you go.

But if any man comes **striding**[2], high and mighty   2.[straiŋ] vi.大踏步
in all he says and does,
no fear of justice, no **reverence**[3]   3.['revərəns] n.尊重
for the temples of the gods—   975
let a rough doom tear him down,
repay his pride, breakneck, ruinous pride!
If he cannot reap his profits fairly
cannot restrain himself from outrage—   980
mad, laying hands on the holy things untouchable!

Can such a man, so desperate, still boast
he can save his life from the flashing bolts of god?
If all such violence goes with honor now
why join the sacred dance?

Never again will I go reverent to Delphi,   985
The **inviolate**[4] heart of Earth   4.[in'vaiələt] adj.无污点的
or Apollo's ancient oracle at Abae
or **Olympia**[5] of the fires—   5.[əu'limpiæ] n.奥林匹亚
unless these prophecies all come true
for all mankind to point toward in wonder.   990
King of kings, if you deserve your titles
Zeus, remember, never forget!
You and your deathless, everlasting reign.

They are dying, the old oracles sent to Laius,
now our masters strike them off the rolls.   995
Nowhere Apollo's golden glory now—
the gods, the gods go down.

* * *   * * *   * * *   * * *   * * *   * * *   * * *   * * *

❁Questions for Discussion

(20) What was the chorus doing in the above sections of the play?

* * *   * * *   * * *   * * *   * * *   * * *   * * *   * * *

(*Enter Jocasta from the palace, carrying a suppliant's
branch wound in wool.*)

Jocasta. Lords of the realm, it occurred to me,
just now, to visit the temples of the gods,
so I have my branch in hand and incense too.   1000

Oedipus is beside himself. **Racked with anguish**[1],   1. 痛苦折磨
no longer a man of sense, he won't admit
the latest prophecies are hollow as the old—
he's at the mercy of every passing voice
if the voice tells of terror.   1005
I urge him gently, nothing seems to help,
so I turn to you, Apollo, you are nearest.
(placing her branch on the altar, while an old herdsman
enters from the side, not the one just summoned by the
king but an unexpected Messenger from Corinth)

I come with prayers and offerings... I beg you,
cleanse[2] us, set us free of **defilement**[3]!   2. [klenz] *v.* 清洗
Look at us, passengers in the grip of fear,   1010   3. [dɪˈfaɪlmənt] *n.* 污秽
watching the **pilot of the vessel go to pieces**[4].   4. 沉船的领航者
Messenger. (*Approaching Jocasta and the Chorus*.)
Strangers, please, I wonder if you could lead us
to the palace of the king... I think it's Oedipus.
Better, the man himself—you know where he is?
Leader. This is his palace, stranger. He's inside.   1015
But here is his queen, his wife and mother
of his children.
Messenger.   Blessings on you, noble queen,
queen of Oedipus crowned with all your family—
blessings on you always!
Jocasta. And the same to you, stranger, you deserve it... 1020
such a greeting. But what have you come for?
Have you brought us news?
Messenger.   Wonderful news—
for the house, my lady, for your husband too.
Jocasta. Really, what? Who sent you?
Messenger.   Corinth.
I'll give you the message in a moment.   1025
You'll be glad of it—how could you help it? —

though it costs a little sorrow in the bargain.

Jocasta. What can it be, with such a double edge?

Messenger. The people there, they want to make your

Oedipus king of Corinth, so they're saying now.　　　1030

Jocasta. Why? Isn't old Polybus still in power?

Messenger. No more. Death has got him in the tomb.

Jocasta. What are you saying? Polybus, dead? —dead?

Messenger.　　　　　　　　　　　　　　　　If not,

if I'm not telling the truth, strike me dead too.

Jocasta (to a servant).

Quickly, go to your master, tell him this!　　　　　1035

You prophecies of the gods, where are you now?

This is the man that Oedipus feared for years,

he fled him, not to kill him—and now he's dead,

quite by chance, a normal, natural death,

not murdered by his son.　　　　　　　　　　1040

Oedipus (*Emerging from the palace.*)

　　　　　　　　　　　　　　　　　　Dearest,

what now? Why call me from the palace?

Jocasta (*Bringing the Messenger closer.*)

Listen to him, see for yourself what all

those awful prophecies of god have come to.

Oedipus. And who is he? What can he have for me?

Jocasta. He's from Corinth, he's come to tell you　　1045

your father is no more—Polybus—he's dead!

Oedipus (Wheeling on the Messenger.)

What? Let me have it from your lips.

Messenger.　　　　　　　　　　　　　　　Well,

if that's what you want first, then here it is:

make no mistake, Polybus is dead and gone.

Oedipus. How—murder? sickness? —what? what killed him?

　　　　　　　　　　　　　　　　　　　　1050

Messenger. A light tip of the scales can put old bones to rest.

Oedipus. sickness then—poor man, it wore him down.

A little disturbance can cause an old person to die.

Messenger.　　　　　　　　　　　　　　　That,

and the long count of years he'd measured out.

Oedipus.   So!

Jocasta, why, why look to the Prophet's hearth,

the fires of the future? Why scan the birds   1055

that scream above our heads? They winged me on

to the murder of my father, did they? That was my doom?

Well look, he's dead and buried, hidden under the earth,

and here I am in Thebes, I never put hand to sword—

unless some longing for me wasted him away,   1060

then in a sense you'd say I caused his death.

But now, all those prophecies I feared—Polybus

packs them off to sleep with him in hell!

They're nothing, worthless.

＊ ＊ ＊　　＊ ＊ ＊　　＊ ＊ ＊　　＊ ＊ ＊　　＊ ＊ ＊　　＊ ＊ ＊　　＊ ＊ ＊　　＊ ＊ ＊

❀Questions for Discussion

(21) What news of Polybus did the messenger from Corinth bring about?

＊ ＊ ＊　　＊ ＊ ＊　　＊ ＊ ＊　　＊ ＊ ＊　　＊ ＊ ＊　　＊ ＊ ＊　　＊ ＊ ＊　　＊ ＊ ＊

Jocasta.   There.

Didn't I tell you from the start?   1065

Oedipus. So you did. I was lost in fear.

Jocasta. No more, sweep it from your mind forever.

Oedipus. But my mother's bed, surely I must fear—

Jocasta.   Fear?

What should a man fear? It's all chance,

chance rules our lives. Not a man on earth   1070

can see a day ahead, groping through the dark.

Better to live at random, best we can.

And as for this marriage with your mother—

have no fear. Many a man before you,

in his dreams, has shared his mother's bed.   1075

Take such things for shadows, nothing at all—

Live, Oedipus,

as if there's no tomorrow!

Oedipus.   Brave words,

and you'd persuade me if mother weren't alive.

But mother lives, so for all your reassurance   1080

I live in fear, I must.

Jocasta.   But your father's death, that, at least, is a great blessing, joy to the eyes!

Oedipus. Great, I know... but I fear her—she's still alive.

Messenger. Wait, who is this woman, makes you so afraid?

Oedipus. Merope, old man. The wife of Polybus.   1085

Messenger. The queen? What's there to fear in her?

Oedipus. A dreadful prophecy, stranger, sent by the gods.

Messenger. Tell me, could you? Unless it's forbidden
other ears to hear.

Oedipus.   Not at all.

Apollo told me once—it is my fate—   1090
I must make love with my own mother,
shed my father's blood with my own hands.
So for years I've **given Corinth a wide berth**[1],   1. 离科斯林很远
and it's been my good fortune too. But still,
to see one's parents and look into their eyes   1095
is the greatest joy I know.

Messenger.   You're afraid of that?
That kept you out of Corinth?

Oedipus.   My father, old man—
so I wouldn't kill my father.

Messenger.   So that's it.
Well then, seeing I came with such good will, my king,
why don't I rid you of that old worry now?   1100

Oedipus. What a rich reward you'd have for that!

Messenger. What do you think I came for, majesty?
So you'd come home and I'd be better off.

Oedipus. Never, I will never go near my parents.

Messenger. My boy, it's clear, you don't know what   1105
you're doing.

Oedipus. What do you mean, old man? For god's sake,
explain.

Messenger. If you ran from them, always **dodging**[2] home...   2. [dɒdʒɪŋ] v. 闪开;避过

Oedipus. Always, terrified Apollo's oracle might come true—

Messenger. And you'd be covered with guilt, from both your
parents.

Oedipus. That's right, old man, that fear is always with me. 1110

Messenger. Don't you know? You've really nothing to fear.

Oedipus. But why? If I'm their son—Merope, Polybus?

Messenger. Polybus was nothing to you，that's why，not in blood.

Oedipus. What are you saying—Polybus was not my father?

Messenger. No more than I am. He and I are equals.   1115

Oedipus.   My father—
how can my father equal nothing? You're nothing to me!

Messenger. Neither was he，no more your father than I am.

Oedipus. Then why did he call me his son?

Messenger.   You were a gift，
years ago—know for a fact he took you
from my hands.   1120

Oedipus.   No，from another's hands?
Then how could he love me so? He loved me，deeply...

Messenger. True，and his early years without a child
made him love you all the more.

Oedipus.   And you，did you...
buy me? find me by accident?

Messenger.   I **stumbled**[1] **on you**，
down the woody **flanks**[2] of Mount Cithaeron.   1125

Oedipus.   So close，
What were you doing here，just passing through?

Messenger. Watching over my **flocks**[3]，**grazing**[4] them on the **slopes.**[5]

Oedipus. A herdsman，were you? A **vagabond**[6]，**scraping for**[7] wages?

Messenger. Your **savior**[8] too，my son，in your worst hour.

Oedipus.   Oh—
when you picked me up，was I in pain? What exactly?   1130

Messenger. Your ankles... they tell the story. Look at them.

Oedipus. Why remind me of that，that old **affliction**?[9]

Messenger. Your ankles were pinned together. I set you free.

Oedipus. That dreadful mark—I've had it from the cradle.

Messenger. And you got your name from that   1135
misfortune too，
the name's still with you.

Oedipus.   Dear god，who did it? —
mother? father? Tell me.

Oedipus' name comes from Greek words meaning "swollen foot."

1. ['stʌmbl] *vi*. 偶然遇见
2. [flæŋk] *n*. 侧面
3. [flɒk] *n*. 羊群
4. ['greɪzɪŋ] *v*. 放牧
5. [sləʊp] *n*. 山坡
6. ['væɡəbɒnd] *v*. 无业游民
7. 为了
8. ['seɪvjə(r)] *n*. 拯救者
9. [ə'flɪkʃən] *n*. 苦恼;痛苦

Messenger.   I don't know.

The one who gave you to me, he'd know more.

Oedipus. What? You took me from someone else?

You didn't find me yourself?   1140

Messenger.   No sir,

another shepherd passed you on to me.

Oedipus. Who? Do you know? Describe him.

Messenger. He called himself a servant of...

if I remember rightly—Laius.

(*Jocasta turns sharply.*)

Oedipus. The king of the land who ruled here long ago?   1145

Messenger. That's the one. That **herdsman**[1] was his man.   1. ['hɜːdzmən] *n.* 牧羊人

Oedipus. Is he still alive? Can I see him?

Messenger. They'd know best, the people of these parts.

(*Oedipus and the Messenger turn to the Chorus.*)

Oedipus. Does anyone know that herdsman,

the one he mentioned? Anyone seen him   1150

in the fields, here in the city? Out with it!

The time has come to reveal this once for all.

Leader. I think he's the very shepherd you wanted to see,

a moment ago. But the queen, Jocasta,

she's the one to say.   1155

Oedipus.   Jocasta,

you remember the man we just sent for?

Is that the one he means?

Jocasta.   That man...

Why ask? Old shepherd, talk, empty nonsense,

don't give it another thought, don't even think—

Oedipus. What—give up now, with a clue like this?   1160

Fail to solve the mystery of my birth?

Not for all the world!

Jocasta. stop—in the name of god,

if you love your own life, call off this search!

My suffering is enough.

Oedipus.   Courage!

Even if my mother turns out to be a slave,   1165

and I a slave, three generations back,

you would not seem common.

Jocasta.   Oh no,

listen to me, I beg you, don't do this.

Oedipus. Listen to you? No more. I must know it all,

must see the truth at last.   1170

Jocasta.   No, please—

for your sake—I want the best for you!

Oedipus. Your best is more than I can bear.

Jocasta.   You're doomed—

may you never **fathom**[1] who you are!   1. ['fæðəm] *v*. 理解

Oedipus. (*To a servant*).

Hurry, fetch me the herdsman, now!

Leave her to glory in her royal birth.   1175

Jocasta. Aieeeeee—

                            man of agony—

that is the only name I have for you,

that, no other—ever, ever, ever!

(*Flinging through the palace doors. A long, tense silence follows.*)

Leader. Where's she gone, Oedipus?

Rushing off, such wild grief...   1180

I'm afraid that from this silence

something monstrous may come bursting forth.

Oedipus. Let it burst! Whatever will, whatever must!

I must know my birth, no matter how common

it may be—I must see my origins face-to-face.   1185

She perhaps, she with her woman's pride

may well be **mortified**[2] by my birth,   2. ['mɔːtɪfaɪ] *v*. 为…感到耻辱

but I, I count myself the son of Chance,

the great goddess, giver of all good things—

I'll never see myself disgraced. She is my mother!   1190

And the moons have marked me out, my blood-brothers,

one moon **on the wane**[3], the next moon great with power.   3. 月亏

That is my blood, my nature—I will never betray it,

never fail to search and learn my birth!

Chorus. Yes—if I am a true prophet   1195

if I can grasp the truth,

by the boundless skies of Olympus,

at the full moon of tomorrow, Mount Cithaeron

you will know how Oedipus glories in you—
you，his birthplace，nurse，his mountain-mother！   1200
And we will sing you，dancing out your praise—
you lift our monarch's heart！
Apollo，Apollo，god of the wild cry
may our dancing please you！

                                    Oedipus—

son，dear child，who bore you？   1205
minor nature goddesses.   1206
the god of forests，pastures，and shepherds.   1207
Who of the **nymphs**[1] who seem to live forever
mated with **Pan**[2]，the mountain-striding Father？
Who was your mother？who，some bride of Apollo
the god who loves the pastures spreading toward
the sun？
Or was it Hermes，king of the lightning ridges？   1210
Or Dionysus，lord of frenzy，lord of the barren

peaks—
did he seize you in his hands，dearest of all his
lucky finds？—
found by the nymphs，their warm eyes dancing，gift
to the lord who loves them dancing out his joy！
（Oedipus strains to see a figure coming from the distance.
Attended by palace guards，an old Shepherd enters slowly，
reluctant to approach the king.）
Oedipus. I never met the man，my friends... still，   1215
if I had to guess，I'd say that's the shepherd，
the very one we've looked for all along.
Brothers in old age，two of a kind，
he and our guest here. At any rate
the ones who bring him in are my own men，   1220
I recognize them.
（Turning to the Leader.）
                        But you know more than I，
you should，you've seen the man before.
Leader. I know him，definitely. One of Laius' men，
a trusty shepherd，if there ever was one.

1. ［nɪmf］*n*. 仙女

2. ［pæn］*n*. 掌管田野、森林、
和洪流的神

Oedipus. You, I ask you first, stranger,   1225

you from Corinth—is this the one you mean?

Messenger. You're looking at him. He's your man.

Oedipus. (to the Shepherd).

You, old man, come over here—

look at me. Answer all my questions.

Did you ever serve King Laius?   1230

Shepherd.   So I did...

a slave, not bought on the block though,

born and reared in the palace.

Oedipus. Your duties, your kind of work?

Shepherd. **Herding**¹ the flocks, the better part of my life.   1. [ˈhɜːdɪŋ] *v*. 放羊

Oedipus. Where, mostly? Where did you do your **grazing**?²   2. [ˈgreɪzɪŋ] *n*. 放牧,吃草

1235

Shepherd.   Well,

Cithaeron sometimes, or the foothills round about.

Oedipus. This man—you know him? Ever see him there?

Shepherd (Confused, glancing from the Messenger to the

King.)

Doing what? —what man do you mean?

Oedipus (Pointing to the Messenger.)   1240

This one here—ever have dealings with him?

Shepherd. Not so I could say, but give me a chance,

my memory's bad...

Messenger. No wonder he doesn't know me, master.

But let me refresh his memory for him.

I'm sure he recalls old times we had

on the slopes of Mount Cithaeron;   1245

he and I, grazing our flocks, he with two

and I with one—we both struck up together,

three whole seasons, six months at a stretch

from spring to the rising of **Arcturus**³ in the fall,   3. [ɑːkˈtjʊərəs] *n*. 大角星

then with winter coming on I'd drive my herds   1250

to my own **pens**⁴, and back he'd go with his   4. [pɒns] *n*. 围栏

to Laius' folds.

(*To the Shepherd*.)

Now that's how it was,

wasn't it—yes or no?

Shepherd.   Yes, I suppose...

it's all so long ago.

Messenger.   Come, tell me,

you gave me a child back then, a boy, remember?   1255

A little fellow to rear, my very own.

Shepherd. What? Why **rake up**[1] that again?   1. 旧事重提

Messenger. Look, here he is, my fine old friend—

the same man who was just a baby then.

Shepherd. Damn you, shut your mouth—quiet!   1260

Oedipus. Don't **lash**[2] out at him, old man—   2. [læʃ] *v.* 抽打

you need lashing more than he does.

Shepherd.   Why,

master, majesty—what have I done wrong?

Oedipus. You won't answer his question about the boy.

Shepherd. He's talking nonsense, wasting his breath.   1265

Oedipus. So, you won't talk willingly—

then you'll talk with pain.

(The guards seize the Shepherd.)

Shepherd. No, dear god, don't **torture**[3] an old man!   3. ['tɔːtʃə(r)] *v.* 扭,拧

Oedipus. **Twist** his arms back, quickly!

Shepherd.   God help us, why? —

what more do you need to know?   1270

Oedipus. Did you give him that child? He's asking.

Shepherd. I did... I wish to god I'd died that day.

Oedipus. You've got your wish if you don't tell the truth.

Shepherd. The more I tell, the worse the death I'll die.

Oedipus. Our friend here wants to stretch things out,   1275

does he?

(Motioning to his men for torture.)

Shepherd. No, no, I gave it to him—I just said so.

Oedipus. Where did you get it? Your house? Someone else's?

Shepherd. It wasn't mine, no, I got it from... someone.

Oedipus. Which one of them?

(Looking at the citizens.)

                         Whose house?

Shepherd.   No—

god's sake, master, no more questions!   1280

Oedipus. You're a dead man if I have to ask again.

Shepherd. Then—the child came from the house...
of Laius.

Oedipus. A slave? or born of his own blood?

Shepherd.　　　　　　　　　　　　　Oh no, I'm
right at the edge, the horrible truth—I've got to say it!

Oedipus. And I'm at the edge of hearing horrors, yes,　　1285
but I must hear!

Shepherd. All right! His son, they said it was—his son!
　　But the one inside, your wife,
　　she'd tell it best.

Oedipus. My wife—
she gave it to you?　　　　　　　　　　　　　　1290

Shepherd. Yes, yes, my king.

Oedipus. Why, what for?

Shepherd. To kill it.

Oedipus. Her own child,
how could she?　　　　　　　　　　　　　　1295

Shepherd. She was afraid—
frightening prophecies.

Oedipus. What?

Shepherd.　　　　　　　　　　　They said—
he'd kill his parents.

Oedipus. But you gave him to this old man—why?　　1300

Shepherd. I pitied the little baby, master,
hoped he'd take him off to his own country,
far away, but he saved him for this, this fate.
If you are the man he says you are, believe me,
you were born for pain.　　　　　　　　　　1035

Oedipus.　　　　　　　　　　　O god—
all come true, all burst to light!
O light—now let me look my last on you!
I stand revealed at last—
cursed in my birth, cursed in marriage,
cursed in the lives I cut down with these hands!　　1310
(Rushing through the doors with a great cry. The
Corinthian Messenger, the Shepherd and attendants exit
slowly to the side.)

＊ ＊ ＊   ＊ ＊ ＊   ＊ ＊ ＊   ＊ ＊ ＊   ＊ ＊ ＊   ＊ ＊ ＊   ＊ ＊ ＊   ＊ ＊ ＊

❖ Questions for Discussion

(22) How did it come about that Oedipus was brought up as Polybus' son? Tell the story in your own words.

(23) What does Oedipus discover about his birth?

(24) Focus on the chorus reacts to Oedipus' discovery of the truth of his birth. Read to find out what the chorus thinks of him now.

＊ ＊ ＊   ＊ ＊ ＊   ＊ ＊ ＊   ＊ ＊ ＊   ＊ ＊ ＊   ＊ ＊ ＊   ＊ ＊ ＊   ＊ ＊ ＊

Chorus. O the generations of men,

the dying generations—adding the total

of all your lives I find they come to nothing...

does there exist, is there a man on earth

who seizes more joy than just a dream, a vision?   1315

And the vision no sooner dawns than dies

blazing into oblivion.

    You are my great example, you, your life

     your destiny, Oedipus, man of misery—

I count no man blest.   1320

      You **outranged**[1] all men! 1. [aʊtˈreɪn(d)ʒ] *vt*. 超过

      Bending your bow to the breaking-point

you captured priceless glory, O dear god,

and the Sphinx came crashing down,

       the virgin, claws hooked

like a bird of omen singing, shrieking death—   1325

like a fortress reared in the face of death

you rose and saved our land.

From that day on we called you king

we crowned you with honors, Oedipus, towering over

all—mighty king of the seven gates of Thebes.   1330

But now to hear your story—is there a man more agonized?

More wed to pain and frenzy? Not a man on earth,

the joy of your life ground down to nothing

O Oedipus, name for the ages—

    one and the same wide harbor served you   1335

       son and father both

son and father came to rest in the same bridal chamber.

How, how could the furrows your father plowed

bear you, your agony, harrowing on

in silence O so long?   1340

But now for all your power

Time, all-seeing Time has dragged you to the light,

judged your marriage monstrous from the start—

the son and the father tangling, both one—

O child of Laius, would to god

I'd never seen you, never never!   1345

Now I weep like a man who **wails**[1] the dead   1. [weɪl] vt. 哀嚎

and the **dirge**[2] comes pouring forth with all my heart!   2. [dɜːdʒ] n. 挽歌

I tell you the truth, you gave me life

my breath leapt up in you

and now you bring down night upon my eyes.   1350

(*Enter a Messenger from the palace.*)

Messenger. Men of Thebes, always first in honor,

what horrors you will hear, what you will see,

what a heavy weight of sorrow you will shoulder...

if you are true to your birth, if you still have

some feeling for the royal house of Thebes.   1355

I tell you neither the waters of the Danube

nor the Nile can wash this palace clean.

Such things it hides, it soon will bring to light—

terrible things, and none done blindly now,

all done with a will. The pains   1360

we **inflict upon**[3] ourselves hurt most of all.   3. [ɪnˈflɪkt] vt. 使…受痛苦,

Leader. God knows we have pains enough already.   给…以(打击、惩罚)

What can you add to them?

Messenger. The queen is dead.

Leader.   Poor lady—how?

Messenger. By her own hand. But you are spared the   1365

worst, you never had to watch... I saw it all,

and with all the memory that's in me

you will learn what that poor woman suffered.

Once she'd broken in through the gates,

dashing past us, **frantic**[4], whipped to fury,   1370   4. [ˈfræntɪk] adj. 疯狂的

ripping her hair out with both hands—

straight to her rooms she rushed, flinging herself
across the bridal-bed, doors slamming behind her—
once inside, she **wailed**[1] for Laius, dead so long,
remembering how she bore his child long ago,　　　　　1375
the life that rose up to destroy him, leaving
its mother to mother living creatures
with the very son she'd borne.
Oh how she wept, mourning the marriage-bed
where she let loose that double brood—monsters—　　　1380
husband by her husband, children by her child.

　　　And then—but how she died is more than I can say.
Suddenly Oedipus burst in, screaming, he stunned us so
we couldn't watch her agony to the end,
our eyes were fixed on him. Circling　　　　　　　　1385
like a maddened beast, stalking, here, there,
crying out to us—
Give him a sword! His wife,
no wife, his mother, where can he find the mother earth
that cropped two crops at once, himself and all his children?
He was raging—one of the dark powers pointing the　　1390
way, none of us mortals crowding around him, no,
with a great shattering cry—someone, something leading
him on—
he hurled at the twin doors and bending the bolts back
out of their sockets, crashed through the chamber.

And there we saw the woman hanging by the neck,　　　1395
cradled high in a woven **noose**[2], spinning,
swinging back and forth. And when he saw her,
giving a low, **wrenching**[3] sob that broke our hearts,
slipping the **halter**[4] from her throat, he eased her down,
in a slow **embrace**[5] he laid her down, poor thing...　　1400
then, what came next, what horror we beheld!

He rips off her **brooches**[6], the long gold pins
holding her robes—and lifting them high,
looking straight up into the points,
he digs them down the sockets of his eyes, crying, "You, 1405

1. [weɪl] *vi.* 哀嚎

2. [nuːs] *n.* 套索；束缚

3. [ˈrentʃɪŋ] *vi.* 使痛苦；使悲痛
4. [ˈhɔːltə] *n.* 绳
5. [ɪmˈbreɪs] *n.* 拥抱

6. [brəʊtʃ] *n.* 胸针

you'll see no more the pain I suffered, all the pain I caused!
Too long you looked on the ones you never should have seen,
blind to the ones you longed to see, to know! Blind
from this hour on! Blind in the darkness—blind!"
His voice like a **dirge**[1], rising, over and over   1410
raising the pins, **raking**[2] them down his eyes.
And at each stroke blood **spurts from the roots**[3],
splashing his beard, a swirl of it, nerves and clots—
black hail of blood pulsing, **gushing down**[4].

These are the griefs that burst upon them both,   1415
coupling man and woman. The joy they had so lately,
the fortune of their old ancestral house
was deep joy indeed. Now, in this one day,
wailing, madness and doom, death, disgrace,
all the griefs in the world that you can name,   1420
all are theirs forever.

Leader.   Oh poor man, the misery—
has he any rest from pain now?
(*A voice within*, *in torment*[5].)

Messenger.   He's shouting,
"Loose the **bolts**[6], someone, show me to all of Thebes!
My father's murderer, my mother's—"
No, I can't repeat it, it's unholy.   1425
Now he'll tear himself from his native earth,
not linger, curse the house with his own curse.
But he needs strength, and a guide to lead him on.
This is sickness more than he can bear.
(*The palace doors open*.)

Look,
he'll show you himself. The great doors are   1430
opening—you are about to see a sight, a horror
even his mortal enemy would pity.
(*Enter Oedipus*, *blinded*, *led by a boy*. *He stands at the
palace steps*, *as if surveying his people once again*.)

Chorus.   O the terror—
the suffering, for all the world to see,
the worst terror that ever met my eyes.

1. [dɜːdʒ] *n*. 挽歌

2. [reɪkɪŋ] *v*. 搜索

3. 喷涌而出

4. [gʌʃ] *v*. 喷涌而出

5. ['tɔːmənt] *n*. 折磨

6. [bəʊlt] *n*. 门闩

What madness swept over you? What god，   1435

what dark power leapt beyond all bounds，

beyond belief，to crush your wretched life？ —

godforsaken，cursed by the gods！

I pity you but I can't bear to look.

I've much to ask，so much to learn，   1440

so much fascinates my eyes，

but you... I **shudder at**[1] the sight.   1.［'ʃʌdə］ *vt*.颤抖，惊恐

Oedipus.   Oh，Ohh—

the agony！I am agony—

where am I going？where on earth？

             where does all this agony hurl me？   1445

where's my voice？ —

winging，swept away on a dark tide—

My destiny，my dark power，what a leap you made！

Chorus. To the depths of terror，too dark to hear，to see.

Oedipus. Dark，horror of darkness   1450

my darkness，drowning，swirling around me

crashing wave on wave—unspeakable，irresistible

headwind，fatal harbor！Oh again，

the misery，all at once，over and over

the stabbing **daggers**[2]，stab of memory   1455   2.［'dægə］ *n*.匕首

raking me insane.

Chorus.   No wonder you suffer

twice over，the pain of your wounds，

the lasting grief of pain.

Oedipus.   Dear friend，still here？

Standing by me，still with a care for me，

the blind man？ Such compassion，   1460

loyal to the last. Oh it's you，

I know you're here，dark as it is

I'd know you anywhere，your voice—   1470

it's yours，clearly yours.

Chorus.   Dreadful，what you've done...

how could you bear it，**gouging out**[3] your eyes？   1465   3.［gaudʒ］ *v*.挖出

What superhuman power drove you on？

Oedipus. Apollo，friends，Apollo—

he **ordained**[4] my agonies—these，my pains on pains！   4.［ɔːdeɪn］ *v*.判定，规定

But the hand that struck my eyes was mine,

mine alone—no one else—   1470

                                   I did it all myself!

What good were eyes to me?

Nothing I could see could bring me joy.

Chorus. No, no, exactly as you say.

Oedipus.   What can I ever see?

What love, what call of the heart   1475

can touch my ears with joy? Nothing, friends.

Take me away, far, far from Thebes,

quickly, cast me away, my friends—

this great murderous ruin, this man cursed to heaven,

the man the deathless gods hate most of all!   1480

Chorus. Pitiful, you suffer so, you understand so much...

I wish you had never known.

Oedipus.   Die, die—

whoever he was that day in the wilds

who cut my ankles free of the ruthless pins,

he pulled me clear of death, he saved my life   1485

for this, this kindness—

                                   Curse him, kill him!

If I'd died then, I'd never have dragged myself,

my loved ones through such hell.

Chorus. Oh if only...would to god.   1490

Oedipus.   I'd never have come to this,

my father's murderer—never been branded

mother's husband, all men see me now! Now,

Loathed[1] by the gods, son of the mother I **defiled**[2]

coupling in my father's bed, **spawning**[3] lives in the **loins**[4]

that spawned my wretched life. What grief can crown   1495

this grief?

It's mine alone, my destiny—I am Oedipus!

Chorus. How can I say you've chosen for the best?

Better to die than be alive and blind.

Oedipus. What I did was best—don't lecture me,

no more advice. I, with my eyes,   1500

how could I look my father in the eyes

when I go down to death? Or mother, so abused...

1. [ləʊθ] *n*. 讨厌

2. [dɪ'faɪl] *v*.污染

3. [spɔːnɪŋ] *vi*. 产卵

4. [lɔɪn] *n*. 腰部

I have done such things to the two of them,
crimes too huge for hanging.

                                   Worse yet,
the sight of my children, born as they were born,   1505
how could I long to look into their eyes?
No, not with these eyes of mine, never.
Not this city either, her high towers,
the sacred glittering images of her gods—
I am misery! I, her best son, reared   1510
as no other son of Thebes was ever reared,
I've stripped myself, I gave the command myself.
All men must cast away the great **blasphemer**[1],   1. [blæs'fi:mə] *n.* 亵渎者
the curse now brought to light by the gods,
the son of Laius—I, my father's son!   1515

Now I've exposed my guilt, **horrendous**[2] guilt,   2. [hɒ'rendəs] *v.* 可怕的
could I **train a level glance on you**[3], my countrymen?   3. 我直盯着你的眼睛
Impossible! No, if I could just block off my ears,
the springs of hearing, I would stop at nothing—
I'd wall up my loathsome body like a prison,   1520
blind to the sound of life, not just the sight.
Oblivion—what a blessing...
for the mind to dwell a world away from pain.
O Cithaeron, why did you give me shelter?
Why didn't you take me, crush my life out on the spot?   1525
I'd never have revealed my birth to all mankind.
O Polybus, Corinth, the old house of my fathers,
so I believed—what a handsome prince you raised—
under the skin, what sickness to the core.
Look at me! Born of **outrage**[4], outrage to the core.   1530   4. ['aʊtreɪdʒ] *n.* 暴行

O triple roads—it all comes back, the secret,
dark ravine, and the oaks closing in
where the three roads join...
You drank my father's blood, my own blood
spilled by my own hands—you still remember me?   1535
What things you saw me do? Then I came here
and did them all once more!

Marriages! O marriage，

you gave me birth，and once you brought me into the

world you brought my sperm rising back，springing to

light fathers，brothers，sons—one murderous breed—   1540

brides，wives，mothers. The blackest things

a man can do，I have done them all!

No more—it's wrong to name what's wrong to do.

Quickly，for the love of god，hide me somewhere，

kill me，hurl me into the sea   1545

where you can never look on me again.

(*Beckoning to the Chorus as they shrink away*).

Closer，

it's all right. Touch the man of grief.   1513

Do. Don't be afraid. My troubles are mine

and I am the only man alive who can **sustain**[1] them.   1. [sə'steɪn] *vt*. 忍受

(*Enter Creon from the palace，attended by palace guards*.)

Leader. Put your requests to Creon. Here he is，   1550

just when we need him. He'll have a plan，he'll act.

Now that he's the sole defense of the country in your place.

Oedipus.   Oh no，what can I say to him?

How can I ever hope to win his trust?

I wronged him so，just now，in every way.   1555

You must see that—I was so wrong，so wrong.

Creon. I haven't come to **mock**[2] you，Oedipus，   2. [mɒk] *vt*. 嘲笑

or to criticize your former failings.

(*Turning to the guards*.)

You there，

have you lost all respect for human feelings?

At least revere the Sun，the holy fire   1560

that keeps us all alive. Never expose a thing

of guilt and holy dread so great it appalls

the earth，the rain from heaven，the light of day!

Get him into the halls—quickly as you can.

Piety demands no less. Kindred alone   1565

should see a kinsman's shame. This is **obscene**[3].   3. [əb'siːn] *adj*. 污秽的

Oedipus. Please，in god's name... you wipe my fears away，

coming so generously to me，the worst of men.

Do one thing more, for your sake, not mine.

Creon. What do you want? Why so insistent?   1570

Oedipus. Drive me out of the land at once, far from sight,

where I can never hear a human voice.

Creon. I'd have done that already, I promise you.

First I wanted the god to **clarify**[1] my duties.   1. [ˈklærɪfaɪ] *vt.* 澄清

Oedipus. The god? His command was clear, every   1575

word: death for the father-killer, the curse—

he said destroy me!

Creon. So he did. Still, in such a crisis

it's better to ask precisely what to do.

Oedipus.   So miserable—

you would consult the god about a man like me?   1580

Creon. By all means. And this time, I assume,

even you will obey the god's decrees.

Oedipus.   I will,

I will. And you, I command you—I beg you...

the woman inside, bury her as you see fit.

It's the only decent thing,   1585

to give your own the last rites. As for me,

never condemn the city of my fathers

to house my body, not while I'm alive, no,

let me live on the mountains, on Cithaeron,

my favorite haunt, I have made it famous.   1590

Mother and father marked out that rock

to be my everlasting tomb—buried alive.

Let me die there, where they tried to kill me.

Oh but this I know: no sickness can destroy me,

nothing can. I would never have been saved   1595

from death—I have been saved

for something great and terrible, something strange.

Well let my destiny come and take me on its way!

About my children, Creon, the boys at least,

don't burden yourself. They're men,   1600

wherever they go, they'll find the means to live.

But my two daughters, my poor helpless girls,

clustering at our table, never without me

hovering[2] near them... whatever I touched,   2. [ˈhɒvə] *v.* 盘旋,徘徊

they always had their share. Take care of them,   1605
I beg you. Wait, better—permit me, would you?
Just to touch them with my hands and take
our fill of tears. Please... my king.
Grant it, with all your noble heart.
If I could hold them, just once, I'd think   1610
I had them with me, like the early days
when I could see their eyes.
(*Antigone and Ismene, two small children, are led in from
the palace by a nurse.*)

                              What's that?

O god! Do I really hear you sobbing? —
my two children. Creon, you've pitied me?
Sent me my darling girls, my own flesh and blood!   1615
Am I right?
Creon.   Yes, it's my doing.
I know the joy they gave you all these years,
the joy you must feel now.
Oedipus.   Bless you, Creon!
May god watch over you for this kindness,
better than he ever guarded me.   1620
                     Children, where are you?
Here, come quickly—
(*Groping for Antigone and Ismene, who approach their
father cautiously, then embrace him.*)

                     Come to these hands of mine,
your brother's hands, your own father's hands
that served his once bright eyes so well—
that made them blind. Seeing nothing, children,
knowing nothing, I became your father,   1625
I fathered you in the soil that gave me life.

How I weep for you—I cannot see you now ...
just thinking of all your days to come, the bitterness,
the life that rough mankind will thrust upon you.
Where are the public gatherings you can join,   1630
the banquets of the clans? Home you'll come,
in tears, cut off from the sight of it all,
the brilliant rites unfinished.

And when you reach perfection，ripe for marriage，
who will he be，my dear ones? Risking all   1635
to shoulder the curse that weighs down my parents，
yes and you too—that wounds us all together.
What more misery could you want?
Your father killed his father，sowed his mother，
one，one and the **selfsame**[1] womb sprang you—   1640   1. ['selfseɪm] *adj*. 完全一样的，
he cropped the very roots of his existence.   相同的
Such disgrace，and you must bear it all!
Who will marry you then? Not a man on earth.
Your doom is clear：you'll **wither away**[2] to nothing，   2. ['wɪðə] *vi*. 萎缩
single，without a child.   1645
(Turning to Creon.)

                                                        Oh Creon，

you are the only father they have now...
we who brought them into the world
are gone，both gone at a stroke—
Don't let them go begging，abandoned，
women without men. Your own flesh and blood!   1650
Never bring them down to the level of my pains.
Pity them. Look at them，so young，so **vulnerable**[3]，   3. ['vʌlnərəbl] *adj*. 脆弱的
shorn of everything—you're their only hope.
Promise me，noble Creon，touch my hand!
(Reaching toward Creon，who draws back.)

You，little ones，if you were old enough   1655
to understand，there is much I'd tell you.
Now，as it is，I'd have you say a prayer.
Pray for life，my children，
live where you are free to grow and season.
Pray god you find a better life than mine，   1660
the father who **begot you**[4].   4. 生下你
Creon.   Enough.
You've wept enough. Into the palace now.
Oedipus. I must，but I find it very hard.
Creon. **Time is the great healer**[5]，you will see.   5. 时间是最伟大的治愈师。
Oedipus. I am going—you know on what condition?   1665

Creon. Tell me. I'm listening.

Oedipus. Drive me out of Thebes, **in exile**[1].

1. 流放

Creon. Not I. Only the gods can give you that.

Oedipus. Surely the gods hate me so much—

Creon. You'll get your wish at once.   1670

Oedipus.   You **consent**?[2]

2. 你同意?

Creon. I try to say what I mean; it's my habit.

Oedipus. Then take me away. It's time.

Creon. Come along, let go of the children.

Oedipus.   No—

don't take them away from me, not now! No no no!

(**Clutching**[3] *his daughters as the guards* **wrench**[4] *them loose*

3. [klʌtʃ] *vt.* 抓住;抓紧

and take them through the palace doors.)

4. [ren(t)ʃ] *vt.* 使劲拽

Creon. Still the king, the master of all things?   1675

No more: here your power ends.

None of your power follows you through life.

(*Exit Oedipus and Creon to the palace. The Chorus comes*

forward to address the audience directly.)

Chorus. People of Thebes, my countrymen, look on Oedipus.

He solved the famous riddle with his brilliance,

he rose to power, a man beyond all power.   1680

Who could **behold**[5] his greatness without envy?

5. [bɪˈhəʊld] *vt.* 注意到

Now what a black sea of terror has overwhelmed him.

Now as we keep our watch and wait the final day,

count no man happy till he dies, free of pain at last.

(*Exit in procession*.)

* * *   * * *   * * *   * * *   * * *   * * *   * * *   * * *

❋Questions for Discussion

(25) Translate the lines 1405—1414 into Chinese.

(26) Write a summary of the play "Oedipus the King". Retell the story of Oedipus in your own words.

(27) By reading this play, we can see very clearly what roles does the chorus play in the drama performance in Ancient Greece. Give a summary of their roles.

(28) There are different interpretations of the play "Oedipus the King". Some critics say this play demonstrates the conflict between "free will and fate". Seen from this view, people even find similarities between the fate of Oedipus and that of Hector

in Homer's *Iliad*. Others hold that the play shows "knowledge and human beings' hubris". Refer to these different interpretations, find out one you are in favor of and give your own comments.

(29) What are your comments on the character of Oedipus in this play? What feelings do you have about him? Aristotle in his *Poetics* comments that in response to the suffering of the characters in the tragedy, the audience experienced a kind of catharsis, or purgation in their emotions as the tragedy evoked in the spectators pity and fear. Do you agree with Aristotle?

* * *   * * *   * * *   * * *   * * *   * * *   * * *   * * *

Chapter Four   The History of the Peloponnesian Wars

Background Knowledge

Thucydides, the second Greek great historian for his great work *History of the Peloponnesian War*, was born in about 460 B.C. about twenty-five years later than Herodotus. Unlike Herodotus, he is an Athenian citizen. He came from an aristocratic family and received very good education along his growth in the Athens. Athens was then at its golden time, prosperous in various aspects of cultural life. Thucydides was greatly influenced by the political speeches of Pericles, dramas of Aeschylus, Sophocles, and Euripides, thoughts of the sophists, historic works of Herodotus. As a youth, we are told, Thucydides heard a reading of Herodotus history at the Olympic Games, and he was moved to tears. Because of these, his work consists of clever speaking, rational deduction, and a

Pericles (495 – 429 BC)

tragic view of the world. When grown up, he, like the other aristocratic offspring, came into politics.

When the Peloponnesian War broke out, he was over 30 years old, and was able to be elected as one of the ten generals of Athens, leading a fleet of 7 warships, stationed at the Thasos Island near Thrace. When the Spartan army attacked Amphipolis, he was requested of help and tried to lead the fleet to help the city, but the city was taken by the Spartans before he arrived. The government blamed him for delaying and exiled him to Thrace, where he lived for the next twenty years.

For the next twenty years, he was always concerned about the ongoing of the Peloponnesian War and took down the process of the war. It was said he often went to the field for observation, and even went to the site of the Peloponnesian army and the island of Sicily. From the very beginning, he had taken care to collect and sort out various data, and made out a writing scheme. It was after the war was ended that he received amnesty and returned to Athens. Then he began to write the book *The Peloponnesian War*. His writing motive came from his deep understanding of the war. He firmly believed it would be a war of much influence to the Greeks, as he wrote in the book,

"Thucydides, an Athenian, wrote the history of the war between the Peloponnesians and the Athenians, beginning at the moment that it broke out, and believing that it would be a great war, and more worthy of relation than any that had preceded it. This belief was not without its grounds. The preparations of both the combatants were in every department in the last state of perfection; and he could see the rest of the Hellenic race taking sides in the quarrel; those who delayed doing so at once having it in contemplation. Indeed this was the greatest movement yet known in history, not only of the Hellenes, but of a large part of the barbarian world—I had almost said of mankind...."

From the structure of the work, Thucydides considered the Peloponnesian War that lasted 27 years as a whole process, which was related chronologically. The book was divided into 8 parts.

Book 1: Introduction, stating the purpose and method of his writing, and traced the causes of the war.

Book 2: The circumstances of the first three years of the war, with the fourth chapter including the famous Pericles' Funeral Oration.

Book 3: Situation from the fourth to the sixth year.

Book 4: Events in the seventh to the ninth year, during which the Athenians won victory and Spartans sued for peace but were refused.

Book 5: Events that went on from the 11th to the 16th year of the war, during which time, Cleon fought dead and there was Peace of Nicias.

Book 6-7: What happened in the 17th year of the war, including the Sicilian Expedition and its total failure.

Book 8: The events that happened in the 18th-19th year.

As the work ended here, and Thucydides mentioned in his work about the Athenians' final loss of the war, he apparently was not able to finish his whole writing plan. His writing stopped at the year 411 B.C. and the last seven years of the Peloponnesian War was not covered.

Thucydides tried to explain the ongoing of history with abstract and permanent "human nature". He believed that, "things which always occur in such times always will occur, so long as human nature remains the same". (*The Peloponnesian War*, 3.82-83) Where Herodotus saw history as an interaction of divine and human forces, Thucydides conceived history as actions of people alone responsible for how things turned out. He also believed historians should try their best to experience what he was putting down. As he said in Book 5, he had experienced the whole process in person and was able to understand the significance of the war. Because of this, he even suggested the ancient history should be left for archaeologists, instead of historians.

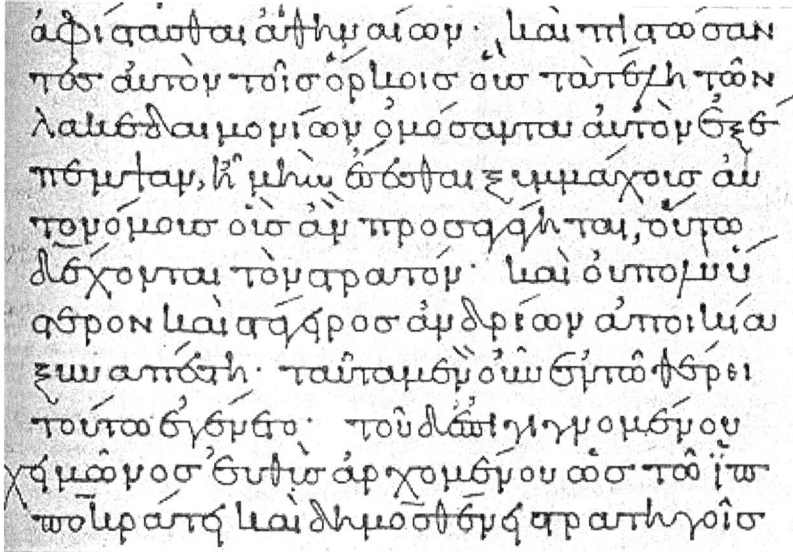

Thucydides manuscript

To obtain truth, Thucydides reminded historians not to be credulous; rather they should be critical and researching and avoid bias. He himself had done much investigation, and he wrote, "As to the events of the war, I have not written them down as I hear them from just anybody, nor as I thought they must have occurred, but have consistently described what I myself saw or have been able to learn from others after going over each event in as much detail as possible. I have found this task to be extremely arduous, since those who were present at these actions gave varying reports on the same event, depending on their sympathies and their memories. My narrative, perhaps, will seem less pleasing to some listeners because it lacks an element of fiction. Those, however, who want to see things clearly as they were and, given human nature, as they will one day be again, more or less, may find this book a useful basis for judgment. My work was composed not as a prizewinning exercise in elocution, to be heard and then forgotten, but as a work of permanent value." (*The Peloponnesian War* 1.21-22, Blanco)

To Thucydides, the cause for the Peloponnesian War was the continuous expansion of Athens after the Persians wars, which aroused envy of Sparta and discontentment of city-states like Corinth; the final failure of Athens was attributed to the internal struggle of the interest groups within Athens, fleeing of the slaves and betraying of allies. He realized that the Peloponnesian war was a tragedy unheard of. On each side there were a group of politicians who involved the whole nations into the unjustified and silly war for their own ambition and selfishness. Meanwhile, the mass did not have any power to stop the war from breaking out and developing, thus drifting with nation to the final destruction.

Thucydides sang highly of the democracy and law of Athens. He summarized and complimented the Athenian democratic principles in Pericles with the Funeral Oration, "Our constitution does not copy the laws of neighboring states; we are rather a pattern to others than imitators ourselves. Its administration favors the many instead of the few; this is why it is called a democracy. If we look to the laws, they afford equal justice to all in their private differences; if no social standing, advancement in public life falls to reputation for capacity, class considerations not being allowed to interfere with merit; nor again does poverty bar the way, if a man is able to serve the state, he is not hindered by the obscurity of his condition. The freedom which we enjoy in our government extends also to our ordinary life." (*The Peloponnesian War*, 2. 34-46, Blanco)

In his writing, Thucydides learned from the orations and rhetoric of the sophists, so that nearly one fourth of the book was speeches. These speeches contained much historic information, and also embodied the Greeks' oration skill, strengthening the inspiration of the book. These speeches, however, were mostly composed by Thucydides, and he frankly admitted, "As to the speeches of the participants, either when they were about to enter the war or after they were already in it, it has been difficult for me and for those who reported to me to remember exactly what was said. I have therefore, written what I thought the speakers must have said given the situation they were in, while keeping as close as possible to the gist of what was actually said." The situation he presumed showed his understanding of the history.

Thucydides was known as the world's first scientific historian, as his work was rather objective. No matter it was the accusation of the enemy, or of Athens, he would give equal description. In his comments of the people or events, whether they were friend or foe of Athens, or whether they were advantageous or disadvantageous to Athens, Thucydides was able to give just comments. Because he related the historic events fairly and fully, his work was highly valued.

* * *　　* * *　　* * *　　* * *　　* * *　　* * *　　* * *　　* * *

❖Questions for Discussion

(1) Compare the writing of Greek historians Herodotus and Thucydides to that of the

Chinese historians like Sima Qian. Do you find any similarities and differences?

(2) In your opinion, what is the greatness of Herodotus and Thucydides?

＊＊＊　　＊＊＊　　＊＊＊　　＊＊＊　　＊＊＊　　＊＊＊　　＊＊＊　　＊＊＊

Pericles' Funeral Oration

In the same winter the Athenians gave a funeral **at the public cost**[1] to those who had first fallen in this war. It was a **custom**[2] of their **ancestors**[3], and the manner of it is as follows. Three days before the **ceremony**[4], the bones of the dead are laid out in a tent which has been **erected**[5]; and their friends bring to their relatives such offerings as they please. In the **funeral procession**[6] **cypress coffins**[7] are borne in cars, one for each **tribe**[8]; the bones of the deceased being placed in the coffin of their tribe. Among these is carried one empty **bier**[9] **decked**[10] for the missing, that is, for those whose bodies could not be recovered.

Any citizen or stranger who pleases, joins in the **procession**[11]; and the female relatives are there to **wail**[12] at the burial. The dead are laid in the public **sepulchre**[13] in the Beautiful suburb of the city, in which those who fall in war are always buried; with the **exception**[14] of those **slain**[15] at Marathon, who for their **singular**[16] and extraordinary **valour**[17] were **interred**[18] on the spot where they fell. After the bodies have been laid in the earth, a man chosen by the state, of approved wisdom and **eminent**[19] reputation, **pronounces**[20] over them an appropriate **panegyric**[21]; after which all retire. Such is the manner of the burying; and throughout the whole of the war, whenever the occasion arose, the established custom was observed. Meanwhile these were the first that had fallen, and **Pericles**[22], son of Xanthippus, was chosen to pronounce their **eulogium**[23]. When the proper time arrived, he advanced from the **sepulchre**[24] to an **elevated platform**[25] in order to be heard by as many of the crowd as possible, and spoke as follows:

1. 国家出钱
2. ['kʌstəm] n. 习俗
3. ['ænsestə(r)] n. 祖先
4. ['serɪmənɪ] n. 典礼, 仪式
5. [ɪ'rekt] vt. 立起来; 支起来
6. 送葬；7. 柏树棺材
8. [traɪb] n. 族
9. [bɪə(r)] n. 棺材
10. ['dek] vt. 装饰; 打扮
11. [prə'seʃən] n. 队列
12. [weɪl] vi. 哭叫, 哀号
13. [sə'pʌlkrəl] 公墓
14. [ɪk'sepʃən] n. 例外
15. [sleɪn] vt. 杀死
16. ['sɪŋɡjʊlə(r)] adj. 非凡的
17. ['vælə(r)] n. 勇气
18. [ɪntərt] vt. 埋葬
19. ['emɪnənt] adj. 杰出的
20. [prə'naʊns] vt. 宣读
21. [ˌpænə'dʒɪrɪk] n. 颂词; 赞美
22. ['perɪklɪs] n. 伯里克利(雅典著名政治家)
23. [juː'ləʊdʒɪəm] n. 颂文
24. ['sepəlkə] n. 公墓
25. 支起的平台

Pericles Spoke to His People

Most of my **predecessors**[1] in this place have **commended**[2] him who made this speech part of the law, telling us that it is well that it should be delivered at the **burial**[3] of those who fall in battle. For myself, I should have thought that the worth which had displayed itself in deeds would be **sufficiently**[4] rewarded by honours also shown by deeds; such as you now see in this funeral prepared at the people's cost. And I could have wished that the reputations of many brave men were not to be **imperilled**[5] in the mouth of a single individual, to stand or fall according as he spoke well or ill. For it is hard to speak

properly upon a subject where it is even difficult to convince your hearers that you are speaking the truth. On the one hand, the friend who is familiar with every fact of the story may think that some point has **not been set forth with that fullness**[6] which he wishes and knows it to deserve; on the other, he who is a stranger to the matter may be led by envy to **suspect exaggeration**[7] if he hears anything above his own nature. For men can **endure**[8] to hear others praised only so long as they can **severally**[9] persuade themselves of their own ability to equal the actions **recounted**[10]: when this point is passed, envy comes in and with it **incredulity**[11]. However, since our ancestors have **stamped**[12] this custom with their **approval**[13], it becomes my duty to obey the law and to try to satisfy your several wishes and opinions as best I may.

1. ['predəsesə(r)] n. 前辈
2. [kə'mend] v. 托付;推荐
3. ['beriəl] n. 埋葬
4. [sə'fɪʃəntlɪ] adv. 足够
5. [ɪm'pɛrəl] vt. 危及;陷于危机
6. 不充分;不足
7. 怀疑夸张
8. [ɪn'djʊə(r)] vi. 容忍
9. ['sev(ə)r(ə)lɪ] adv. 各自地;分别地
10. [rɪ'kaʊnt] vt. 讲述
11. [ˌɪnkrɪ'djuːlətɪ] n. 怀疑;
12. [stæm'piːd] vt. 规定
13. [ə'pruːvəl] n. 同意;赞许

＊＊＊　　＊＊＊　　＊＊＊　　＊＊＊　　＊＊＊　　＊＊＊　　＊＊＊　　＊＊＊

✤Questions for Discussion

(1) Pericles begins his speech by praising the custom of the public funeral for the war dead，but criticizes the inclusion of the speech. Why?

＊＊＊　　＊＊＊　　＊＊＊　　＊＊＊　　＊＊＊　　＊＊＊　　＊＊＊　　＊＊＊

I shall begin with our ancestors：it is both just and proper that they should have the honour of the first mention on an occasion like the present. They **dwelt in**[1] the country without break in the **succession**[2] from generation to generation，and handed it down free to the present time by their **valour**[3]. And if our more **remote**[4] ancestors deserve praise，much more do our own fathers，who added to their **inheritance**[5] the empire which we now possess，and **spared no pains**[6] to be able to leave their **acquisitions**[7] to us of the present generation. Lastly，there are few parts of our **dominions**[8] that have not been **augmented**[9] by those of us here，who are still more or less in **the vigour of life**[10]；while the mother country has been **furnished**[11] by us with everything that can enable her to depend on her own resources whether for war or for peace. That part of our history which tells of the military achievements which gave us our several **possessions**[12]，or of the ready valour with which either we or our fathers **stemmed**[13] the tide of Hellenic or foreign **aggression**[14]，is a theme too familiar to my hearers for me to **dilate on**[15]，and I shall therefore pass it by. But what was the road by which we reached our position，what the form of government under which our greatness grew，what the national habits out of which it sprang；these are questions which I may try to solve before I proceed to my **panegyric**[16] upon these men；since I think this to be a subject upon which on the present occasion a speaker may properly **dwell**[17]，and to which the whole **assemblage**[18]，whether citizens or foreigners，may listen with advantage.

1. 居住在
2. [sək'seʃn] n. 接连
3. ['vælə] n. 勇气
4. [rɪ'məʊt] adj. 久远的
5. [ɪn'herɪtəns] n. 遗产
6. 不遗余力
7. [ˌækwɪ'zɪʃən] n. 兼并；获得
8. [də'mɪnɪən] n. 版图；领土
9. [ɔːg'ment] vt. 扩张
10. 壮年
11. ['fɜːnɪʃ] vt. 布置；装修

12. [pə'zeʃən] n. 领地；财产
13. [stemd] vt. 阻止
14. [ə'greʃən] n. 入侵
15. [daɪ'leɪt] v. 详述

16. [ˌpænə'dʒɪrɪk] n. 颂词

17. [dwel] v. 思考
18. [ə'semblɪdʒ] n. 聚集(会)

＊＊＊　　＊＊＊　　＊＊＊　　＊＊＊　　＊＊＊　　＊＊＊　　＊＊＊　　＊＊＊

✤Questions for Discussion

(2) Pericles next praised ancestors of the Athenians，their fathers，and their own contemporaries. On what points does he think they all deserve praises and respects of the present day Athenians?

(3) Pericles says "either we or our fathers stemmed the tide of Hellenic or foreign aggression，is a theme too familiar to my hearers for me to dilate on...". What does

"foreign aggression" here refer to?

* * *   * * *   * * *   * * *   * * *   * * *   * * *   * * *

Our **constitution**[1] does not copy the laws of neighbouring states; we are rather a pattern to others than **imitators**[2] ourselves. Its **administration**[3] favours the many instead of the few; this is why it is called a democracy. If we look to the laws, they afford equal justice to all in their private differences; if no social standing, advancement in public life falls to **reputation**[4] for capacity, class considerations not being allowed to **interfere**[5] with **merit**[6]; nor again does poverty **bar**[7] the way, if a man is able to serve the state, he is not **hindered**[8] by the **obscurity**[9] of his condition. The freedom which we enjoy in our government extends also to our ordinary life. There, far from exercising a jealous **surveillance**[10] over each other, we do not feel called upon to be angry with our neighbour for doing what he likes, or even to **indulge in**[11] those **injurious**[12] looks which cannot fail to be offensive, although they **inflict**[13] no positive penalty. But all this ease in our private relations does not make us lawless as citizens. Against this fear is our chief safeguard, teaching us to obey the **magistrates**[14] and the laws, particularly such as regard the protection of the injured, whether they are actually on the **statute**[15] book, or belong to that **code**[16] which, although unwritten, yet cannot be broken without acknowledged disgrace.

1. [ˌkɒnstɪˈtjuːʃən] *n*. 政治制度
2. [ˈɪmɪteɪtə(r)] *n*. 模仿者
3. [ədˌmɪnɪˈstreɪʃən] *n*. 政府

4. [ˌrepjʊˈteɪʃən] *n*. 名声
5. [ˌɪntəˈfɪə(r)] *n*. 干扰
6. [ˈmerɪt] *n*. 优点
7. [bɑː(r)] *vt*. 阻止
8. [ˈhɪndə(r)] *vt*. 阻碍
9. [əbˈskjʊərəti] *n*. 困难
10. [sɜːˈveɪləns] *n*. 监视

11. [ɪnˈdʌldʒ] *v*. 沉溺于
12. [ɪnˈdʒʊərɪəs] *adj*. 中伤的
13. [ɪnˈflɪkt] *vt*. 把…强加于

14. [ˈmædʒɪstreɪt] *n*. 大法官

15. [ˈstætʃuːt] *n*. 法令；法规
16. [kəʊd] *n*. 法典；准则

* * *   * * *   * * *   * * *   * * *   * * *   * * *   * * *

❋Questions for Discussion

(4) Pericles thinks highly of their own political systems. On the basis of what he says, what are the distinctive features of their administration?

* * *   * * *   * * *   * * *   * * *   * * *   * * *   * * *

Further, we provide plenty of means for the mind to **refresh**[17] itself from business. We celebrate games and sacrifices all the year round, and the **elegance**[18] of our private **establishments**[19] forms a daily source of pleasure and helps to **banish**[20] the **spleen**[21]; while the magnitude of our city draws the produce of the world into our **harbour**[22], so that to the Athenian the fruits of other countries are as familiar a **luxury**[23] as those of his own.

If we turn to our **military**[24] policy, there also we differ from our **antagonists**[25]. We throw open our city to the world, and never by **alien**[26] acts exclude foreigners from any opportunity of learning or observing, although the eyes of an enemy may

17. [rɪˈfreʃ] *vt*. 使…恢复活力

18. [ˈelɪɡəns] *n*. 优雅
19. [ɪsˈtæblɪʃmənt] *n*. 建设；建立
20. [ˈbænɪʃ] *vt*. 驱逐
21. [spliːn] *n*. 怒气
22. [ˈhɑːbə(r)] *n*. 海港
23. [ˈlʌkʃəri] *n*. 享受；奢侈
24. [ˈmɪlɪtəri] *adj*. 军事的
25. [ænˈtægənɪst] *n*. 对手；敌人
26. [ˈeɪlɪən] *n*. 外国的

occasionally profit by our **liberality**[1] ; trusting less in system and policy than to the native spirit of our citizens; while in education, where our **rivals**[2] from their very **cradles**[3] by a painful **disciplines**[4] eek after **manliness**[5] , at Athens we live exactly as we please, and yet are just as ready to **encounter**[6] every **legitimate**[7] danger. In proof of this it may be noticed that the Lacedaemonians do not **invade**[8] our country alone, but bring with them all their **confederates**[9] ; while we Athenians advance unsupported into the **territory**[10] of a neighbour, and fighting upon a foreign soil usually **vanquish**[11] with ease men who are defending their homes. Our united force was never yet encountered by any enemy, because we have at once to attend to our **marine**[12] and to **dispatch**[13] our citizens by land upon a hundred different services; so that, wherever they engage with some such **fraction**[14] of our strength, a success against a **detachment**[15] is **magnified**[16] into a victory over the nation, and a defeat into a reverse suffered at the hands of our entire people. And yet if with habits not of labour but of ease, and courage not of art but of nature, we are still willing to encounter danger, we have the double advantage of escaping the experience of **hardships**[17] in **anticipation**[18] and of facing them in the hour of need as fearlessly as those who are never free from them.

1. [ˌlɪbəˈræləti] n. 慷慨

2. [ˈraɪvəl] n. 对手

3. [ˈkrædls] n. 摇篮

4. [ˈdɪsɪplɪn] n. 纪律

5. [ˈmænlɪnɪs] n. 男子气概；勇敢

6. [ɪnˈkaʊntə(r)] vt. 直面

7. [lɪˈdʒɪtɪmət] adj. 合理的；可能的

8. [ɪnˈveɪd] vt. 入侵

9. [kənˈfedərət] n. 联盟

10. [ˈterɪtərɪ] n. 领土

11. [ˈvæŋkwɪʃ] vt. 战胜；征服

12. [məˈriːn] n. 海军

13. [dɪsˈpætʃ] vt. 派遣

14. [ˈfrækʃən] n. 一小部分

15. [dɪˈtætʃmənt] n. 派遣

16. [ˈmæɡnɪfaɪə(r)] vi. 扩大

17. [ˈhɑːdʃɪp] n. 困难；艰难

18. [ˌænˌtɪsɪˈpeɪʃən] n. 预期

✳ ✳ ✳   ✳ ✳ ✳   ✳ ✳ ✳   ✳ ✳ ✳   ✳ ✳ ✳   ✳ ✳ ✳   ✳ ✳ ✳   ✳ ✳ ✳

❀Questions for Discussion

(5) On what points is Athens said to be an open city by Pericles?

(6) What details Pericles gives to support that Athens is a military strong city?

✳ ✳ ✳   ✳ ✳ ✳   ✳ ✳ ✳   ✳ ✳ ✳   ✳ ✳ ✳   ✳ ✳ ✳   ✳ ✳ ✳   ✳ ✳ ✳

Nor are these the only points in which our city is worthy of admiration. We **cultivate**[19] **refinement**[20] without **extravagance**[21] and knowledge without **effeminacy**[22] ; wealth we employ more for use than for show, and place the real **disgrace**[23] of poverty not in owning to the fact but in declining the struggle against it. Our public men have, besides politics, their private affairs to attend to, and our ordinary citizens, though **occupied**[24] with the pursuits of industry, are still fair judges of public matters; for, unlike any other nation, regarding him who takes no part in these duties not as unambitious but as useless, we Athenians are able to judge at all events if we cannot originate, and, instead

19. [ˈkʌltɪveɪt] n. 培育

20. [rɪˈfaɪnmənt] n. 精致

21. [ɪksˈtrævəɡəns] n. 奢华

22. [ɪˈfemɪnəsi] n. 柔弱；女人气

23. [dɪsˈɡreɪs] n. 耻辱

24. [ˈɒkjʊpaɪd] vt. 占用

of looking on discussion as a stumbling—**block**[1] in the way of action, we think it an **indispensable**[2] **preliminary**[3] to any wise action at all. Again, in our enterprises we present the **singular**[4] **spectacle**[5] of daring and **deliberation**[6], each carried to its highest point, and both united in the same persons; although usually decision is the fruit of ignorance, **hesitation**[7] of **reflection**[8]. But the **palm**[9] of courage will surely be **adjudged**[10] most justly to those, who best know the difference between hardship and pleasure and yet are never tempted to **shrink**[11] from danger. In **generosity**[12] we are equally **singular**[13], acquiring our friends by **conferring**[14], not by receiving, favours. Yet, of course, the doer of the favour is the firmer friend of the two, in order by continued kindness to keep the **recipient**[15] in his debt; while the debtor feels less keenly from the very **consciousness**[16] that the return he makes a payment, not a free gift. And it is only the Athenians, who, fearless of consequences, confer their benefits not from **calculations**[17] of **expediency**[18], but in the confidence of **liberality**[19].

1. [blɒk] vt. 阻止
2. [ˌɪndɪsˈpensəbl] adj. 不可或缺的
3. [prɪˈlɪmɪnəri] n. 预备
4. [ˈsɪŋɡjʊlə(r)] adj. 非凡的
5. [ˈspektəkl] n. 壮观
6. [dɪˌlɪbəˈreɪʃən] n. 深思熟虑
7. [ˌhezɪˈteɪʃən] n. 犹豫
8. [rɪˈflekʃ(ə)n] n. 反思
9. [pɑːm] n. 手掌
10. [əˈdʒʌdʒ] vt. 判决
11. [ʃrɪŋk] vi. 退缩
12. [ˌdʒenəˈrɒsəti] n. 大方
13. [ˈsɪŋɡjʊlə(r)] adj. 非凡的
14. [kənˈfɜːrɪŋ] v. 给予
15. [rɪˈsɪpɪənt] n. 接受者
16. [ˈkɒnʃəsnɪs] n. 意识
17. [ˌkælkjʊˈleɪʃən] n. 计算
18. [ɪksˈpiːdɪənsi] n. 方便
19. [ˌlɪbəˈræləti] n. 慷慨

* * *   * * *   * * *   * * *   * * *   * * *   * * *   * * *

❊ Questions for Discussion

(7) Translate the following sentences into Chinese: "We cultivate refinement without extravagance and knowledge without effeminacy; wealth we employ more for use than for show, and place the real disgrace of poverty not in owning to the fact but in declining the struggle against it."

(8) "Again, in our enterprises we present the singular spectacle of daring and deliberation, each carried to its highest point, and both united in the same person; although usually decision is the fruit of ignorance, hesitation of reflection." Translate these words into Chinese. Why does Pericles say "usually decision is the fruit of ignorance?"

* * *   * * *   * * *   * * *   * * *   * * *   * * *   * * *

In short, I say that as a city we are the school of Hellas, while I doubt if the world can produce a man who, where he has only himself to depend upon, is equal to so many **emergencies**[20], and graced by so happy a **versatility**[21], as the Athenian. And that this is no mere **boast**[22] thrown out for the occasion, but

20. [ɪˈmɜːdʒənsi] n. 紧急情况
21. [ˌvɜːsəˈtɪləti] n. 多才多艺
22. [bəʊst] n. 吹嘘

plain matter of fact, the power of the state acquired by these habits proves. For Athens alone of her **contemporaries**[1] is found when tested to be greater than her reputation, and alone gives no occasion to her **assailants**[2] to **blush**[3] at the antagonist by whom they have been worsted, or to her subjects to question her **title**[4] by **merit**[5] to rule. Rather, the admiration of the present and succeeding ages will be ours, since we have not left our power without witness, but have shown it by mighty **proofs**[6]; and far from needing a Homer for our panegyrist, or other of his **craft**[7] whose **verses**[8] might **charm**[9] for the moment only for the impression which they gave to melt at the touch of fact, we have forced every sea and land to be the highway of our daring, and everywhere, whether for evil or for good, have left **imperishable**[10] monuments behind us. Such is the Athens for which these men, in the **assertion**[11] of their **resolve**[12] not to lose her, nobly fought and died; and well may every one of their survivors be ready to suffer in her cause.

1. ［kən'tempərərɪ］ n. 当代；同代

2. ［ə'seɪlənt］ n. 进攻者

3. ［blʌʃ］ vi. 脸红

4. ［'taɪtl］ n. 头衔

5. ［'merɪt］ n. 优点

6. ［pruːf］ n. 证据

7. ［huːz］ n. 技艺

8. ［vɜːs］ n. 诗歌

9. ［tʃɑːm］ vi. 有魅力

10. ［ɪm'perɪʃəbl］ adj. 永不消失的

11. ［ə'sɜːʃn］ n. 断言；主张

12. ［rɪ'zɒlv］ n. 决心

* * *   * * *   * * *   * * *   * * *   * * *   * * *   * * *

❋Questions for Discussion

（9）What details does Pericles give to support his viewpoint that "as a city we are the school of Hellas"?

（10）Homer is described by Plato in his "Republic" as "teacher of all Greece". But here, Pericles says Athens does not need a Homer for panegyric. What does he mean? For any nation or any culture persons like Homer are very important. Why does Pericles say Homer is not needed?

* * *   * * *   * * *   * * *   * * *   * * *   * * *   * * *

Indeed if I have **dwelt**[13] at some length upon the character of our country, it has been to show that our **stake**[14] in the struggle is not the same as theirs who have no such **blessings**[15] to lose, and also that the **panegyric**[16] of the men over whom I am now speaking might be by definite proofs established. That panegyric is now in a great measure complete; for the Athens that I have celebrated is only what the **heroism**[17] of these and their like have made her, men whose fame, unlike that of most Hellenes, will be found to **be only commensurate with**[18] their deserts. And if a test of worth be wanted, it is to be found in their closing scene, and this not only in cases in which it **set the final seal**[19] upon their merit, but also in those in which it gave

13. ［dwelt］ vi. 思考

14. ［steɪk］ n. 重大利益

15. ［'blesɪŋ］ n. 赐福

16. ［ˌpænə'dʒɪrɪk］ n. 颂歌

17. ［'herəʊɪzəm］ n. 英雄主义

18. 仅与…相当的

19. 盖棺定论

the first **intimation**[20] of their having any. For there is justice in the claim that **steadfastness**[1] in his country's battles should be as a **cloak**[2] to cover a Man's other imperfections; since the good action has **blotted**[3] out the bad, and his merit as a citizen more than **outweighed**[4] his demerits as an individual. But none of these allowed either wealth with its prospect of future enjoyment to **unnerve**[5] his spirit, or poverty with its hope of a day of freedom and riches to tempt him to **shrink**[6] from danger. No, holding that **vengeance**[7] upon their enemies was more to be desired than any personal blessings, and reckoning this to be the most **glorious**[8] of hazards, they joyfully determined to accept the risk, to make sure of their vengeance, and to let their wishes wait; and while **committing to**[9] hope the uncertainty of final success, in the business before them they thought fit to act **boldly**[10] and trust in themselves. Thus choosing to die resisting, rather than to live **submitting**[11], they fled only from dishonour, but met danger face to face, and after one brief moment, while at the summit of their fortune, escaped, not from their fear, but from their glory.

20. [ˌɪntɪˈmeɪʃən] n. 暗示；通知
1. [ˈstedfɑːstnɪs] n. 坚定
2. [kləʊk] n. 斗篷，掩盖物
3. [ˈblɒtə(r)] vt. 扔掉
4. [ˌaʊtˈweɪ] vt. 比…更重

5. [ʌnˈnɜːv] vt. 使…失去勇气
6. [ʃrɪŋk] vi. 退缩
7. [ˈvendʒəns] n. 报仇

8. [ˈglɔːrɪəs] adj. 光荣的

9. 把…投入

10. [ˈbɔːldlɪ] adv. 大胆地
11. [səbˈmɪtɪŋ] vi. 投降

＊＊＊　　＊＊＊　　＊＊＊　　＊＊＊　　＊＊＊　　＊＊＊　　＊＊＊　　＊＊＊

❀Questions for Discussion

（11） Do you agree with Pericles on the point that "...steadfastness in his country's battles should be as a cloak to cover a man's other imperfections"?

（12） That last sentence of this paragraph seems very hard to make sense. Please try to translate it into Chinese: "Thus choosing to die resisting, rather than to live submitting, they fled only from dishonour, but met danger face to face, and after one brief moment, while at the summit of their fortune, escaped, not from their fear, but from their glory."

＊＊＊　　＊＊＊　　＊＊＊　　＊＊＊　　＊＊＊　　＊＊＊　　＊＊＊　　＊＊＊

So died these men as became Athenians. You, their survivors, must determine to have as **unfaltering**[12] a **resolution**[13] in the field, though you may pray that it may have a happier issue. And not contented with ideas **derived**[14] only from words of the advantages which are bound up with the defence of your country, though these would **furnish**[15] a valuable text to a speaker even before an audience so alive to them as the present, you must yourselves realize the power of Athens, and feed your eyes upon her from day to day, till love of her fills

12. [ʌnˈfɔːltərɪŋ] adj. 坚定的
13. [ˌrezəˈluːʃən] n. 决心
14. [dɪˈraɪv] vi. 得到

15. [ˈfɜːnɪʃ] vt. 装饰

your hearts; and then, when all her greatness shall break upon you, you must reflect that it was by courage, sense of duty, and a keen feeling of honour in action that men were enabled to win all this, and that no personal failure in an enterprise could make them consent to deprive their country of their **valour**,[1] but they laid it at her feet as the most glorious contribution that they could offer. For this offering of their lives made in common by them all they each of them individually received that renown which never grows old, and for a **sepulchre**[2], not so much that in which their bones have been **deposited**[3], but that noblest of **shrines**[4] wherein their glory is laid up to be **eternally**[5] remembered upon every occasion on which deed or story shall call for its **commemoration**[6]. For heroes have the whole earth for their tomb; and in lands far from their own, where the column with its **epitaph**[7] declares it, there is enshrined in every breast a record unwritten with no **tablet**[8] to preserve it, except that of the heart. These take as your model and, judging happiness to be the fruit of freedom and freedom of valour, never decline the dangers of war. For it is not the miserable that would most justly be **unsparing**[9] of their lives; these have nothing to hope for: it is rather they to whom continued life may bring reverses as yet unknown, and to whom a fall, if it came, would be most tremendous in its consequences. And surely, to a man of spirit, the **degradation**[10] of **cowardice**[11] must be immeasurably more **grievous**[12] than the unfelt death which strikes him in the midst of his strength and **patriotism**[13]!

1. ['vælə] n. 勇气

2. ['sepəlkə(r)] n. 坟墓
3. [dɪ'pɒzɪt] vt. 放置;埋葬
4. [ʃraɪn] n. 神龛
5. [ɪ'tɜːnəli] adv. 永久地
6. [kəˌmeməˈreɪʃən] n. 纪念仪式
7. ['epɪtɑːf] n. 墓志铭

8. ['tæblɪt] n. 片状物

9. [ʌnˈspeərɪŋ] adj. 慷慨大方的;毫不留情的

10. [ˌdegrəˈdeɪʃən] n. 堕落
11. ['kaʊədɪs] n. 懦弱
12. ['griːvəs] adj. 悲痛的
13. ['peɪtrɪətɪzəm] n. 爱国主义

* * *　　* * *　　* * *　　* * *　　* * *　　* * *　　* * *　　* * *

❖Questions for Discussion

(13) Translate this sentence into Chinese: "and then, when all her greatness shall break upon you, you must reflect that it was by courage, sense of duty, and a keen feeling of honour in action that men were enabled to win all this, and that no personal failure in an enterprise could them consent to deprive their country of their valour, but they laid it at her feet as the most glorious contribution that they could offer."

(14) Translate this sentence into Chinese: "These take as your model and, judging happiness to be the fruit of freedom and freedom of valour, never decline the dangers of war."

* * *　　* * *　　* * *　　* * *　　* * *　　* * *　　* * *　　* * *

Comfort, therefore, not **condolence**[14], is what I have to

14. [kənˈdəʊləns] n. 哀悼;吊唁

offer to the parents of the dead who may be here. Numberless are the chances to which, as they know, the life of man is subject; but fortunate indeed are they who draw for their lot a death so glorious as that which has caused your mourning, and to whom life has been so exactly measured as to terminate in the happiness in which it has been passed. Still I know that this is a hard saying, especially when those are in question of whom you will constantly be reminded by seeing in the homes of others blessings of which once you also boasted: for grief is felt not so much for the want of what we have never known, as for the loss of that to which we have been long accustomed. Yet you who are still of an age to **beget children**[1] must bear up in the hope of having others in their stead; not only will they help you to forget those whom you have lost, but will be to the state at once a **reinforcement**[2] and a **security**[3]; for never can a fair or just policy be expected of the citizen who does not, like his fellows, bring to the decision the interests and **apprehensions**[4] of a father. While those of you who have passed your **prime**[5] must congratulate yourselves with the thought that the best part of your life was fortunate, and that the brief span that remains will be cheered by the fame of the **departed**[6]. For it is only the love of honour that never grows old; and honour it is, not gain, as some would have it, that **rejoices**[7] the heart of age and helplessness.

1. 生小孩

2. [ˌriːɪnˈfɔːsmənt] n. 加强

3. [sɪˈkjʊərɪtɪ] n. 安全

4. [ˌæprɪˈhenʃən] n. 忧虑；领悟

5. 这里指适合生孩子的年龄

6. [dɪˈpɑːtɪd] vi. 离开的

7. [rɪˈdʒɔɪs] vt. 使…快乐

* * *　* * *　* * *　* * *　* * *　* * *　* * *　* * *

❖ Questions for Discussion

(15) "for grief is felt not so much for the want of what we have never known, as for the loss of that to which we have been long accustomed." Translate this sentence into Chinese. Do you agree with Pericles on this point? Support your viewpoints.

(16) Translate this sentence into Chinese: "For it is only the love of honour that never grows old; and honour it is, not gain, as some would have it, that rejoices the heart of age and helplessness."

* * *　* * *　* * *　* * *　* * *　* * *　* * *　* * *

Turning to the sons or brothers of the dead, I see an arduous struggle before you. When a man is gone, all **are wont to**[8] praise him, and should your merit be ever so **transcendent**[9], you will still find it difficult not merely to **overtake**[10], but even to approach their renown. The living have envy to contend with, while those who are no longer in our path are honoured with a goodwill

8. 习惯

9. [trænˈsendənt] adj. 至高无上的

10. [ˌəʊvəˈteɪk] vt. 赶上；超越

into which rivalry does not enter. On the other hand, if I must say anything on the subject of female excellence to those of you who will now be in **widowhood**[1], it will be all comprised in this brief **exhortation**[2]. Great will be your glory in not falling short of your natural character; and greatest will be hers who is least talked of among the men, whether for good or for bad.

    My task is now finished. I have performed it to the best of my ability, and in word, at least, the requirements of the law are now satisfied. If deeds be in question, those who are here **interred**[3] have received part of their honours already, and for the rest, their children will be brought up till **manhood at the public expense**[4]: the state thus offers a valuable prize, as the **garland**[5] of victory in this race of valour, for the reward both of those who have fallen and their survivors. And where the rewards for merit are greatest, there are found the best citizens.

    And now that you have brought to a close your **lamentations**[6] for your relatives, you may depart.

1. ['wɪdəʊhʊd] *n.* 寡妇
2. [ˌegzɔːˈteɪʃən] *n.* 演讲
3. [ɪnˈtɜːd] *vt.* 埋葬
4. 国家出钱
5. [ˈɡɑːlənd] *n.* 花环；花冠；花园
6. [ˌlæmenˈteɪʃən] *n.* 悲痛；哀悼

* * *　　* * *　　* * *　　* * *　　* * *　　* * *　　* * *　　* * *

❖Questions for Discussion

(17) David Cartwright describes this speech by Pericles as "a eulogy of Athens itself…". Do you agree with him? What points are listed by Pericles to glorify Athens' achievements? This funeral oration was held in honor of the dead in the war for their country, but why did Pericles depart from the typical formula of Athenian funeral speeches and, instead, sing highly of their city Athens?

(18) People often compare Abraham Lincoln's Gettysburg Address with Pericles' funeral oration. Are these two speeches comparable?

* * *　　* * *　　* * *　　* * *　　* * *　　* * *　　* * *　　* * *

The Address by Abraham Lincoln

(November 19, 1863)

Four score and seven years ago our fathers brought forth on this continent, a new nation, conceived in Liberty, and dedicated to the proposition that all men are created equal.

Now we are engaged in a great civil war, testing whether that nation, or any nation so conceived and so dedicated, can long endure. We are met on a great battle-field of that war. We have come to dedicate a portion of that field, as a final resting place for those who here gave their lives that that nation might live. It is altogether fitting and proper that we should do this.

But, in a larger sense, we can not dedicate — we can not consecrate — we can not hallow — this ground. The brave men, living and dead,

Abraham Lincoln (November 19, 1863)

who struggled here, have consecrated it, far above our poor power to add or detract. The world will little note, nor long remember what we say here, but it can never forget what they did here. It is for us the living, rather, to be dedicated here to the unfinished work which they who fought here have thus far so nobly advanced. It is rather for us to be here dedicated to the great task remaining before us — that from these honored dead we take increased devotion to that cause for which they gave the last full measure of devotion — that we here highly resolve that these dead shall not have died in vain — that this nation, under God, shall have a new birth of freedom — and that government of the people, by the people, for the people, shall not perish from the earth.

* * *　　* * *　　* * *　　* * *　　* * *　　* * *　　* * *　　* * *

❉Questions for discussion:

(1) In the beginning, Lincoln says "Four score and seven years ago...". Why not just say "eighty-seven years ago"?

(2) Look up in a dictionary these words like "brought forth", "conceived", and "proposition". What do these words imply? What actually did Lincoln want to say?

(3) Lincoln used the word "great" twice. Why doesn't he come up with a synonym?

(4) "Dedicate", "Consecrate", "Hallow". What kind of words are those? How many times is God invoked? Lincoln's speech is seen as a profoundly religious speech, do you agree?

(5) In the beginning, Lincoln used the word "liberty", but in the end, he used another word "freedom". Is this just a search for synonyms?

(6) Did Lincoln clearly tell his countrymen in this speech why the civil was fought (or what the war was about)?

(7) Read this speech by Lincoln very carefully. Do you think Lincoln was, in one way or another, influenced by Pericles' Funeral Oration? Give support for your viewpoints.

＊＊＊　　＊＊＊　　＊＊＊　　＊＊＊　　＊＊＊　　＊＊＊　　＊＊＊　　＊＊＊

Sixteenth Year of the War—The Melian Conference—Fate of Melos

The next summer Alcibiades sailed with twenty ships to Argos and seized the suspected persons still left of the **Lacedaemonian**[1] faction to the number of three hundred, whom the Athenians **forthwith**[2] **lodged**[3] in the neighbouring islands of their empire. The Athenians also made an **expedition**[4] against the isle of Melos with thirty ships of their own, six Chian, and two Lesbian vessels, sixteen hundred heavy **infantry**[5], three hundred **archers**[6], and twenty mounted archers from Athens, and about fifteen hundred heavy infantry from the allies and the islanders. The Melians are a colony of Lacedaemon that would not **submit to**[7] the Athenians like the other islanders, and at first remained **neutral**[8] and took no part in the struggle, but afterwards upon the Athenians using violence and **plundering**[9] their territory, **assumed**[10] an attitude of open **hostility**[11]. Cleomedes, son of Lycomedes, and Tisias, son of Tisimachus, the generals, **encamping**[12] in their territory with the above **armament**[13], before doing any harm to their land, sent **envoys**[14] to negotiate. These the Melians did not bring before the people, but **bade**[15] them **state**[16] the object of their **mission**[17] to the **magistrates**[18] and the few; upon which the Athenian envoys spoke as follows:

Athenians. Since the negotiations are not to go on before the people, in order that we may not be able to speak straight on without interruption, and **deceive**[19] the ears of the **multitude**[20] by **seductive**[21] arguments which would pass without refutation (for we know that this is the meaning of our being brought before the few), what if you who sit there were to pursue a method more **cautious**[22] still? Make no set speech yourselves, but take us up at whatever you do not like, and settle that before going any farther. And first tell us if this **proposition**[23] of ours suits you. The Melian **commissioners**[24] answered:

Melians. To the fairness of quietly instructing each other as you propose there is nothing to object; but your military preparations are too far advanced to agree with what you say,

1. [ˌlæsɪdɪˈməunɪən] *n*. 斯巴达人
2. [ˌfɔːθˈwɪð] *adv*. 立刻；马上
3. [lɒdʒ] *vt*. 安顿
4. [ˌekspɪˈdɪʃ(ə)n] *n*. 远征
5. [ˈɪnfəntri] *n*. 步兵
6. [ˈɑːtʃə(r)] *n*. 弓箭兵
7. [ˈsəbˈmɪt] *vi*. 投降
8. [ˈnjuːtrəl] *adj*. 中立的
9. [ˈplʌndə(r)] *vt*. 掠夺
10. [əˈsjuːmd] *vt*. 采取
11. [hɒˈstɪləti] *n*. 敌对；敌意
12. [ɪnˈkæmp] *vi*. 扎营
13. [ˈɑːməmənt] *n*. 军备
14. [ˈenvɔi] *n*. 大使
15. [beɪd] *vt*. 叮嘱
16. [steɪt] *vt*. 陈述
17. [ˈmɪʃn] *n*. 使命
18. [ˈmædʒɪstreɪt] *n*. 行政官
19. [dɪˈsiːv] *vt*. 欺骗
20. [ˈmʌltɪtjuːd] *n*. 大众
21. [sɪˈdʌktɪv] *adj*. 诱惑的；引人注意的

22. [ˈkɔːʃəs] *adj*. 小心谨慎

23. [ˌprɒpəˈzɪʃn] *n*. 提议
24. [kəˈmɪʃənə(r)] *n*. 专员

as we see you are come to be judges in your own cause，and that all we can reasonably expect from this negotiation is war，if we prove to have right on our side and refuse to **submit**[1]，and in the contrary case，slavery.

Athenians. If you have met to reason about **presentiments**[2] of the future，or for anything else than to **consult**[3] for the safety of your state upon the facts that you see before you，we will **give over**[4]；otherwise we will go on.

Melians. It is natural and excusable for men in our position to turn more ways than one both in thought and **utterance**[5]. However，the question in this conference is，as you say，the safety of our country；and the discussion，if you please，can **proceed**[6] in the way which you propose.

Athenians. For ourselves，we shall not trouble you with **specious**[7] **pretences**[8]—either of how we have a right to our empire because we **overthrew**[9] the **Mede**[10]，or are now attacking you because of wrong that you have done us—and make a long speech which would not be believed；and in return we hope that you，instead of thinking to influence us by saying that you did not join the Lacedaemonians，although their colonists，or that you have done us no wrong，will aim at what is **feasible**[11]，holding in view the real **sentiments**[12] of us both；since you know as well as we do that right，as the world goes，is only in question between equals in power，while the strong do what they can and the weak suffer what they must.

Melians. As we think，at any rate，it is **expedient**[13]—we speak as we are obliged，since you **enjoin**[14] us to let right alone and talk only of interest—that you should not destroy what is our common protection，the **privilege**[15] of being allowed in danger to **invoke**[16] what is fair and right，and even to profit by arguments not strictly valid if they can be got to **pass current**[17]. And you are as much interested in this as any，as your fall would be a signal for the heaviest **vengeance**[18] and an example for the world to **meditate**[19] upon.

Athenians. The end of our empire，if end it should，does not frighten us：a rival empire like Lacedaemon，even if Lacedaemon was our real antagonist，is not so terrible to the **vanquished**[20] as subjects who by themselves attack and **overpower**[21]

1.［səbˈmɪt］*vi*. 投降,屈服

2.［prɪˈzentɪmənt］*n*. 预感

3.［kənˈsʌlt］*vi*. 商谈

4. 中止

5.［ˈʌtərəns］*n*. 谈话；辩论

6.［prəˈsiːd］*vi*. 继续进行

7.［ˈspiːʃəs］*adj*. 似是而非的

8.［prɪˈtens］*n*. 借口

9.［ˌəʊvəˈθrəʊ］*vt*. 推翻

10.［miːd］*n*. 波斯人

11.［ˈfiːzəbl］*adj*. 可行的

12.［ˈsentɪmənt］*n*. 意见；观点；感情

13.［ɪksˈpiːdɪənt］*adj*. 便利的；应急有效的

14.［ɪnˈdʒɔɪn］*vt*. 命令

15.［ˈprɪvɪlɪdʒ］*n*. 特权

16.［ɪnˈvəʊk］*vt*. 提出；祈求

17. 流行；流传

18.［ˈvendʒəns］*n*. 报仇

19.［ˈmedɪteɪt］*vt*. 沉思

20.［ˈvæŋkwɪʃ］*vt*. 征服；击败

21.［ˌəʊvəˈpaʊə(r)］*vt*. 压倒；制服

their rulers. This, however, is a risk that we are content to take. We will now proceed to show you that we are come here in the interest of our empire, and that we shall say what we are now going to say, for the preservation of your country; as we would **fain**[1] exercise that empire over you without trouble, and see you **preserved**[2] for the good of us both.

Melians. And how, pray, could it turn out as good for us to serve as for you to rule?

Athenians. Because you would have the advantage of **submitting**[3] before suffering the worst, and we should gain by not destroying you.

Melians. So that you would not **consent to**[4] our being **neutral**[5], friends instead of enemies, but **allies**[6] of neither side.

Athenians. No; for your **hostility**[7] cannot so much hurt us as your friendship will be an **argument**[8] to our subjects of our weakness, and your **enmity**[9] of our power.

Melians. Is that your subjects' idea of **equity**[10], to put those who have nothing to do with you in the same **category**[11] with peoples that are most of them your own colonists, and some conquered **rebels**?[12]

Athenians. As far as right goes they think one has as much of it as the other, and that if any maintain their independence it is because they are strong, and that if we do not **molest**[13] them it is because we are afraid; so that besides extending our empire we should gain in security by your subjection; the fact that you are islanders and weaker than others **rendering**[14] it all the more important that you should not succeed in **baffling**[15] the masters of the sea.

Melians. But do you consider that there is no security in the policy which we indicate? For here again if you **debar**[16] us from talking about justice and invite us to obey your interest, we also must explain ours, and try to persuade you, if the two happen to **coincide**[17]. How can you avoid making enemies of all existing **neutrals**[18] who shall look at case from it that one day or another you will attack them? And what is this but to make greater the enemies that you have already, and to force others to **become so**[19] who would otherwise have never thought of it?

Athenians. Why, the fact is that **continentals**[20] generally give

1. [feɪn] *vt*. 乐意;不得不
2. [prɪˈzɜːv] *vt*. 保存

3. [səbˈmɪt] *vi*. 压服

4. 同意
5. [ˈnjuːtrəl] *adj*. 中立的
6. [ˈælaɪ] *n*. 同盟
7. [hɒsˈtɪlɪti] *n*. 敌意
8. [ˈɑːɡjʊmənt] *n*. 论据
9. [ˈenməti] *n*. 敌意
10. [ˈekwɪti] *n*. 平等
11. [ˈkætɪɡəri] *n*. 同类(类别)
12. [ˈrebl] *n*. 反叛者

13. [məʊˈlest] *vt*. 骚扰;干扰

14. [ˈrendərɪŋ] *vi*. 使得…

15. [ˈbæflɪŋ] *vt*. 使…为难

16. [dɪˈbɑː(r)] *vt*. 禁止;阻止

17. [ˌkəʊɪnˈsaɪd] *vi*. 一致;相符

18. [ˈnjuːtrəl] *n*. 中立者

19. 成为你们的敌人

20. [ˌkɒntɪˈnentl] *n*. 大陆军士兵

us but little alarm; the liberty which they enjoy will long prevent their **taking precautions**[1] against us; it is rather islanders like yourselves, outside our empire, and subjects **smarting**[2] under the **yoke**[3], who would be the most likely to take a **rash**[4] step and lead themselves and us into obvious danger.

Melians. Well then, if you risk so much to retain your empire, and your subjects to get rid of it, it were surely great **baseness**[5] and **cowardice**[6] in us who are still free not to try everything that can be tried, before **submitting**[7] to your **yoke**.

Athenians. Not if you are well advised, the contest not being an equal one, with honour as the prize and shame as the penalty, but a question of self-preservation and of not resisting those who are far stronger than you are.

Melians. But we know that the fortune of war is sometimes more **impartial**[8] than the **disproportion**[9] of numbers might lead one to suppose; to submit is to give ourselves over to despair, while action still preserves for us a hope that we may **stand erect**[10].

Athenians. Hope, danger's comforter, may be indulged in by those who have abundant resources, if not without loss at all events without ruin; but its nature is to be extravagant, and those who go so far as to put their all upon the venture see it in its true colours only when they are ruined; but so long as the discovery would enable them to guard against it, it is never found wanting. Let not this be the case with you, who are weak and hang on a single turn of the **scale**[11]; nor be like the **vulgar**[12], who, abandoning such security as human means may still afford, when visible hopes fail them in **extremity**[13], turn to invisible, to prophecies and oracles, and other such inventions that **delude**[14] men with hopes to their destruction.

Melians. You may be sure that we are as well aware as you of the difficulty of contending against your power and fortune, unless the terms be equal. But we trust that the gods may grant us fortune as good as yours, since we are just men fighting against unjust, and that what we want in power will be made up by the **alliance**[15] of the Lacedaemonians, who are bound, if only for very shame, to come to the aid of their **kindred**[16]. Our confidence, therefore, after all is not so **utterly**[17] **irrational**[18].

1. 预防
2. [smɑːtɪŋ] *vi.* 疼痛
3. [jəʊk] *n.* 牛轭
4. [ræʃ] *adj.* 轻率的

5. [ˈbeɪsnɪs] *n.* 下贱
6. [ˈkaʊdɪs] *n.* 懦弱
7. [səbˈmɪt] *n.* 臣服

8. [ɪmˈpɑːʃəl] *adj.* 无偏颇的；公正的
9. [ˌdɪsprəˈpɔːʃən] *n.* 不成比例
10. 直立

11. [skeɪl] *n.* 天平
12. [ˈvʌlɡə(r)] *n.* 粗人；平民
13. [ɪkˈstremɪti] *n.* 极端

14. [dɪˈluːd] *n.* 蛊惑；欺骗

15. [əˈlaɪəns] *n.* 同盟
16. [ˈkɪndrɪd] *n.* 亲戚关系
17. [ˈʌtə(r)] *adv.* 完全
18. [ɪˌræʃəˈnæl] *adj.* 非理性的

Athenians[18]. When you speak of the favour of the gods, we may as fairly hope for that as yourselves; neither our **pretensions**[1] nor our conduct being in any way contrary to what men believe of the gods, or practise among themselves. Of the gods we believe, and of men we know, that by a necessary law of their nature they rule wherever they can. And it is not as if we were the first to make this law, or to act upon it when made: we found it existing before us, and shall leave it to exist for ever after us; all we do is to make use of it, knowing that you and everybody else, having the same power as we have, would do the same as we do. Thus, as far as the gods are concerned, we have no fear and no reason to fear that we shall be at a disadvantage. But when we come to your notion about the Lacedaemonians, which leads you to believe that shame will make them help you, here we bless your simplicity but do not envy your **folly**[2]. The Lacedaemonians, when their own interests or their country's laws are in question, are the worthiest men alive; of their conduct towards others much might be said, but no clearer idea of it could be given than by shortly saying that of all the men we know they are most **conspicuous**[3] in considering what is agreeable honourable, and what is **expedient**[4] just. Such a way of thinking does not promise much for the safety which you now unreasonably **count upon**[5].

Melians. But it is for this very reason that we now trust to their respect for **expediency**[6] to prevent them from betraying the Melians, their colonists, and thereby losing the confidence of their friends in Hellas and helping their enemies.

Athenians. Then you do not adopt the view that expediency goes with security, while justice and honour cannot be followed without danger; and danger the Lacedaemonians generally court as little as possible.

Melians. But we believe that they would be more likely to face even danger for our sake, and with more confidence than for others, as our nearness to Peloponnese makes it easier for them to act, and our common blood ensures our fidelity.

Athenians. Yes, but what an intending ally trusts to is not the goodwill of those who ask his aid, but a decided **superiority**[7] of power for action; and the Lacedaemonians look to this even

1. [prɪˈtenʃən] *n*. 声称;自负;狂妄

2. [ˈfɒli] *n*. 愚蠢

3. [kənˈspɪkjʊəs] *adj*. 明显的
4. [ɪksˈpiːdɪənt] *adj*. 便利的

5. 指望;依靠

6. [ɪksˈpiːdɪənsɪ] *n*. 权宜;方便;便利

7. [sjuːˌpɪərɪˈɒrɪtɪ] *n*. 优越;高级

more than others. At least, such is their distrust of their home resources that it is only with numerous allies that they attack a neighbour; now is it likely that while we are masters of the sea they will cross over to an island?

Melians. But they would have others to send. The Cretan Sea is a wide one, and it is more difficult for those who command it to **intercept**[1] others, than for those who wish to **elude**[2] them to do so safely. And should the Lacedaemonians **miscarry**[3] in this, they would fall upon your land, and upon those left of your **allies**[4] whom Brasidas did not reach; and instead of places which are not yours, you will have to fight for your own country and your own confederacy.

Athenians. Some **diversion**[5] of the kind you speak of you may one day experience, only to learn, as others have done, that the Athenians never once yet withdrew from a **siege**[6] for fear of any. But we are struck by the fact that, after saying you would **consult**[7] for the safety of your country, in all this discussion you have mentioned nothing which men might trust in and think to be saved by. Your strongest arguments depend upon hope and the future, and your actual resources are too **scanty**[8], as compared with those **arrayed**[9] against you, for you to come out victorious. You will therefore show great blindness of judgment, unless, after allowing us to retire, you can find some **counsel**[10] more **prudent**[11] than this. You will surely not be caught by that idea of disgrace, which in dangers that are disgraceful, and at the same time too plain to be mistaken, proves so fatal to mankind; since in too many cases the very men that have their eyes perfectly open to what they are rushing into, let the thing called disgrace, by the mere influence of a seductive name, lead them on to a point at which they become so **enslaved**[12] by the phrase as in fact to fall willfully into hopeless disaster, and **incur**[13] disgrace more disgraceful as the companion of error, than when it comes as the result of misfortune. This, if you are well advised, you will guard against; and you will not think it dishonourable to submit to the greatest city in Hellas, when it makes you the moderate offer of becoming its **tributary**[14] **ally**[15], without ceasing to enjoy the country that belongs to you; nor when you have the choice

1. [ˌɪntəˈsept] *vt*. 拦截
2. [ɪˈluːd] 逃避
3. [ˌmɪsˈkærɪ] *vi*. 流产；失败
4. [ˈælaɪs] *n*. 同盟

5. [daɪˈvɜːʃən] *n*. 转移；分散

6. [siːdʒ] *n*. 包围

7. [kənˈsʌlt] *vi*. 商讨

8. [ˈskæntɪ] *adj*. 空洞；缺乏的
9. [əˈreɪ] *n*. 排队；列队

10. [ˈkaʊnsəl] *n*. 建议
11. [ˈpruːdənt] *adj*. 谨慎的

12. [ɪnˈsleɪv] *vt*. 被奴役
13. [ɪnˈkɜː(r)] *vt*. 招致；惹起

14. [ˈtrɪbjʊtərɪ] *adj*. 进贡的
15. [ˈælaɪ] *n*. 同盟

given you between war and security, will you be so blinded as to choose the worse. And it is certain that those who do not **yield to**[1] their equals, who keep terms with their **superiors**[2], and are moderate towards their **inferiors**[3], on the whole succeed best. Think over the matter, therefore, after our withdrawal, and reflect once and again that it is for your country that you are consulting, that you have not more than one, and that upon this one **deliberation**[4] depends its prosperity or ruin.

The Athenians now **withdrew**[5] from the conference; and the Melians, left to themselves, came to a decision **corresponding with**[6] what they had maintained in the discussion, and answered: "Our resolution, Athenians, is the same as it was at first. We will not in a moment deprive of freedom a city that has been inhabited these seven hundred years; but we put our trust in the fortune by which the gods have preserved it until now, and in the help of men, that is, of the Lacedaemonians; and so we will try and save ourselves. Meanwhile we invite you to allow us to be friends to you and **foes**[7] to neither party, and to retire from our country after making such a treaty as shall seem fit to us both."

Such was the answer of the Melians. The Athenians now **departing**[8] from the conference said: "Well, you alone, as it seems to us, judging from these **resolutions**[9], regard what is future as more certain than what is before your eyes, and what is out of sight, in your eagerness, as already coming to pass; and as you have **staked most on**[10], and trusted most in, the Lacedaemonians, your fortune, and your hopes, so will you be most completely **deceived**[11]."

The Athenian envoys now returned to the army; and the Melians showing no signs of yielding, the generals at once **betook**[12] themselves to hostilities, and drew a line of **circumvallation**[13] round the Melians, dividing the work among the different states. Subsequently the Athenians returned with most of their army, leaving behind them a certain number of their own citizens and of the allies to keep guard by land and sea. The force thus left stayed on and **besieged**[14] the place.

About the same time the Argives invaded the territory of Phlius and lost eighty men cut off in an **ambush**[15] by the Phliasians

1. [jiːld] *vt.* 屈服

2. [sjuːˈpɪərɪə(r)] *n.* 上级

3. [ɪnˈfɪərɪə(r)] *adj.* 低级的

4. [dɪˌlɪbəˈreɪʃən] *n.* 考虑;深思熟虑

5. [wɪðˈdruː] *vi.* 撤出

6. 与……一致的

7. [fəʊ] *n.* 敌人

8. [dɪˈpɑːtɪŋ] *vi.* 离开

9. [ˌrezəˈluːʃən] *n.* 决议

10. 看得很重的

11. [dɪˈsiːv] *vt.* 欺骗

12. [bɪˈtuk] *vt.* 去;赴;致力于

13. [ˌsɜːkəmvəˈleɪʃən] *n.* 城墙,围墙

14. [bɪˈsiːdʒ] *vt.* 包围

15. [ˈæmbʊʃ] *n.* 埋伏

and Argive exiles. Meanwhile the Athenians at Pylos took so much **plunder**[1] from the Lacedaemonians that the latter，although they still **refrained**[2] from breaking off the treaty and going to war with Athens，yet **proclaimed**[3] that any of their people that chose might plunder the Athenians. The Corinthians also **commenced**[4] hostilities with the Athenians for private quarrels of their own；but the rest of the Peloponnesians stayed quiet. Meanwhile the Melians attacked by night and took the part of the Athenian lines over against the market，and killed some of the men，and brought in corn and all else that they could find useful to them，and so returned and kept quiet，while the Athenians took measures to keep better guard in future.

1. ['plʌndə(r)] *n*. 掠夺

2. [rɪ'freɪn] *vi*. 克制

3. [prə'kleɪm] *vi*. 宣称

4. [kə'mens] *vi*. 开始

Summer was now over. The next winter the Lacedaemonians intended to invade the Argive territory，but arriving at the frontier found the sacrifices for crossing unfavourable，and went back again. This intention of theirs gave the Argives **suspicions**[5] of certain of their fellow citizens，some of whom they arrested；others，however，escaped them. About the same time the Melians again took another part of the Athenian lines which were but **feebly**[6] **garrisoned**[7]. Reinforcements afterwards arriving from Athens in consequence，under the command of Philocrates, son of Demeas, the siege was now pressed **vigorously**[8]；and some treachery taking place inside，the Melians surrendered at **discretion**[9] to the Athenians, who put to death all the grown men whom they took，and sold the women and children for slaves，and subsequently sent out five hundred **colonists**[10] and **inhabited**[11] the place themselves.

5. [sə'spɪʃən] *n*. 怀疑

6. ['fiːbl] *adv*. 很弱地

7. ['gærɪsən] *vt*. 布防

8. ['vɪgərəs] *adv*. 热烈地

9. [dɪs'kreʃən] *n*. 谨慎；慎重

10. ['kɒlənɪst] *n*. 殖民者

11. [ɪn'hæbɪt] *vt*. 居住

* * *　　* * *　　* * *　　× × ×　　× × ×　　× × ×　　× × ×　　× × ×

❈Questions for discussion

(1) Interpret "Might makes right" by citing what the Athenian negotiator says in the beginning of the dialogue.

(2) The Melians argue that they are a neutral city and not an enemy，so Athens has no need to conquer them. How do the Athenians counter it?

(3) The Melians argue that an invasion will alarm the other neutral Greek states，who will become hostile to Athens for fear of being invaded themselves. How do the Athenians counter it?

(4) The Melians argue that it would be shameful and cowardly of them to submit without a fight.How do the Athenians counter it?

(5) The Melians argue that though the Athenians are far stronger, there is at least a slim chance that the Melians could win, and they will regret not trying their luck. How do the Athenians counter it?

(6) The Melians believe that they will have the assistance of the gods because their position is morally just. How do the Athenians counter it?

(7) The Melians argue that their Spartan kin will come to their defense. How do the Athenians counter it?

(8) What is the goal of the Athenians in this negotiation? And what is the goal of the Melians? What fate did the Melians suffer in the end? Who, do you think, is the winner of this negotiation between the Athenians and the Melians? Are there any better solutions? What lessons do you think we can learn from this negotiation?

(9) This dialogue is frequently cited by political scientists and diplomats as a classic case study in political realism. What is political realism? Find references and provide a definition for this term. People comment that this dialogue demonstrates the foolishness of pride and hope, and that selfish and pragmatic concerns drive wars. Do you agree? Can we find other examples to support this view?

* * *   * * *   * * *   * * *   * * *   * * *   * * *   * * *

Chapter Five   Greek Philosophy

Background Knowledge

1. An Overview

The ancient Greeks were curious about many things. They enquired about the universe, searching for its underlying principles. Ancient Greek thinkers had taken delight in challenging or dropping established ideas, using their imagination, and forming their own conclusion. Those thinkers devoted themselves to their pursuits in different shapes. Hesiod tried to explain in his *Theogony* that the world was created and run by the Olympian gods. Thales, the great thinker, concentrated on the natural world. Herodotus and Thucydides, the two Greek great historians, utilized the writing of history as a vehicle conveying their ideas about the human condition. Greek dramatists like Aeschylus, Sophocles, and Euripides, on the other hand, expressed them by writing tragedies. Xenophon and Plato, in the fourth century B.C., would write dialogues and Aristotle treatise. These creative and innovative thinkers were committed to the areas that still make up philosophy today.

What is philosophy? The word itself is Greek in origin. It comes from two words "philia" which means love, and "sophia" which means wisdom. And so, philosophy is the "love of wisdom". Since love is familiar to us all, what, then, is wisdom? In a Greek sense, wisdom is being able to answer the "perennial" and "fundamental" questions. In summary, the ancient Greeks were trying to find answers to the following questions: Is anything stable and permanent, or is reality always changing? Are human beings capable of understanding reality as it is in itself? Or is reality always seen from a human perspective, which distorts it? Must reality remain a mystery? Are ethical values, such as justice and courage, relative? Do they depend on the individual or group that holds them? Or are there some absolute values that are independent of who holds them, ones that are simply and forever right and true? What sort of political community is most just? Is any political system better than democracy? Is freedom the highest and most important political value, or are their higher ones? What is the proper relationship between human beings and the natural world? Does the natural world exist for human consumption? Should it be revered? Can it be understood? Should it be conquered? These were the questions asked and answered by the ancient Greek philosophers and these are still probed into by modern thinkers.

By seeking answers to these questions, Greek philosophy has shaped the entire Western thought since its birth. Alfred Whitehead said, "The safest general characterization of the European Philosophical tradition is that it consists of a series of footnotes to Plato." In other words, Plato asked all the fundamental questions for the philosophers to answer in his over 25 dialogues. Later, Aristotle, Plato's pupil, would write treatises. Aristotle, was also very influential. In the Middle Ages, he was known simply as "the philosopher". His writings became the organizing principle of the western institutions till today. Plato, with Socrates and Aristotle, laid the foundation of the Western intellectual tradition.

Traditionally, ancient Greek philosophy is divided into four distinctive periods or units: First, the Pre-Socratics, the thinkers before and during the life of Socrates, the first thinker being Thales of Miletus, whose date is traditionally given as 585 BC. Second, Socrates, who lived from 469 to 399 BC. Third, Plato, Socrates' best student, from 429 to 347 BC; and fourth, Aristotle, student of Plato, from 384 to 322 BC.

2. The Trial of Socrates (399 B.C.)

In 399 B.C., a trial, one of the most famous of all time, was in progress in Athens. The accused, Socrates, seventy years old, Athenian greatest thinker and teacher, was convicted and later on, executed. The specific charges against him were that "Socrates is guilty of impiety, not recognizing the gods the polis recognizes; in addition, he is guilty of corrupting young men." The trial is regarded as the most infamous episode in Athenian history in the aftermath of the Peloponnesian War.

What caused such intensity of hatred as to put an old man, a famous Athenian, on trial and for such severe charges?

We do not have many sources available representing a reasonable portrait of the real Socrates. Socrates himself never wrote anything. What we do have as direct evidence are two divergent portraits of Socrates. One came from Aristophanes' comedy *The Clouds*, the other from two of Socrates' well-known pupils, Xenophon and Plato, whose lives were shaped by their teacher, and from Aristotle, father of the university, who was also influenced by the ideas of Socrates through his teacher, Plato.

Aristophanes' comedy *The Clouds* was produced in 423 B.C. It is said that the feeling that Socrates could be a danger to Athenian traditional society gave Aristophanes the inspiration for this comedy. In the play, Socrates is presented as a cynical sophist. For a fee, he offers instruction in his "Thinking Shop" to his disciples by using the Protagorean technique. Socrates is such a person "who can make a good argument seem bad and a bad

argument seem good." His pupils were taught how to argue effectively for any position, even an outrageously immoral one. A vivid scene presented in the comedy is the protagonist's son, a Socrates' pupil, argues against his father that a son has the right to beat his parents. By attending Socrates' "Thinking Shop", the young men of Athens showed their disrespect for tradition and for their elders. This makes an indelible impression on the Athenians, especially the old generation. They felt that Socrates could be a danger to the conventional conception that the son was supposed to be educated by the father. Then the protagonist ends the comedy by burning down Socrates' "Thinking Shop". Therefore, from the play, we can see one important source of Athenians' hostility against Socrates. And elements of the legal charges made against him in 399 B.C. were already present in this comedy.

The other direct evidence we have is the portrait by Xenophon and Plato, whose lives were forever shaped by the trial of their teacher. You want to look today the legacy of Socrates, Xenophon and Plato and the pupil of Plato, Aristotle, for if a teacher be judged by the enduring greatness of his pupils, who can equal Socrates? Plato who was the very foundation of philosophy, it has been said all the western philosophy would be a series of footnotes to Plato and his pupils Aristotle, who is the intellectual father of all the universities of the world today and Xenophon, less influential but a man of action as well as ideas like Plato, devoted to his teacher.

A totally different portrait of Socrates is from his pupils, Plato and Xenophon, and Plato's pupil, Aristotle, father of the university. Both Plato and Xenophon were in their late twenties at the time of Socrates' trial. They belonged to the same upper class of Athenians from which most of Socrates' admirers were drawn. All of the three intellectual figures, Xenophon, Plato and Aristotle, were forever molded by what happened on a single day in the year of 399 B.C. For Plato, Socrates' trial and execution were the beginning of his whole intellectual pursuit of truth. Plato paid his great tributes to his teacher, Socrates, by putting his ideas into the mouth of Socrates (Plato's Dialogues), and devoted first four dialogues to the events surrounding that trial: *The Euthyphro*, *Apology*, *Crito*, *and Phaedo*.

Euthyphro

By Plato

PERSONS OF THE DIALOGUE：

 · **SOCRATES**

 · **EUTHYPHRO**

SCENE：The **Porch**[1] of the **King Archon**[2].

Euthyphro and Socrates meet at the Porch of the King Archon. *Both have* ***legal business***[3] *on hand*.

EUTHYPHRO   Why have you left the Lyceum，Socrates? And what are you doing in the Porch of the King Archon? Surely you cannot be **concerned**[4] in a **suit**[5] before the King，like myself?

SOCRATES   Not in a suit，Euthyphro；**impeachment**[6] is the word which the Athenians use.

EUTHYPHRO   What! I suppose that some one has been **prosecuting**[7] you，for I cannot believe that you are the **prosecutor**[8] of another.

SOCRATES   Certainly not.

EUTHYPHRO   Then some one else has been prosecuting you?

SOCRATES   Yes.

EUTHYPHRO   And who is he?

SOCRATES   A young man who is little known，Euthyphro；and I hardly know him：his name is Meletus，and he is of the **deme**[9] of Pitthis. Perhaps you may remember his appearance；he has a **beak**[10]，and long straight hair，and a **beard**[11] which is ill grown.

EUTHYPHRO   No，I do not remember him，Socrates. But what is the **charge**[12] which he brings against you?

SOCRATES   What is the charge? Well，a very serious charge，which shows a good deal of character in the young man，and for which he is certainly not to be **despised**[13]. He says he knows how the youth are **corrupted**[14] and who are their corruptors. I fancy that he must be a wise man，and seeing that I am **the reverse**[15]

1．［pɔːtʃ］*n*．门廊，走廊

2．［ɑːkən］*n*．执政官；统治者（king archon 指古希腊审理案子的地方）

3．法律事务；官司

4．［kən'sɜːnd］*vt*．涉及，关系到

5．［sjuːt］*n*．官司

6．［ɪm'piːtʃmənt］*n*．控告；弹劾

7．［'prɒsɪkjuːtɪŋ］*vt*．起诉

8．［'prɒsɪkjuːtə(r)］*n*．检举人

9．［diːm］*n*．市区，地名

10．［biːk］*n*．鹰钩鼻

11．［bɪəd］*n*．胡子

12．［tʃɑːdʒ］*n*．指控

13．［'dɪspaɪzd］*vt*．小看；蔑视

14．［kə'rʌpt］*vt*．被腐蚀

15．［rɪ'vɜːs］*n*．相反

of a wise man, he has found me out, and is going to accuse me of corrupting his young friends. And of this our mother **the state**[1] is to be the **judge**[2]. Of all our political men he is the only one who seems to me to begin in the right way, with the cultivation of **virtue**[3] in youth; like a good **husbandman**[4], he makes the **young shoots**[5] his first care, and clears away us who are the destroyers of them. This is only the first step; he will afterwards attend to the elder branches; and if he goes on as he has begun, he will be a very great public **benefactor.**[6]

EUTHYPHRO   I hope that he may; but I rather fear, Socrates, that the opposite will turn out to be the truth. My opinion is that in attacking you he is simply aiming **a blow**[7] at the **foundation**[8] of the state. But in what way does he say that you corrupt the young?

SOCRATES   He brings a wonderful **accusation**[9] against me, which at first hearing excites surprise: he says that I am a poet or maker of gods, and that I invent new gods and deny the existence of old ones; this is the ground of his **indictment**[10].

EUTHYPHRO   I understand, Socrates; he means to attack you about the familiar sign which occasionally, as you say, comes to you. He thinks that you are a **neologian**[11], and he is going to have you up before the court for this. He knows that such a charge is readily received by the world, as I myself know too well; for when I speak in the **assembly**[12] about **divine**[13] things, and **foretell**[14] the future to them, they laugh at me and think me a madman. Yet every word that I say is true. But they are **jealous**[15] of us all; and we must be brave and go at them.

SOCRATES   Their laughter, friend Euthyphro, is not a matter of much **consequence**[16]. For a man may be thought wise; but the Athenians, I suspect, do not much trouble themselves about him until he begins to **impart**[17] his wisdom to others; and then for some reason or other, perhaps, as you say, from **jealousy**[18], they are angry.

EUTHYPHRO   I am never likely to try their **temper**[19] in this way.

SOCRATES   I dare say not, for you are **reserved**[20] in your behaviour, and seldom **impart**[21] your wisdom. But I have a

1. [steɪt] n. 国家
2. [dʒʌdʒ] n. 法官;裁判
3. [ˈvɜːtʃuː] n. 德行
4. [ˈhʌzbəndmən] n. 农夫
5. 幼芽,秧苗
6. [ˈbenɪfæktə(r)] n. 施惠者
7. [bləʊ] n. 攻击
8. [faʊnˈdeɪʃn] n. 根基
9. [ˌækjuˈzeɪʃn] n. 指控
10. [ɪnˈdaɪtmənt] n. 起诉书;控告
11. [nɪ(ː)əʊˈləʊdʒɪən] n. 使用新义者
12. [əˈsembli] n. 公民大会
13. [dɪˈvaɪn] adj. 神的
14. [fɔːˈtel] vt. 预言
15. [ˈdʒeləs] adj. 嫉妒的
16. [ˈkɒnsɪkwəns] n. 后果
17. [ɪmˈpɑːt] vt. 传授;教授
18. [ˈdʒeləsi] n. 嫉妒
19. [ˈtempə(r)] n. 脾气;性情
20. [rɪˈzɜːvd] vt. 保留
21. [ɪmˈpɑːt] vt. 传授

benevolent[1] habit of pouring out myself to everybody，and would even pay for a listener，and I am afraid that the Athenians may think me too talkative. Now if，as I was saying，they would only laugh at me，as you say that they laugh at you，the time might pass **gaily**[2] enough in the court；but perhaps they may be in earnest，and then what the end will be you **soothsayers**[3] only can predict.

EUTHYPHRO　I dare say that the affair will end in nothing，Socrates，and that you will win your cause；and I think that I shall win my own.

SOCRATES　And what is your suit，Euthyphro? Are you the **pursuer**[4] or the **defendant**?[5]

EUTHYPHRO　I am the pursuer.

SOCRATES　Of whom?

EUTHYPHRO　You will think me mad when I tell you.

SOCRATES　Why，has the **fugitive**[6] wings?

EUTHYPHRO　Nay，he is not very **volatile**[7] at his time of life.

SOCRATES　Who is he?

EUTHYPHRO　My father.

SOCRATES　Your father! My good man?

EUTHYPHRO　Yes.

SOCRATES　And of what is he accused?

EUTHYPHRO　Of murder，Socrates.

SOCRATES　By the powers，Euthyphro! How little does the **common herd**[8] know of the **nature**[9] of right and truth. A man must be an extraordinary man，and have made great **strides**[10] in wisdom，before he could have seen his way to bring such an action.

EUTHYPHRO　Indeed，Socrates，he must.

SOCRATES　I suppose that the man whom your father murdered was one of your relatives—clearly he was；for if he had been a stranger you would never have thought of **prosecuting**[11] him.

EUTHYPHRO　I am amused，Socrates，at your **making a distinction**[12] between one who is a relation and one who is not a relation；for surely the pollution is the same in either case，if you knowingly associate with the murderer when you ought to clear yourself and him by proceeding against him. The real

1．[bɪˈnevələnt] *adj*. 仁慈的

2．[ˈɡeɪli] *adv*. 快乐地

3．[ˈsuːθseɪə(r)] *n*. 预言者

4．[pəˈsjuː] *n*. 原告

5．[dɪˈfendənt] *n*. 被告

6．[ˈfjuːdʒɪtɪv] *n*. 逃亡者

7．[ˈvɒlətaɪl] *adj*. 易变的；不稳定的；轻快的

8．普通大众

9．[ˈneɪtʃə(r)] *n*. 本质

10．[straɪd] *n*. 大踏步

11．[ˈprɒsɪkjuːt] *v*. 起诉

12．作出区分

question is whether the murdered man has been justly **slain**[1]. If justly, then your duty is to let the matter alone; but if unjustly, then even if the murderer lives under the same roof with you and eats at the same table, proceed against him. Now the man who is dead was a poor dependant of mine who worked for us as a field labourer on our farm in Naxos, and one day in a fit of drunken passion he got into a quarrel with one of our **domestic**[2] servants and slew him. My father bound him hand and foot and threw him into a **ditch**[3], and then sent to Athens to ask of a **diviner**[4] what he should do with him. Meanwhile he never attended to him and took no care about him, for he regarded him as a murderer; and thought that no great harm would be done even if he did die. Now this was just what happened. For such was the effect of cold and hunger and **chains**[5] upon him, that before the messenger returned from the diviner, he was dead. And my father and family are angry with me for taking the part of the murderer and **prosecuting**[6] my father. They say that he did not kill him, and that if he did, the dead man was but a murderer, and I ought not to take any notice, for that a son is **impious**[7] who prosecutes a father. Which shows, Socrates, how little they know what the gods think about piety and impiety.

SOCRATES　　Good heavens, Euthyphro! and is your knowledge of religion and of things **pious**[8] and **impious**[9] so very exact, that, supposing the circumstances to be as you **state**[10] them, you are not afraid lest you too may be doing an impious thing in bringing an action against your father?

EUTHYPHRO　　The best of Euthyphro, and that which **distinguishes**[11] him, Socrates, from other men, is his exact knowledge of all such matters. What should I be good for without it?

SOCRATES　　Rare friend! I think that I cannot do better than be your **disciple**[12]. Then before the trial with Meletus comes on I shall challenge him, and say that I have always had a great interest in religious questions, and now, as he charges me with **rash**[13] imaginations and innovations in religion, I have become your disciple. You, Meletus, as I shall say to him, **acknowledge**[14] Euthyphro to be a great **theologian**[15], and sound in his opinions; and if you approve of him you ought to approve of me, and not

1. [sleɪn] vt. 杀死(slay 的过去分词)

2. [dəˈmestɪk] adj. 家里的

3. [ˈdɪtʃ] n. 渠沟

4. [dɪˈvaɪnə(r)] n. 通晓法典的僧侣

5. [tʃeɪn] n. 束缚

6. [ˈprɒsɪkjuːtɪŋ] v. 起诉

7. [ˈɪmpɪəs] adj. 不虔诚

8. [ˈpaɪəs] adj. 虔诚的
9. [ˈɪmpɪəs] adj. 不虔诚的
10. [steɪt] vt. 陈述

11. [dɪsˈtɪŋgwɪʃt] vt. 区分,区别

12. [dɪˈsaɪpl] n. 门徒;学生

13. [ræʃ] adj. 鲁莽的;轻率的
14. [əkˈnɒlɪdʒ] vt. 承认
15. [ˌθɪəˈlɒdʒɪən] n. 神学家

have me into court; but if you disapprove, you should begin by **indicting**[1] him who is my teacher, and who will be the **ruin**[2], not of the young, but of the old; that is to say, of myself whom he instructs, and of his old father whom he **admonishes**[3] and **chastises**[4]. And if Meletus refuses to listen to me, but will go on, and will not shift the **indictment**[5] from me to you, I cannot do better than repeat this challenge in the court.

EUTHYPHRO Yes, indeed, Socrates; and if he attempts to indict me I am mistaken if I do not find a **flaw**[6] in him; the court shall have a great deal more to say to him than to me.

SOCRATES And I, my dear friend, knowing this, am desirous of becoming your disciple. For I observe that no one appears to notice you—not even this Meletus; but his sharp eyes have found me out at once, and he has indicted me for impiety. And therefore, I **adjure**[7] you to tell me the nature of piety and impiety, which you said that you knew so well, and of murder, and of other offences against the gods. What are they? Is not piety in every action always the same? and impiety, again—is it not always the opposite of piety, and also the same with itself, having, as impiety, one **notion**[8] which includes whatever is impious?

EUTHYPHRO To be sure, Socrates.

SOCRATES And what is piety, and what is impiety?

EUTHYPHRO Piety is doing as I am doing; that is to say, **prosecuting**[9] any one who is **guilty**[10] of murder, **sacrilege**[11], or of any similar crime—whether he be your father or mother, or whoever he may be—that makes no difference; and not to prosecute them is impiety. And please to consider, Socrates, what a notable **proof**[12] I will give you of the truth of my words, a proof which I have already given to others:—of the principle, I mean, that the impious, whoever he may be, ought not to go unpunished. For do not men regard Zeus as the best and most **righteous**[13] of the gods? —and yet they admit that he bound his father [Cronos] because he **wickedly**[14] **devoured**[15] his sons, and that he too had punished his own father *n*. [Uranus] for a similar reason, in a nameless manner. And yet when I proceed against my father, they are angry with me. So

1. [ɪnˈdaɪtɪŋ] *n*. 指控
2. [ˈruːn] *n*. 破坏
3. [ədˈmɒnɪʃ] *vt*. 警告
4. [tʃæˈstaɪz] *vt*. 惩罚；严责
5. [ɪnˈdaɪtmənt] *n*. 指控
6. [flɔː] *n*. 缺点；缺陷
7. [əˈdʒʊə(r)] *vt*. 恳求；祈求
8. [ˈnəʊʃən] *n*. 理念；概念
9. [ˈprɒsɪkjuːtɪŋ] *vt*. 指控
10. [ˈɡɪlti] *adj*. 有罪的
11. [ˈsækrɪlɪdʒ] *n*. 渎圣行为
12. [pruːf] *n*. 证据
13. [ˈraɪtʃəs] *adj*. 正义的；正直的；正确的
14. [ˈwɪkɪd] *adv*. 邪恶地
15. [dɪˈvaʊə] *vt*. 吞吃

inconsistent[1] are they in their way of talking when the gods are concerned, and when I am concerned.

SOCRATES   May not this be the reason, Euthyphro, why I am charged with impiety—that I cannot away with these stories about the gods? and therefore I suppose that people think me wrong. But, as you who are well informed about them approve of them, I cannot do better than **assent**[2] to your **superior**[3] wisdom. What else can I say, **confessing**[4] as I do, that I know nothing about them? Tell me, for the love of Zeus, whether you really believe that they are true.

EUTHYPHRO   Yes, Socrates; and things more wonderful still, of which the world is in **ignorance**[5].

SOCRATES   And do you really believe that the gods fought with one another, and had **dire**[6] quarrels, battles, and the like, as the poets say, and as you may see **represented**[7] in the works of great artists? The temples are full of them; and notably the robe of Athene, which is carried up to the Acropolis at the great Panathenaea, is **embroidered**[8] with them. Are all these tales of the gods true, Euthyphro?

EUTHYPHRO   Yes, Socrates; and, as I was saying, I can tell you, if you would like to hear them, many other things about the gods which would quite amaze you.

SOCRATES   I dare say; and you shall tell me them at some other time when I have leisure. But just at present I would rather hear from you a more precise answer, which you have not as yet given, my friend, to the question, What is 'piety'? When asked, you only replied, Doing as you do, charging your father with murder.

EUTHYPHRO   And what I said was true, Socrates.

SOCRATES   No doubt, Euthyphro; but you would admit that there are many other **pious**[9] acts?

EUTHYPHRO   There are.

SOCRATES   Remember that I did not ask you to give me two or three examples of **piety**[10], but to explain the general idea which makes all pious things to be pious. Do you not **recollect**[11] that there was one idea which made the impious impious, and the pious pious?

1. [ˌɪnkənˈsɪstənt] adj. 不一致的

2. [əˈsent] vi. 同意

3. [sjuːˈpɪərɪə(r)] adj. 更好的

4. [kənˈfesɪŋ] vi. 坦白

5. [ˈɪɡnərəns] n. 无知;愚昧

6. [ˈdaɪə(r)] n. 可怕的;极端的

7. [reprɪˈzentɪd] v. 表现

8. [ɪmˈbrɔɪdə] vt. 装饰

9. [ˈpaɪəs] n. 虔诚的,信神的

10. [ˈpaɪətɪ] n. 虔诚

11. [ˌrekəˈlekt] vt. 想起;回忆

EUTHYPHRO   I remember.

SOCRATES   Tell me what is the nature of this idea, and then I shall have a standard to which I may look, and by which I may measure actions, whether yours or those of any one else, and then I shall be able to say that such and such an action is pious, such another impious.

EUTHYPHRO   I will tell you, if you like.

SOCRATES   I should very much like.

EUTHYPHRO   Piety, then, is that which **is dear to**[1] the gods, and **impiety**[2] is that which is not dear to them.

1. 对…而言是珍贵的

2. [ɪmˈpaɪəti] *n.* 不虔诚

SOCRATES   Very good, Euthyphro; you have now given me the sort of answer which I wanted. But whether what you say is true or not I cannot as yet tell, although I make no doubt that you will prove the truth of your words.

（What the gods love）

EUTHYPHRO   Of course.

SOCRATES   Come, then, and let us **examine**[3] what we are saying. That thing or person which is dear to the gods is pious, and that thing or person which is hateful to the gods is impious, these two being the extreme opposites of one another. Was not that said?

3. [ɪgˈzæmɪn] *vt.* 审查

EUTHYPHRO   It was.

SOCRATES   And well said?

EUTHYPHRO   Yes, Socrates, I thought so; it was certainly said.

SOCRATES   And further, Euthyphro, the gods were **admitted to**[4] have **enmities**[5] and **hatreds**[6] and differences?

4. 承认

5. [ˈenməti] *n.* 敌意

6. [ˈheɪtrɪd] *n.* 仇恨

EUTHYPHRO   Yes, that was also said.

SOCRATES   And what sort of difference creates enmity and anger? Suppose for example that you and I, my good friend, differ about a **number**[7]; do differences of this sort make us enemies and set us at **variance**[8] with one another? Do we not go at once to **arithmetic**[9], and put an end to them by a sum?

7. [ˈnʌmbə(r)] *n.* 数字

8. [ˈveərɪəns] *n.* 不一致；变化

9. [əˈrɪθmətɪk] *n.* 算术

EUTHYPHRO   True.

SOCRATES   Or suppose that we differ about **magnitudes**[10], do we not quickly end the difference by measuring?

10. [ˈmæɡnɪtjuːd] *n.* 大小；级数

EUTHYPHRO   Very true.

SOCRATES And we end a **controversy**[1] about heavy and light by **resorting to**[2] a weighing machine?

EUTHYPHRO To be sure.

SOCRATES But what differences are there which cannot be thus decided，and which therefore make us angry and set us at enmity with one another? I dare say the answer does not occur to you at the moment，and therefore I will suggest that these enmities arise when the matters of difference are the **just**[3] and **unjust**[4]，good and evil，honourable and dishonourable. Are not these the points about which men differ，and about which when we are unable satisfactorily to decide our differences，you and I and all of us quarrel，when we do quarrel?

EUTHYPHRO Yes，Socrates，the nature of the differences about which we quarrel is such as you describe.

SOCRATES And the quarrels of the gods，noble Euthyphro，when they occur，are of a like nature?

EUTHYPHRO Certainly they are.

SOCRATES They have differences of opinion，as you say，about good and evil，just and unjust，honourable and dishonourable：there would have been no **quarrels**[5] among them，if there had been no such differences—would there now?

EUTHYPHRO You are quite right.

SOCRATES Does not every man love that which he deems noble and just and good，and hate the opposite of them?

EUTHYPHRO Very true.

SOCRATES But，as you say，people regard the same things，some as just and others as unjust，—about these they **dispute**[6]；and so there arise wars and fightings among them.

EUTHYPHRO Very true.

SOCRATES Then the same things are hated by the gods and loved by the gods，and are both hateful and dear to them?

EUTHYPHRO True.

SOCRATES And upon this view the same things，Euthyphro，will be pious and also impious?

EUTHYPHRO So I should suppose.

SOCRATES Then，my friend，I **remark**[7] with surprise that you have not answered the question which I asked. For I certainly did not ask you to tell me what action is both pious and

1. ['kɒntrəvɜːsɪ] *n*. 争吵
2. 诉诸

3. [dʒʌst] *adj*. 正义的
4. [ʌn'dʒʌst] *adj*. 非正义的

5. ['kwɒrəl] *n*. 争吵

6. [dɪs'pjuːt] *vi*. 争论；争端；争吵

7. [rɪ'mɑːk] *vi*. 评论；说话

impious; but now it would seem that what is loved by the gods is also hated by them. And therefore, Euthyphro, in thus **chastising**[1] your father you may very likely be doing what is agreeable to Zeus but disagreeable to Cronos or Uranus, and what is acceptable to Hephaestus but unacceptable to Hera, and there may be other gods who have similar differences of opinion.

EUTHYPHRO But I believe, Socrates, that all the gods would be agreed as to the **propriety**[2] of punishing a murderer: there would be no difference of opinion about that.

SOCRATES Well, but speaking of men, Euthyphro, did you ever hear any one arguing that a murderer or any sort of evil-doer ought to be let off?

EUTHYPHRO I should rather say that these are the questions which they are always arguing, especially in courts of law: they **commit all sorts of crimes**[3], and there is nothing which they will not do or say in their own defence.

SOCRATES But do they admit their guilt, Euthyphro, and yet say that they ought not to be punished?

EUTHYPHRO No; they do not.

SOCRATES Then there are some things which they **do not venture**[4] to say and do: for they do not venture to argue that the **guilty**[5] are to be unpunished, but they deny their **guilt**[6], do they not?

EUTHYPHRO Yes.

SOCRATES Then they do not argue that the evil-doer should not be punished, but they argue about the fact of who the evil-doer is, and what he did and when?

EUTHYPHRO True.

SOCRATES And the gods are in the same case, if as you **assert**[7] they quarrel about just and unjust, and some of them say while others deny that injustice is done among them. For surely neither God nor man will ever **venture**[8] to say that the doer of injustice is not to be punished?

EUTHYPHRO That is true, Socrates, in the main.

SOCRATES But they join issue about the **particulars**[9]—gods and men alike; and, if they dispute at all, they **dispute**[10] about some act which is called in question, and which by some is

1. [tʃæ'staɪz] n. 惩罚
2. [prə'praɪəti] n. 适当;正当
3. 犯下各种罪
4. 不敢
5. ['ɡɪlti] adj. 有罪的
6. [ɡɪlt] n. 有罪
7. [ə'sɜːt] vt. 断言
8. ['ventʃə(r)] vi. 斗胆
9. [pə'tɪkjʊlə(r)] n. 具体
10. [dɪs'pjuːt] vt. 争吵;争论

affirmed[1] to be just，by others to be unjust. Is not that true?

EUTHYPHRO   Quite true.

SOCRATES   Well then，my dear friend Euthyphro，do tell me，for my better instruction and information，what **proof**[2] have you that in the opinion of all the gods a servant who **is guilty of**[3] murder，and is put in **chains**[4] by the master of the dead man，and dies because he is put in chains before he who bound him can learn from the interpreters of the gods what he ought to do with him，dies unjustly；and that on behalf of such an one a son ought to proceed against his father and accuse him of murder. How would you show that all the gods absolutely agree in approving of his act? Prove to me that they do，and I will **applaud**[5] your wisdom as long as I live.

EUTHYPHRO   It will be a difficult task；but I could make the matter very clear indeed to you.

SOCRATES   I understand；you mean to say that I am not so quick of **apprehension**[6] as the judges：for to them you will be sure to prove that the act is unjust，and hateful to the gods.

EUTHYPHRO   Yes indeed，Socrates；at least if they will listen to me.

SOCRATES   But they will be sure to listen if they find that you are a good speaker. There was a notion that came into my mind while you were speaking；I said to myself，'Well，and what if Euthyphro does prove to me that all the gods regarded the death of the **serf**[7] as unjust，how do I know anything more of the nature of piety and impiety? for granting that this action may be hateful to the gods，still piety and impiety are not adequately defined by these **distinctions**[8]，for that which is hateful to the gods has been shown to be also pleasing and dear to them.' And therefore，Euthyphro，I do not ask you to prove this；I will suppose，if you like，that all the gods **condemn**[9] and **abominate**[10] such an action. But I will **amend**[11] the **definition**[12] so far as to say that what all the gods hate is **impious**[13]，and what

1. [əˈfɜːm] *vt.* 证实

2. [pruːf] *n.* 证据

3. 有…罪的
4. [tʃeɪn] *n.* 锁链

5. [əˈplɔːd] *vt.* 为…鼓掌

6. [ˌæprɪˈhenʃən] *n.* 理解；了解

7. [sɜːf] *n.* 仆人

8. [dɪsˈtɪŋkʃən] *n.* 区别

9. [kənˈdem] *vt.* 指责
10. [əˈbɒmɪneɪt] *vt.* 痛恨；憎恶
11. [əˈmend] *vt.* 修改
12. [ˌdefɪˈnɪʃən] *n.* 定义
13. [ˈɪmpɪəs]

they love pious or holy; and what some of them love and others hate is both or neither. Shall this be our definition of piety and impiety?

EUTHYPHRO   Why not，Socrates?

SOCRATES   Why not! Certainly，as far as I am concerned，Euthyphro，there is no reason why not. But whether this **admission**[1] will greatly assist you in the task of instructing me as you promised，is a matter for you to consider.

EUTHYPHRO   Yes，I should say that what all the gods love is pious and holy，and the opposite which they all hate，impious.

SOCRATES   Ought we to **enquire**[2] into the truth of this，Euthyphro，or simply to accept the mere statement on our own **authority**[3] and that of others? What do you say?

EUTHYPHRO   We should enquire；and I believe that the statement will **stand**[4] the test of **enquiry**[5].

SOCRATES   We shall know better，my good friend，in a little while. The point which I should first wish to understand is whether the pious or holy is beloved by the gods because it is **holy**[6]，or holy because it is beloved of the gods.

EUTHYPHRO   I do not understand your meaning，Socrates.

SOCRATES   I will **endeavour**[7] to explain：we speak of carrying and we speak of being carried，of leading and being led，seeing and being seen. You know that in all such cases there is a difference，and you know also in what the difference lies?

EUTHYPHRO   I think that I understand.

SOCRATES   And is not that which is beloved **distinct**[8] from that which loves?

EUTHYPHRO   Certainly.

SOCRATES   Well；and now tell me，is that which is carried in this state of carrying because it is carried，or for some other reason?

EUTHYPHRO   No；that is the reason.

SOCRATES   And the same is true of what is led and of what is seen?

1. ['ɪmpɪəs] *n*. 承认

2. [ɪn'kwaɪə(r)] *vi*. 询问；调查

3. [ɔː'θɒrəti] *n*. 权威

4. [stænd] *vt*. 经受住
5. [ɪn'kwaɪəri] *n*. 询问

6. ['həʊli] *adj*. 神圣的；至善的
7. [ɪn'devə(r)] *vt*. 努力

8. [dɪs'tɪŋkt] *adj*. 有区别的

EUTHYPHRO　True.

SOCRATES　And a thing is not seen because it is visible, but **conversely**[1], visible because it is seen; nor is a thing led because it is in the state of being led, or carried because it is in the state of being carried, but the **converse**[2] of this. And now I think, Euthyphro, that my meaning will be **intelligible**[3]; and my meaning is, that any state of action or passion **implies**[4] previous action or passion. It does not become because it is becoming, but it is in a state of becoming because it becomes; neither does it suffer because it is in a state of suffering, but it is in a state of suffering because it suffers. Do you not agree?

EUTHYPHRO　Yes.

SOCRATES　Is not that which is loved in some state either of becoming or suffering?

EUTHYPHRO　Yes.

SOCRATES　And the same holds as in the previous instances; the state of being loved follows the act of being loved, and not the act the state.

EUTHYPHRO　Certainly.

SOCRATES　And what do you say of piety, Euthyphro: is not piety, according to your definition, loved by all the gods?

EUTHYPHRO　Yes.

SOCRATES　Because it is pious or holy, or for some other reason?

EUTHYPHRO　No, that is the reason.

SOCRATES　It is loved because it is holy, not holy because it is loved?

EUTHYPHRO　Yes.

SOCRATES　And that which is dear to the gods is loved by them, and is in a state to be loved of them because it is loved of them?

EUTHYPHRO　Certainly.

SOCRATES　Then that which is dear to the gods, Euthyphro, is not holy, nor is that which is holy loved of God, as you **affirm**[5]; but they are two different things.

EUTHYPHRO　How do you mean, Socrates?

SOCRATES　I mean to say that the holy has been **acknowledged**[6] by us to be loved of God because it is holy, not to

1. ['kɒnvɜːsli] *adv.* 相反地

2. [kən'vɜːs] *n.* 相反

3. [ɪn'telɪdʒəbl] *adj.* 可理解的

4. [ɪm'plaɪd] *vt.* 暗示;暗含

5. [ə'fɜːm] *v.* 确认,证实

6. [ək'nɒlɪdʒd] *vt.* 承认;认可

be holy because it is loved.

EUTHYPHRO　Yes.

SOCRATES　But that which is dear to the gods is dear to them because it is loved by them, not loved by them because it is dear to them.

EUTHYPHRO　True.

SOCRATES　But, friend Euthyphro, if that which is holy is the same with that which is dear to God, and is loved because it is holy, then that which is dear to God would have been loved as being dear to God; but if that which is dear to God is dear to him because loved by him, then that which is holy would have been holy because loved by him. But now you see that the **reverse**[1] is the case, and that they are quite different from one another. For one (theophiles) is of a kind to be loved because it is loved, and the other (osion) is loved because it is of a kind to be loved. Thus you appear to me, Euthyphro, when I ask you what is the **essence**[2] of **holiness**[3], to offer an **attribute**[4] only, and not the essence—the attribute of being loved by all the gods. But you still refuse to explain to me the nature of holiness. And therefore, if you please, I will ask you not to hide your treasure, but to tell me once more what holiness or piety really is, whether dear to the gods or not (for that is a matter about which we will not quarrel); and what is impiety?

EUTHYPHRO　I really do not know, Socrates, how to express what I mean. For somehow or other our arguments, on whatever ground we rest them, seem to turn round and walk away from us.

SOCRATES　Your words, Euthyphro, are like the **handiwork**[5] of my ancestor Daedalus; and if I were the sayer or **propounder**[6] of them, you might say that my **arguments**[7] walk away and will not remain fixed where they are placed because I am a **descendant**[8] of his. But now, since these notions are your own, you must find some other **gibe**[9], for they certainly, as you yourself allow, show an **inclination**[10] to be on the move.

EUTHYPHRO　Nay, Socrates, I shall still say that you are the Daedalus who sets arguments in **motion**[11]; not I, certainly, but you make them move or go round, for they would never have **stirred**[12], as far as I am concerned.

SOCRATES　Then I must be a greater than Daedalus: for

1. [rɪ'vɜːs] *n.* 相反

2. ['esəns] *n.* 精髓

3. ['həʊlɪnɪs] *n.* 神圣;敬神

4. [ə'trɪbjuːt] *n.* 属性

5. ['hændɪwɜːk] *n.* 手工艺

6. [prə'paʊnd] *n.* 提议者

7. ['ɑːɡjʊmənt] *n.* 论据;争吵;争论

8. [dɪ'sendənt] *n.* 后代;后裔

9. [dʒaɪb] *n.* 嘲笑;嘲讽话

10. [ˌɪnklɪ'neɪʃn] *n.* 倾向;意愿

11. ['məʊʃən] *n.* 运动

12. ['stɜːrə(r)] *vi.* 激起;引起

whereas he only made his own inventions to move，I move those of other people as well. And the beauty of it is，that I would rather not. For I would give the wisdom of Daedalus，and the wealth of Tantalus，to be able to **detain**[1] them and keep them fixed. But enough of this. As I **perceive**[2] that you are lazy，I will myself **endeavour**[3] to show you how you might instruct me in the **nature**[4] of piety；and I hope that you will not **grudge**[5] your labour. Tell me，then，—Is not that which is pious necessarily just?

EUTHYPHRO　Yes.

SOCRATES　And is，then，all which is just pious? or，is that which is pious all just，but that which is just，only in part and not all，pious?

EUTHYPHRO　I do not understand you，Socrates.

SOCRATES　And yet I know that you are as much wiser than I am，as you are younger. But，as I was saying，**revered**[6] friend，the **abundance**[7] of your wisdom makes you lazy. Please to **exert**[8] yourself，for there is no real difficulty in understanding me. What I mean I may explain by an illustration of what I do not mean. The poet ［Stasinus］ sings—'Of Zeus，the author and creator of all these things，You will not tell：for where there is fear there is also **reverence**[9].'

Now I disagree with this poet. Shall I tell you in what respect?

EUTHYPHRO　**By all means**[10].

SOCRATES　I should not say that where there is fear there is also reverence；for I am sure that many persons fear poverty and disease，and the like evils，but I do not **perceive**[11] that they reverence the objects of their fear.

EUTHYPHRO　Very true.

SOCRATES　But where reverence is，there is fear；for he who has a feeling of reverence and shame about the **commission**[12] of any action，fears and is afraid of an ill reputation.

EUTHYPHRO　No doubt.

SOCRATES　Then we are wrong in saying that where there is fear there is also reverence；and we should say，where there is reverence there is also fear. But there is not always reverence where there is fear；for fear is a more **extended**[8] notion，and reverence is a part of fear，just as the **odd**[9] is a part of number，and number is a more extended notion than the odd. I suppose

1. ［dɪˈteɪn］ vt. 拘留；耽搁；拘押
2. ［pəˈsiːv］ vt. 觉得
3. ［ɪnˈdevə(r)］ vi. 努力
4. ［ˈneɪtʃə(r)］ n. 本质
5. ［grʌdʒ］ vt. 吝惜；不愿
6. ［rɪˈvɪə(r)］ adj. 尊敬的
7. ［əˈbʌndəns］ n. 丰富；充足
8. ［ɪgˈzɜːt］ vt. 施加；运用
9. ［ˈrevərəns］ n. 敬畏；尊敬
10. 一定，务必
11. ［pəˈsiːv］ v. 察觉
7. ［kəˈmɪʃən］ n. 犯罪；委托；委任
8. ［ɪksˈtendɪd］ adj. 延展的
9. ［ɒd］ n. 奇数

that you follow me now?

EUTHYPHRO　Quite well.

SOCRATES　That was the sort of question which I meant to raise when I asked whether the just is always the pious, or the pious always the just; and whether there may not be justice where there is not piety; for justice is the more extended notion of which piety is only a part. Do you **dissent**?[1]

1. [dɪˈsent] *n*. 不同意

EUTHYPHRO　No, I think that you are quite right.

SOCRATES　Then, if piety is a part of justice, I suppose that we should enquire what part? If you had pursued the **enquiry**[2] in the previous cases; for instance, if you had asked me what is an even number, and what part of number the even is, I should have had no difficulty in replying, a number which **represents**[3] a figure having two equal sides. Do you not agree?

2. [ɪnˈkwaɪəri] *n*. 询问

3. [ˌreprɪˈzent] *vt*. 代表

EUTHYPHRO　Yes, I quite agree.

SOCRATES　In like manner, I want you to tell me what part of justice is piety or holiness, that I may be able to tell Meletus not to do me injustice, or **indict**[4] me for impiety, as I am now **adequately**[5] instructed by you in the nature of piety or holiness, and their opposites.

4. [ɪnˈdaɪt] *n*. 告发

5. [ˈædɪkwɪtli] *adv*. 足够地

EUTHYPHRO　Piety or holiness, Socrates, appears to me to be that part of justice which attends to the gods, as there is the other part of justice which attends to men.

SOCRATES　That is good, Euthyphro; yet still there is a little point about which I should like to have further information, What is the meaning of 'attention'? For attention can hardly be used in the same sense when **applied to**[6] the gods as when applied to other things. For instance, horses are said to require attention, and not every person is able to attend to them, but only a person skilled in **horsemanship**[7]. Is it not so?

6. 应用到

7. [ˈhɔːsmənʃɪp] *n*. 马术；骑术

EUTHYPHRO　Certainly.

SOCRATES　I should suppose that the art of horsemanship is the art of attending to horses?

EUTHYPHRO　Yes.

SOCRATES　Nor is every one qualified to attend to dogs, but only the **huntsman**[8]?

8. [ˈhʌntsmən] *n*. 猎人

EUTHYPHRO　True.

SOCRATES　And I should also **conceive**[1] that the art of the huntsman is the art of attending to dogs?

EUTHYPHRO　Yes.

SOCRATES　As the art of the oxherd is the art of attending to **oxen**?[2]

EUTHYPHRO　Very true.

SOCRATES　In like manner holiness or piety is the art of attending to the gods? —that would be your meaning, Euthyphro?

EUTHYPHRO　Yes.

SOCRATES　And is not attention always designed for the good or benefit of that to which the attention is given? As in the case of horses, you may observe that when attended to by the horseman's art they are benefited and improved, are they not?

EUTHYPHRO　True.

SOCRATES　As the dogs are benefited by the huntsman's art, and the **oxen** by the art of the oxherd, and all other things are tended or attended for their good and not for their hurt?

EUTHYPHRO　Certainly, not for their hurt.

SOCRATES　But for their good?

EUTHYPHRO　Of course.

SOCRATES　And does piety or holiness, which has been defined to be the art of attending to the gods, benefit or improve them? Would you say that when you do a holy act you make any of the gods better?

EUTHYPHRO　No, no; that was certainly not what I meant.

SOCRATES　And I, Euthyphro, never supposed that you did. I asked you the question about the nature of the attention, because I thought that you did not.

EUTHYPHRO　You do me justice, Socrates; that is not the sort of attention which I mean.

SOCRATES　Good, but I must still ask what is this attention to the gods which is called piety?

EUTHYPHRO　It is such, Socrates, as servants show to their masters.

SOCRATES　I understand—a sort of **ministration**[3] to the gods.

EUTHYPHRO　Exactly.

SOCRATES　Medicine is also a sort of ministration or service,

1. [kən'siːv] *vt.* 构思；想像，设想

2. [ɒksə] *n.* 牛

3. [ˌmɪnɪs'treɪʃən] *n.* 帮助；服务

having in view the **attainment**[1] of some object—would you not say of health?

EUTHYPHRO   I should.

SOCRATES   Again, there is an art which ministers to the ship-builder with a view to the attainment of some result?

EUTHYPHRO   Yes, Socrates, with a view to the building of a ship.

SOCRATES   As there is an art which ministers to the house-builder with a view to the building of a house?

EUTHYPHRO   Yes.

SOCRATES   And now tell me, my good friend, about the art which ministers to the gods: what work does that help to accomplish? For you must surely know if, as you say, you are of all men living the one who is best instructed in religion.

EUTHYPHRO   And I speak the truth, Socrates.

SOCRATES   Tell me then, oh tell me—what is that fair work which the gods do by the help of our ministrations?

EUTHYPHRO   Many and fair, Socrates, are the works which they do.

SOCRATES   Why, my friend, and so are those of a general. But the chief of them is easily told. Would you not say that victory in war is the chief of them?

EUTHYPHRO   Certainly.

SOCRATES   Many and fair, too, are the works of the **husbandman**[2], if I am not mistaken; but his chief work is the production of food from the earth?

EUTHYPHRO   Exactly.

SOCRATES   And of the many and fair things done by the gods, which is the chief or **principal**[3] one?

EUTHYPHRO   I have told you already, Socrates, that to learn all these things accurately will be very **tiresome**[4]. Let me simply say that piety or holiness is learning how to please the gods in word and deed, by prayers and sacrifices. Such piety is the **salvation**[5] of families and states, just as the impious, which is unpleasing to the gods, is their **ruin**[6] and **destruction**[7].

SOCRATES   I think that you could have answered in much fewer words the chief question which I asked, Euthyphro, if you had chosen. But I see plainly that you are not **disposed**[8] to

1. [əˈteɪnmənt] *n.* 获得

2. *n.* 农夫

3. [ˈprɪnsəpəl] *adj.* 重要的

4. [ˈtaɪəsəm] *adj.* 疲劳的

5. [sælˈveɪʃən] *n.* 救赎

6. [ˈruːɪn] *n.* 破坏

7. [dɪˈstrʌkʃən] *n.* 毁灭

8. [dɪsˈpəʊzd] *v.* 愿意,有意于

instruct me—clearly not: else why, when we reached the point, did you turn aside? Had you only answered me I should have truly learned of you by this time the nature of piety. Now, as the asker of a question is necessarily dependent on the answerer, whither he leads I must follow; and can only ask again, what is the pious, and what is piety? Do you mean that they are a sort of science of praying and sacrificing?

EUTHYPHRO   Yes, I do.

SOCRATES   And sacrificing is giving to the gods, and prayer is asking of the gods?

EUTHYPHRO   Yes, Socrates.

SOCRATES   Upon this view, then, piety is a science of asking and giving?

EUTHYPHRO   You understand me **capitally**[1], Socrates.

1. [ˈkæpɪtəl] *adv.* 佳妙地；极佳地

SOCRATES   Yes, my friend; the reason is that I am a **votary**[2] of your science, and give my mind to it, and therefore nothing which you say will be thrown away upon me. Please then to tell me, what is the nature of this service to the gods? Do you mean that we prefer requests and give gifts to them?

2. [ˈvəʊtəri] *n.* 崇拜者；信徒

EUTHYPHRO   Yes, I do.

SOCRATES   Is not the right way of asking to ask of them what we want?

EUTHYPHRO   Certainly.

SOCRATES   And the right way of giving is to give to them **in return**[3] what they want of us. There would be no meaning in an art which gives to any one that which he does not want.

3. 回报

EUTHYPHRO   Very true, Socrates.

SOCRATES   Then piety, Euthyphro, is an art which gods and men have of doing business with one another?

EUTHYPHRO   That is an expression which you may use, if you like.

SOCRATES   But I have no particular liking for anything but the truth. I

wish, however, that you would tell me what benefit **accrues**[4] to the gods from our gifts. There is no doubt about what they give to us; for there is no good thing which they do not give; but how we can give any good thing to them in return is far from

4. [əˈkruː] *vi.* 积累；增加

being equally clear. If they give everything and we give nothing, that must be an affair of business in which we have very greatly the advantage of them.

EUTHYPHRO   And do you imagine, Socrates, that any benefit accrues to the gods from our gifts?

SOCRATES   But if not, Euthyphro, what is the meaning of gifts which are **conferred**[1] by us upon the gods?

EUTHYPHRO   What else, but **tributes**[2] of honour; and, as I was just now saying, what pleases them?

SOCRATES   Piety, then, is pleasing to the gods, but not beneficial or dear to them?

EUTHYPHRO   I should say that nothing could be dearer.

SOCRATES   Then once more the **assertion**[3] is repeated that piety is dear to the gods?

EUTHYPHRO   Certainly.

SOCRATES   And when you say this, can you wonder at your words not standing firm, but walking away? Will you **accuse**[4] me of being the Daedalus who makes them walk away, not **perceiving**[5] that there is another and far greater artist than Daedalus who makes them go round in a circle, and he is yourself; for the argument, as you will perceive, comes round to the same point. Were we not saying that the holy or pious was not the same with that which is loved of the gods? Have you forgotten?

EUTHYPHRO   I quite remember.

SOCRATES   And are you not saying that what is loved of the gods is holy; and is not this the same as what is dear to them—do you see?

EUTHYPHRO   True.

SOCRATES   Then either we were wrong in our former assertion; or, if we were right then, we are wrong now.

EUTHYPHRO   One of the two must be true.

SOCRATES   Then we must begin again and ask, What is piety? That is an **enquiry**[6] which I shall never **be weary of**[7] pursuing as far as in me lies; and I **entreat**[8] you not to **scorn**[9] me, but to apply your mind to the utmost, and tell me the truth. For, if any man knows, you are he; and therefore I must

1. [kənˈfɜːrə(r)] vt. 商讨;授予;赐予

2. [ˈtrɪbjuːt] n. 贡品;礼物

3. [əˈsɜːʃn] n. 诊断;主张

4. [əˈkjuːz] vt. 指控…;指责

5. [pəˈsiːv] vt. 觉察到

6. [ɪnˈkwaɪərɪ] n. 询问
7. 厌烦,不耐烦
8. [ɪnˈtriːt] vt. 请求
9. [skɔːn] vt. 嘲笑

detain[1] you, like Proteus, until you tell. If you had not certainly known the nature of piety and impiety, I am confident that you would never, on behalf of a **serf**[2], have charged your aged father with murder. You would not have run such a risk of doing wrong in the sight of the gods, and you would have had too much respect for the opinions of men. I am sure, therefore, that you know the nature of piety and impiety. Speak out then, my dear Euthyphro, and do not hide your knowledge.

EUTHYPHRO   Another time, Socrates; for I am in a hurry, and must go now.

SOCRATES   Alas! My **companion**[3], and will you leave me in despair? I was hoping that you would instruct me in the nature of piety and impiety; and then I might have cleared myself of Meletus and his **indictment**[4]. I would have told him that I had been **enlightened**[5] by Euthyphro, and had given up **rash**[6] innovations and **speculations**[7], in which I **indulged**[8] only through ignorance, and that now I am about to lead a better life.

1. [dɪˈteɪn] *vt.* 拘留

2. [sɜːf] *n.* 仆人

3. [kəmˈpænjən] *n.* 伙伴

4. [ɪnˈdaɪtmənt] *n.* 指控
5. [ɪnˈlaɪtənd] *vt.* 启蒙
6. [ræʃ] *adj.* 轻率的
7. [ˌspekjʊˈleɪʃən] *n.* 推测
8. [ɪnˈdʌldʒ] *vt.* 沉溺于; 纵情于

＊ ＊ ＊   ＊ ＊ ＊   ＊ ＊ ＊   ＊ ＊ ＊   ＊ ＊ ＊   ＊ ＊ ＊   ＊ ＊ ＊   ＊ ＊ ＊

❈**Questions for discussion**:

(1) Why did Socrates choose Euthyphro to discuss "piety"? Do you think Euthyphro is the ideal to discuss "What is piety?"

(2) What was the first definition of piety did Euthyphro give? According to Socrates, what's wrong with this definition?

(3) What was the second definition of piety did Euthyphro give? How did Socrates refute this second definition?

(4) Euthyphro modified his second definition of piety and came up with a third definition. What was it? How did Socrates refute that definition again?

(5) What was the last definition of piety that Socrates came up with? What is wrong with it?

(6) By reading this dialogue, do you understand what are "Socrates' questions"? Why are "Socrates' questions" very important?

(7) In this dialogue, by goading Euthyphro to define "piety", Socrates is seeking a definition which is universally true and covers all the particular instances of piety. Do you think so? This dialogue typically features what is called "Socratic Method". Summarize in your own words, what are Socratic Method?

(8) Did you read the famous saying by Socrates "The unexamined life is not worth living"? Read this dialogue carefully and figure out what this saying means.

* * *　　* * *　　* * *　　* * *　　* * *　　* * *　　* * *　　* * *

References

阿波罗多洛斯. 希腊神话[M]. 周作人, 译. 北京: 中国对外翻译出版公司, 1998.

埃斯库罗斯. 普罗米修斯[M]//罗念生. 罗念生全集(第二卷). 上海: 上海人民出版社, 2004.

奥斯温·默里. 早期希腊[M]. 晏绍详, 译. 上海: 上海人民出版社, 2008.

布克哈特. 希腊人和希腊文明[M]. 王大庆, 译. 上海: 上海人民出版社, 2008.

程志敏. 荷马史诗导读[M]. 上海: 华东师范大学出版社, 2007.

邓晓芒. 古希腊罗马哲学讲演录[M]. 北京: 世界图书出版公司, 2007.

弗雷泽. 金枝[M]. 徐育新, 等, 译. 北京: 大众文艺出版社, 1998.

荷马. 奥德赛[M]. 王焕生, 译. 南京: 人民文学出版社, 1997.

荷马. 奥德赛[M]. 陈中梅, 译注. 南京: 译林出版社, 2003.

荷马. 伊利亚特[M]. 罗念生, 译. 上海: 上海人民出版社, 2007.

赫西俄德. 工作与时日·神谱[M]. 张竹明, 蒋平, 译. 北京: 商务印书馆, 1991.

克莱门. 劝勉希腊人[M]. 王来法, 译. 北京: 生活·读书·新知三联书店, 2002.

利奇德. 古希腊风华史[M]. 杜之, 常鸣, 译. 沈阳: 辽宁教育出版社, 2000.

欧里庇得斯. 美狄亚[M]//罗念生. 罗念生全集(第三卷). 上海: 上海人民出版社, 2004.

色诺芬. 回忆苏格拉底[M]. 吴永泉, 译. 北京: 商务印书馆, 1986.

索福克勒斯. 安提戈涅[M]//罗念生. 罗念生全集(第二卷). 上海: 上海人民出版社, 2004.

索福克勒斯. 俄狄浦斯王[M]// 罗念生. 罗念生全集(第二卷). 上海: 上海人民出版社, 2004.

温克尔曼. 希腊人的艺术[M]. 邵大箴, 译. 桂林: 广西师范大学出版社, 2001.

王以欣. 神话与历史: 古希腊英雄故事的历史和文化内涵[M]. 北京: 商务印书馆, 2006.

吴诗玉, 涂鸣华. 古希腊神话的现代解读: 理性和神性[M]. 北京: 北京大学出版社 & 上海: 上海交通大学出版社, 2014.

吴诗玉, 葛明永. 古希腊文明演绎(英文)[M]. 上海: 上海交通大学出版社, 2012.

希罗多德. 历史[M]. 王以铸, 译. 北京: 商务印书馆, 2011.

亚里士多德. 诗学[M]. 陈中梅, 译注. 北京: 商务印书馆, 1996.

EURIPIDES. Ten Plays[M]. Translated by Paul Roche. New York: New American Library, 1998.

HARD, R. The Routledge Handbook of Greek Mythology[M]. New York: Routledge, 2004.

SOPHOCLES. the Complete Plays[M]. Translated by Paul Roche. New York: New American Library, 2001.

HOMER. The Homeric Hymns[M]. Apostolos N. Athanassakis (translation, introduction and notes), Baltimore: Johns Hopkins University Press, 1976.

HOMER. The Iliad[M]. Translated by Robert Fagles. London: the Penguin Group, 1990.

HOMER. The Odyssey[M]. Translated by Robert Fagles. London: the Penguin Group, 1990.

JEAN-PIERRE V. Myth and Thought among the Greeks[M]. Cambridge: Zone books, 2006.